The Raj And After

The Raj And After

Krishna P. Bahadur

Ess Ess Publications

4837/24, Ansari Road
Daryaganj,
New Delhi - 110 002
Ph: 3260807

First published 1996

ISBN 81-7000-170-6

Rs. **400.00**

Published by
Ess Ess Publications
4837/24, Ansari Road,
Daryaganj
New Delhi - 110002.
Phone : 3260807

Composed by :
Academy of Computer Studies
BG-1/42, Paschim Vihar
New Delhi - 110063
Phone : 5580312

Printed By :
Mehra Offset Press
New Delhi

To my son

Sanjay

24 February 1958 – 26 March 1980

and

my daughter

Sandhya

16 October 1963 – 17 March 1979

Alas, that Spring should vanish with the Rose !
That Youth's sweet-scented Manuscript should close!
The Nightingale that in the Branches sang
Ah, whence, and wither flown again, who knows!

OMAR KHAYYAM: FITZGERALD

The author wishes to make it clear that in this book he has no intention of running down or stygmatizing any class or community, for he believes that all persons are equal before God, and that the evils of society are not universal, and no class can be wholly condemnable as it consists of individuals both good and evil. The spirit behind the book is to point out that this is the time for introspection and correction, so that this nation may be admired and respected the world over.

CONTENTS

PREFACE

It was the best of times, it was the worst
of times, it was the age of wisdom, it
was the age of foolishness, it was the
epoch of belief, it was the epoch of
incredulity, it was the season of Light, it
was the season of Darkness, it was the
spring of hope, it was the winter of
despair, we had everything before us, we
had nothing before us, we were all going
direct to Heaven, we were all going direct the
other way - in short, the period was so far
like the present period, that some of the
noisiest authorities insisted on its being
received, for good or for evil, in the
superlative degree of comparison only.

CHARLES DICKENS: A TALE OF TWO CITIES

Creatures are born in this world, live their allotted years and then go the way of all flesh. They have no choice in the kind of their birth, the place, the house, the family, and in the case of humans their wealth and position. Shankaracharya says in the 'Crest-Jewel of Wisdom' that among sentient creatures birth as a human being is difficult of attainment. According to Hindu traditional belief it is only after passing through eighty-four lakh births in inferior wombs, one gets human birth. Having got it, the pursuit of soul-knowledge ought to be its quest. Dr S. Radhakrishnan compares life to a game of cards. The players have no choice in the cards dealt to them, but a good player could win the game with bad cards and a bad player lose it with a good hand. Thus even though here people worship the rising sun, only, greatness is no passport to goodness. A corrupt prime minister or chief minister plays life's game badly while an honest peon plays it well. Nonetheless, whatever may be the divine parameter, here the world courts greatness and the journalists' cameras click only for the big wheels. Many bedrooms must have secrets, but what engages the attention of the British intelligentsia are those of the royalty. So much so that lensmen lurk behind curtained bedroom windows to get snaps of holidaying princesses! While the deaths of the great are celebrated by public holidays and the sounding of bugles, and if they are very great by firing guns and canons, the small fry have to be burnt in government crematoriums or lie in nondescript graves - Taj Mahals are for queens only - and remembered in paid obituaries. Therefore as I proceeded with this book I realized that it should be mere than an autobiography and turned towards the objective point of view, about matters that would be of universal concern, not merely personal.

I have sought to relate what researehers have tried to uncover about afterlife and out-of-the-body experiences, about sages true and false, and whether this existence of ours is governed by chance or destiny or the divine will, basing my conclusions on my own experiences. I have had the opportunity of seeing the working of the Raj and in that period of the Quit India movement launched by Gandhi, the Partition and its aftermath and thereafter the forty-seven years of our independence.

The Raj had its faults and follies. The British always considered Indians to be inferior and untrustworthy, loathing the 'heathen heart' as much as the Moslem, the *kaffirs*. They were bothered only about the maintenance of law and order and making money from the country they had subdued for that was of primary importance for the 'nation of shopkeepers'. Incidentally they gave us gifts like the railway, telegraph, the telephone and canals, but most of these were not so much for the people's good but to assist them in ruling India. Unfortunately even when the Raj packed up and went, we continued these gifts in the same colonial manner with only this difference that while before the Raj usurped the benefits of these conveniences for itself, now our domineering governments, not giving a hoot for its citizens, ride roughshod over those whom these benefits should serve. This you-be-damned attitude of departments like the railways, airlines, telecommunications and many others towards the consumer is a continuation of the old imperious spirit of the Raj. Nonetheless the Raj had an administrative machinery much superior to what we have been able to evolve over the five decades of freedom. It could deliver while our governments merely dither. It had a strong bureaucracy because there were no politicians to coerce it and the British ICS officers seldom bothered about transfers because their home was in England and one place here was as alien as another. They did not believe in ponderous files and mammoth meetings, but talked accross the table to settle their problems. They had but one master to please, their own British government, and so there was no question of forming narrow affinities. They lived and worked fearlessly without carbine-totting cops and did not think it necessary to find security within huge walls and gates. They were reasonably honest and prized integrity. Our administration is not only weak and unable to turn the trick, it also reeks of corruption and the grease becomes thicker to keep pace with the rising cost of living. It is difficult to find an honest man in this country now for honesty is scarcer than ice water in hell. Then there is inefficiency largely due to sloth and unconcern. While in the developed nations people are busier than a one-armed paper hanger, we have innumerable holidays, quite a few to honour the long dead and gone, the dying and doubtless many[VIPs] awaiting death; and since we are secular [non-religious] we must have holidays for the various religious festivals - Hindu, Moslem, Christian, Jain, Buddhist and so forth. It is so bad that exasperated over almost a week's closure of banks, the Reserve Bank of India, solicitous for our affluent citizens, ordered them to open full day on a Saturday (usually they work till two only on this day). But what happens to the small beer? Here's how the police the citizens' protectors, handle them: 'In the process [of chasing agitators sore over a 'fake' encounter] innocent officer-goers, shopkeepers and children playing in the vicinity were roughed up by the police. Sushil Kumar Singh a medical representative suffered head injuries when he was beaten up by some PAC and CRPF jawans Satish, a Parag milk vendor, Jhabbulal a panwala, Sadde, a scooter mechanic were just a few of those who were beaten for daring to open their shops... Sadde's tool box was thrown on the street' [The *Pioneer* 14 April 1995]. In lanes which were spotlessly clean, now there is the stench of human excreta and urine, and pigs roam about grunting. The British ICS had able handpicked men, merit being the only criterion, a good few belonging to the nobility. In Independent India merit is no longer the criterion with reservations going as high as 85 per cent and in utter disregard to court decisions fixing 50 per cent as the maximum. So many persons are now in the saddle whose caste or class is the only qualification and our administration in fields both technical and non-technical is flooded with mediocrity. The IAS as we have it now is a cheesy copy of the British ICS. As for the Indian politician, the less said the better. The mutual vilification and cussing out are often muckerish and devoid of all refinement, as for example an episode about an ex-minister in the Congress government: 'Some newsmen witnessed with disbelief on Tuesday a physical and verbal assault by Mr Kalpnath Rai on Janata Dal leader Mr S.Jaipal Reddy. Mr Reddy who suffers from permanent impairment of his legs, walks with the help of crutches. On Tuesday after addressing a press conference in the party office in

Parliament, he was walking back with some reporters around 5 pm. As he passed by the prime minister's chamber, Mr Rai, who was apparently waiting for an audience with the PM, came from behind and hit Mr Reddy hard on his shoulders with both his hands. Mr Reddy nearly collapsed, according to a reporter accompanying him [Mr Reddy]. When he managed to recover from this assault, Mr Rai loudly asked, *kyon Jaipal tumhari doosri tang kab tootegi*? ['Jaipal {Reddy}, when will your other leg also break?'] Mr Reddy, who had by now recovered his composure, replied, *agar tumse nahin tootee to kabhi nahin tootegi* ['If it could not be broken by you, it'll never break'?] After this Mr Rai started shouting generally at everyone: *yeh tumhare VP Singh, Narasimha Rao (the PM), VC Shukla koi bhi ajaye aur mere akele se chunao ladke mujhe harai to janoon* ['I defy any of your VP Singh, Narasimha Rao, VC Shukla; anyone; to stand against me and win the election']. But an unruffled Mr Reddy just walked away [The *Pioneer.* Friday 31 March 1995]. There are no longer elections in this country. They are political feuds fought with unremitting violence, bloodshed, shoot-outs, rigging, booth-capturing, intimidating voters and selfishly seeking vote-banks resembling more battlefields than sanctuaries of human rights. A report says that revolvers at a little above half their price are being hogged by grabby legislators and MPs *to whom alone they are being offered.* The reason given by an ex-MLA is ' Politcs today has become dangerous and one doesn't know when and where it will be required.!' [Legislators, MPs gunning for a gun. The *Pioneer* 21 June 1995]. And the astounding thing is that some prestigious magazines seem to feel that such elections are better than no elections at all! If democracy is to be achieved by such violent disorder, it is certainly not democracy. The situation is no doubt very critical today with religion controlled by fanatics, administration by second and third raters, lazyboots and sleepyheads abounding, corruption spreading like a fog enveloping everyone, the population shooting like a satellite, absence of work-culture, poor implementation of plans and policies, a patched-up constitution which has taken away most of the fundamental rights, disorderly conduct, a plethora of political parties, elections by the bullet, poverty, malnutrition and unemployment, careless doctors maiming and blinding and conscious of nothing but money, women raped and children abused, law and order extinct and scant regard for the security of the land, provinces trying to break away, and an enslaved and partisan media. Will we be able to reverse all this and put our derailed democracy back on the rails? The answer could be both no and yes, for in the government by the people everything depends on the people:

> 'The fault, clear Brutus, is not in our stars
> But in ourselves, that we are underlings'.

The grim reality, however, that stares us in the face, is that the chances of retrieving our democracy from going downhill are receding. This is a pity. Japan was almost destroyed by the atomic bomb near about the time when our ancestors, maybe some of us too, were dancing about the streets, over the moon to see freedom come [while others lay brutally mauled by mobs with cruelty which only the Oriental can perpetrate - the women committing harakiri to save there honour]. Yet that small island country, tinier than our smallest province, is leading the world in industrial development while we are still in the developing group and with each passing year sliding down So as the days flit by, more and more it seems the answer is going to be, no.

The book has been written in the spirit of friendly criticism and there is no intention to hurt the feelings of anyone, rather to emphasize wherein we have failed to achieve and to suggest ways of improvement. Slang words which might seem unfamiliar have been italicized. I am grateful to my publisher for bringing out the book despite the hard times and for the excellent format.

1

THE LIGHT OF DAY

Our birth is but a sleep and a forgetting
The Soul that rises with us, our life's star
Hath had elsewhere its setting.

WILLIAM WORDSWORTH

The old sage lay on a matress spread on the ground, clean-shaven with greying eyebrows and a face innocent as a child's. He could have been eighty or a hundred, but the years did not seem to have any effect on him. He was known as Mouni Baba, the Silent Sage, and lived in Ayodhya. He seldom spoke and never about worldly matters, but this was one of those rare occasions, for in the woman before him he recognized the presence of devotion to God. 'Babaji, this girl was married thirteen years ago, but she is childless. We don't know whether she's going to have a child'. The old sage closed his eyes for a second, then opened them. They were reddish as of a man filled with anger. His white eyebrows contracted as he spoke. 'Why do you say she will have no children. She is bound to have them. Go and see what happens hereafter'. Next year his words came true and her first child was born. That woman was my mother. It was a day of rejoicing, for in the first half of the twentieth century a childless woman was considered inauspicious in India, which is amazing for the population in this country is expected to touch 1,278 million by the turn of the century.[1] People, even members of the family would turn aside at a barren woman's approach. Other women who had half a dozen mouths to feed, wouldn't look at the faces of such a couple in the morning. They would heap insults on the poor childless woman. Women have always been victimized not only in India but the world over, which is very strange for it is from the womb of a woman that male babes are born. It is as though the sapling should despise its root, the river its source and the stars and planets the heavens that hold them.

2

UNSAINTLY SAINTS - DESTINY

Saints should always be judged guilty
until they are proved innocent

GEORGE ORWELL

Is the world governed by chance or is there a Maker? The question is not new. It was raised almost eight centuries before the advent of Christ: 'Discoursers on the *Brahman* (the Absolute) ask, is it that which is the cause of the universe? From where do we come, by what do we live, where do we go after death, who is the dispenser of our joys and sorrows? Someone might say it's time or nature, or necessity, or chance, or the elements or even the soul; or any of these or all of them put together. He'd be wrong, for how can they act of themselves? Nor can it be the soul for that experiences the consequence of good and evil deeds. The sages discovered that the unseen power of God himself directs each and all of these causes.[2] Chance is something erratic without regularity, order and system. Our experience shows that there is harmony in the sequence of day and night, the coming of the seasons, the stages of life–birth, childhood, youth, age and death. The earth gets just enough heat to sustain life, the rivers always flow into seas and the whirling planets and the star-studded sky have been in their places for millions of years. There is an unseen Intelligence which controls the universe, but what it really is, no one has ever known. However most religions and researches point to that Supreme Controller being light, perhaps a Light and a Voice, neither of which is met with anywhere in the world. The seers of the Upanishads said:

'The sun does not shine there, nor the moon and stars,
Nor these lightnings, and much less this fire.
When the Supreme shines then shines everything else
By its light alone is all illumined.'[3]

In the *Bhagavadgita,* the most religious scripture of the Hindus and perhaps a record of the world's highest philosophy, Sanjaya described this light as that of a thousand suns shining all at once[4]. In the Holy Bible we are told that God appeared to Moses in the form of fire in a bush which lighted up with it but was not burnt[5]. While

Arjuna not only saw the Lord's form, but also vividly described it. Moses hid his face for he was afraid to look on God. The reason for this appears to be that religions like Islam and Christianity which conceive a formless God (known as *Brahman* to Hinduism) are loath to give any description of him. As the Holy Bible puts it: 'Thou shalt have no other gods before me. Thou shalt not make unto thee any graven images, or any likeness of anything that is in heaven above, or that is in the earth beneath, or that is in the water under the earth: thou shalt not bow to them: for I the LORD thy God am a jealous God...'[6] The Holy Quran considers the worshippers of idols unclean.[7] The other world religions propagate their own doctines, but refrain from condemning those of others. Modern research is probably nearer to the truth about who God really is, and the conclusion of most of the researchers are, firstly that he is a 'Being-of-Light', light of infinite intensity but not dazzling; secondly that this 'Being-of-Light' can communicate but it is not in any of the languages of human beings, but in a kind of thought-language which the disembodied soul can understand; thirdly that the soul-out-of-the-body is shown a flashback of the entire life in which it has been involved prior to leaving it, and this flashback is not just the kind we see in movies, but has a certain reality and is like the whole life relived, and takes just a few seconds; fourthly the 'Being-of-Light' keeps on pointing out the faults one had committed in the previous existence, but without rancour or accusation [in other words merely as a kind of corrective for the future]; fifthly that the experience of the disembodied soul is one of overpowering joy, peace, exhilaration and delight, and is so wonderful indeed that scarcely anyone wishes to go back to the world; and sixthly that the 'Being-of-Light' stresses two things, one that people should show love to all fellow-beings and try to assist them in every way and two, that one should gather knowledge [of the spiritual] and that this process of knowledge was a continuous one that went on from one life to another. These facts have been confirmed by researchers who have studied hundreds of Out-of-the-Body experiences (O.B.E) of persons who were declared clinically dead but came to life.[8]

It might seem strange that one should begin an account of one's birth by speaking about death, but birth and death are the back and front of the same coin, as the poet says.

Death is the veil which those who live call life;
They sleep and it is lifted.[9]

OR as a writer says: 'I consider all human beings to be immortal, or rather to possess an immortal component, with what we call birth and death as mere points on the graph of our personal evolution'.[10]

Mouni Baba, who in a way predicted my birth, lived in Ayodha, that peaceful pilgrim township which today looks more like a battlefield with all varieties of armed poliçe personnel guarding what is now a rubble with a makeshift temple on if housing the idol of 'Rama-lala'. This tiny place has been agitating politicians and governments for the last few years, as though it was the ace show of the Indian circus. In a country where people are dying like rats in epidemics, where trains run twenty hours late, go off the rails, ran into each other and bogies catch fire, where often one can reach where he has to go, by a car earlier than by plane, where most people can't get two meals a day and all their literary acumen is confined to putting thumb impressions on papers they know nothing about; it is this small spot which is constantly under attack. Maybe I had a glimpse of Mauni Baba sometime after my birth, and as childhood memories are vivid, I seem to recollect his golden-yellow complexion and his faraway look as though musing on something in the world beyond. He was doubtless a very holy man. The *Gita* tells us to seek wisdom at the feet of saints.[11] The saints are in a way God-men as they have advanced on the spiritual path much beyond ordinary beings. A writer who has investigated psychic phenomena accepts the Hindu concept of sages and avatars: ' I believe that certain individual human beings have been reincarnated to serve as mediums of the supreme intelligence for the purpose of correcting the course of humanity.'[12] But it is as difficult to single out saints from imposters as to distinguish a fake bank note or imitation jewellery from the real. There has been a mushrooming of saints in our times, saints having unsaintly liaisons with buxom girls whom they euphemistically call 'secretaries', saints who are careful to pander to the noveaux riches and the elite and hobnobbing with ambitious politicians and who, pretending to be otherworldly, are out to establish world governments and heaven-on-earth. The first 'saint' I saw was perched on a bamboo platform held by a thick pole sunk deep into the ground. It seemed to be a kind of machan for shikarees. It was the Kumbha in Allahabad, the biggest religious gathering in the world, held once in twelve years, when devout Hindus come to wipe away their sins by a dip in the Sangam and the not so devout to commit some more. A colleague of mine who was a disciple of the *baba* took me to have his *darshan* [that's what seeing a holy man is called]. It was a little hard to talk to him for he was almost twelve feet away on his machan, but his first words didn't click with my impression of a saint at all. 'It is because of me' he said 'that this boy [pointing to my colleague] became a deputy collector. I made him so'. That sounded like what a swellhead would say. He tossed me an apple and then a banana which I caught deftly and promptly handed them to the poor ill-clad urchins with bony bodies crowding expectantly round me. The great man shook his head disapproving my magnanimity and tossed me an apple, pointing his finger accusingly, so this time I let the urchins wail. Such overpowering conceit couldn't be a saintly attribute, but he was a hot favourite with the bigwigs. The next holy man I met was an improvement for he was firmly on the ground lying on a mat as Mouni Baba was. I saw him at Niemsar a place in Lakhimpur, where sadhus reposed in the loneliness of caves and grottos. This sadhu seemed to be a European for he was very fair with the rosiness showing through his skin. I began a greeting in English but he silenced me, saying '*Ham ne angrezi das sal se bolna chor diya* ('I ceased speaking English ten years back'). That was an effective snub and I looked a fool for not speaking in my mother tongue. 'If I gave you the whole of Lucknow' he said [in Hindi of course], 'would you take it?' It was a hypothetical question, for the municipal corporation of Lucknow where I lived were always goading me about my house tax and to be the nabob of Lucknow was beyond imagination, but just to see his response I said 'Sure, I'll take it'. That put the old man in a tantrum and he told me I wasn't a candidate for the spiritual quest, which incidentally I knew already. The *Gita* says about the sage: 'The man who is untroubled in the midst of sorrows and is free from eager desire amid pleasures, he from whom passion, fear and *rage* have passed away, is a sage of settled intelligence[13]. The first holy man was an egotist, this one hadn't got over rage. So they did not at all confirm to my impression of saints. There is one thing, however. I have found remarkable. Almost all westerners in saintly garb discard English, while we seem to pride ourselves in discarding our mother tongue! One day I was on an evening stroll in Hazrutgang (Lucknow) where there was a van with Hare–Krishna devotees who had set up a small table on which they had stacked books on Krishnaism and other Hindu holy scriptures. They were all Americans, shaven–headed and dressed in saffron I said to the one who was selling the books 'Good evening'. 'Hare-Krishna' he smiled and said. That made me hang my head in shame and I hastily departed. I will have something to say about the Indian tangle of tongues, but I'll hurry on to the next 'saint' I met, the last and the greatest of imposters. A friend of mine who was a disciple of this *baba* urged me to meet him. I had lost two young children, my daughter sixteen who died after just after five day's illness and a year after, my son, twenty-three who shot himself with my own pistol, so I readily agreed to meet this holy man, who, I thought might alleviate my sorrow. I bought some bananas on the way for, as my friend told me, one should not go to a saint empty-handed. We went in and sat with a number of other devotees who were awaiting the *baba's darshan*. An hour, two hours and three, yet no *baba*. After a long wait a man came and asked us to accompany him. Apparently the holy man had made a special concession to my friend who was a regular visitor. The man led us to an anteohamber where the saffron-clad *baba* sat. The smell of incense was strong. I put the bananas on the wooden dais and we bowed, the holy man extending his hand in a gesture of blessing. My friend told him about my bereavement. 'Could I have done anything to prevent my son shooting himself' I asked, 'You ? oh what could you do; yet you could have, if you had come to the right person'. With that enigmatic observation he resumed the sphinx - like silence. After a pause he said 'your elder son (who was turning thirty) is likely to meet with an accident. It can be prevented by performing a diamond-*yajna*, and you can have it done, but it's better if you leave it to me, for its a long ritual. The cost will be five thousand rupees'. And seeing me upset he threw me a black string-garland to wear. We rose and bowing, went out, while he asked his assistant to note down my name and address, apparently he was a methodical sadhu who kept a record of those from whom he hoped to extort some money. I had gone to the holy man to find comfort in my sorrow, he had done nothing to give it and only left me more disturbed. Such is the holiness of the holy! Anyway I had the string-garland with his blessing and I put it round my neck. I have often wondered if there is any significance in rings and talismans. One hardly comes across a man wearing at least one ring with a lucky-stone, emerald, sapphire, ruby, diamond , any that the astrologer or palmist recommends; some wear two or three, each to ward off some particular evil. There are amulets to wear and talismans to hang round the neck, like the one the *baba* gave me, which has an interesting story. I would wear it sleeping or awake, or wherever I went. It became with me, a kind of thing which if I thought I ever ceased wearing, would surely bring disaster. Soon I made a kind of compromise. As I hated going to bed with rings and beads, I would put it away under my pillow taking care to wear it as soon as I woke. One day I had to reach a relation to Kanpur to catch a train. As I was in service then I made out a day's programme for work there. Our car had gone on the Lucknow-Kanpur highway about eight or ten kilometers, when my hand went to my neck and I was dismayed to find it bare, I had forgotten to wear the string-garland, which lay under my pillow. My son, who was with me, saw my discomfiture and offered me his Shiva-image emblem which he wore on a string round his neck, but it was no use. There was no way to calm my tension and anxiety except to get *babaji's* good-luck charm, and back we all went to Lucknow. It was only when I picked up the black string–garland and put it round my neck, that I was at peace with myself. We again took the road to Kanpur managing to reach by the train-time, so vital it had become for me to wear that thing. When I would go out for my evening stroll I would wear it, or as I later began to do, put it in my trouser-pocket. One day, by chance, I wore trousers with a pocket having a hole and while I was on the road, the string-garland slipped down it and fell somewhere, and that was the end to it. It was also the end to my unreasoned faith in it, or perhaps I should call it, superstition. That's all what rings and amulets mean. They create an unreasoned faith, a vain trust, a canker of the diseased mind which thinks that the colour of a stone can change the course of destiny. But is destiny something inexorable, unalterable and rigid? What function does karma have in destiny? The question is difficult to answer, for the matter is abstruse. The *Gita*, which is unalloyed philosophy, says at one place 'seated in the hearts of all beings, God makes them go round and round by the power of his maya, as though mounted on a lathe' [14] and at another place, 'Your right is to works only, never to the fruit of works, therefore do not work with desire for the fruit, and also shun the urge to desist from works.'[15] Thus fate is predetermined and we only work it out, as Shakespeare says:

All the world's a stage
And all the men and women merely players:
They have their exists and their entrances'.[16]

Omar is right about the Moving Finger, and I will relate some incidents in my own life to illustrate this. I was additional district magistrate, when there was a confrontation between students and the management of a cinema-house and in their fury the students were determined to set the cinema-house on fire. The district magistrate sent a note to the other additional district magistrate (there were two) who was concerned, to send four magistrates to the cinema which was on a road-crossing. One of the magistrates asked me if I would like to come too. Though I had nothing to do with it, I agreed to go with them, and on the way we thought it prudent to take a posse of armed cops with us from the concerned police-station. When we had done so and four armed policemen were on the brand-new police pick-up, it just wouldn't start. The driver raised the bonnet, there was nothing wrong, but after about a ten minute wait, when he pressed the starter the engine came alive. Meanwhile, as we learnt later, the situation at the cinema was critical. The cinema was at the intersection of three roads and the students, and as usually happens, joined by same hoodlums who had snaked in, were ranged on all the three roads, practically surrounding the cinema, and politicians (*netas*) who can sniff trouble from a long way off, had promptly come to exploit it. There wasn't any magistrate till then, the district magistrate was on the way but hadn't reached. One of the prominent *netas* said to the deputy superintendent of police there, 'You are the senior most officer here, you should talk to these people and try to persuade them to disperse'. The dy. S.P. went to address them and as soon as he began, a man rushed out of the crowd and thrust a sharp iron bar into his stomach. The dy. S.P. fell down bleeding and immediately the police opened fire, which they always do under such circumstances, the magisterial order for it being obtained afterwards as a matter of formality. Now all this took place in those ten minutes or so when our pick-up for no accountable reason, failed to start, otherwise it would have been me who got hit by the iron spike, not the dy. S.P. for then I would have been the 'seniormost' present–we reached just when the firing had started. Of course this could have been merely a coincidence, but one bead or two are merely beads, a whole lot of them together, make a rosary, and there have been enough 'coincidences' with me, some leading to a good end, others to a bad one, to convince me that destiny indeed shapes our ends. When I was sixty I was knocked down by a speeding scooterist, and got five fractures, breaking my right wrist and right leg. I was on my usual evening stroll and on the way I stopped to buy some medicines I needed, from a chemist's shop. It was my favourite shop, and whenever I went there I would chat for at least ten or fifteen minutes with the salesman-cum-proprietor with whom I had become friendly. While I was chatting with him in the breaks between one customer and another, my son who had gone there to buy *his* medicines, also, arrived, and it was the one and the only occasion when the two of us were there together. He cut short our talk and said 'Papa, I'll take your medicines also, give me your list and you carry on with your walk'. I protested that I would like to stay on and talk some time more with my friend, but nothing doing, he insisted that I should go, why delay my stroll. So I walked out, and just after three or four minutes – the crossing where the accident took place was that close – I was hit by the scooter. Had not my son thus unexpectedly come to the chemist, I would have been there at that moment, not crossing the road. But it all happened as though timed precisely by the clock. By whom? I would say it was by that Hidden Hand, that Moving Finger which some may call chance, but I would prefer to call destiny. I go back a few years when I was working as inspector general of prisons and was trying to find a suitable boy for my daughter. All the girl-and-boy affairs we see on the Indian TV movies are sheer nonsense, much different from the arranged marriages which are still the Indian social norm. In fact it's much like the slave-markets of old, except that it's boys on sale, not girls, each with a price tag and instead of lusty sheikhs with fat purses, it's the harried parents with worry-creased brows who go round to spot some lad for their daughter, whose price they can afford. There are a few love affairs, too, which end in wedlock, but they are only exceptions to the general rule. I had been to a distant town, talked over, shown my daughter who was fair with a very charming personality, all part of what we call a 'marriage negotiation', and was assured that she was acceptable. Soon after I got a letter from the boy's father asking me to come for a full one day's talk. A 'one-day-talk' sounded more like a conference to me, anyway a girl's father is always at the receiving end, so I went. It was all round and round the mulberry bush of dowry, the man having three unmarried daughters wanted to extract enough for the dower of all of them; so exasperated, I finally let him have the figure of 40,000 cash down, more I couldn't give. Later I got his final reply that he was sorry the 'boy and the girl were not compatible', which indeed they weren't for my daughter was very fair and his son very dark, so his letter was more a relief to my guilty conscience rather than bad news, but I was back to square one. Getting an arranged marriage through is as tough as getting a child's admission in a good school, securing a decent job or even winning a lottery; and that too when according to the last census of 1991 the sex ratio in India was 929 women to 1000 men! But every father with a grown-up daughter has to go through the mill and so I was sitting rather glum in my office room with the brown redtape-tied files stacked on my table, when this man came. He was known as Jhariwale Baba [*jhari* meaning 'bush'] and was said to have lived hid in the bushes stark naked in his early youth. A short dark man with dense black hair and deep penetrating eyes, he could speak Sanskrit fluently and like the usual run of holy men, loved to hobnob with high-ups, but basically he was a simple man and, as I discovered he had the gift of prophecy. He had asked me before, about my daughter's marriage, and I had told him about the person whom I had approached. He had said then 'Look, this won't come off. And I'll tell you frankly the impediment will be dowry. So now when he came, I said he had been right, the matter had fallen through, and it was, just as he had said, dowry. 'Ah that's why you're so crestfallen' he said 'but don't worry, by March next year your daughter will be married in a much better family and you *won't need to go out of your house'*. 'But that's impossible' I said, thinking of all the places I had been wandering about for it. He said 'That's how it'll be, I'm telling you'. And he was absolutely right. It happened just that way. He had said by March, my daughter was married that January. Next he came some months before I was to retire from service. 'You'll have to leave this job in September'.; he said [it was June 1981]. 'But how can that be?' I said, 'I'm retiring in February next year, and it's smooth sailing, why should there be a change at the fag end?' 'It has to be thus', he said. 'Look, what I say can never be wrong, *agar hamari bat galat nikal jaye to ap log hame kyon puchem, yah galat ho hi nahi sakta* [if what we say turns out wrong why would you people ever give us any importance]. What I am saying must happen. You'll get a more peaceful job,' he added 'but you'll have to go. Circumstances will be created for it'. I dismissed it all as moonshine and soon forgot all about it. Some time after the minister in charge of jails wanted me to do something which was irregular and I refused. We were at a meeting in his room. 'You are afraid' he said 'because you have soon to retire'. I keep quiet at his silly remark, but the flush of anger on my face made him say 'something is disturbing you?' 'Look' I said 'you ask me to do what's wrong. Why should I do it? and even if I had six years left instead of six months, I still wouldn't do such a thing ?' Next day I got my walking papers. It was a local posting and true enough, just as the *baba* had said, a more peaceful job, but it happened exactly as he had foretold. Although there wasn't anything saintly about him nor was he particularly wise, there were moments when he could divine the future. The last time I saw him he said 'I have got all my teeth extracted'. 'Why? I asked him, 'were they all bad? 'No, I was advised by a dentist to have them all out' was his incredible reply. That was that, there was nothing wrong with his teeth, yet he was foolish enough to get them extracted!

The conclusion from these incidents is that I am sure there is destiny, fixed and irrevocable. But then why do we work, what is the incentive to endeavour if we are only chessmen on the board of life? Ramana Maharshi, perhaps the last genuine sage of the twentieth century (b. 1879. d. 1948), was a firm believer in destiny. The message he gave was 'The Ordainer controls the fate of souls in accordance with their *prarabdha* karma (destiny to be worked out in this life resulting from the balance-sheet of actions in past lives). Whatever is destined not to happen will not happen, try as you may. Whatever is destined to happen will happen, do what you may to prevent it. The best course therefore is silence.' He said explicitly 'All actions that the body is to perform are already decided upon at the time it comes into existence: the only freedom you have is whether or not to identify yourself with the body. But as beings reap the fruit of their actions in accordance with God's laws, the responsibility is theirs not his'.[18] This being so, why should one still make effort and work, why not just sit quiet, inactive, and let destiny take its course? The Maharshi said that though it is vain to oppose destiny, to 'kick against the pricks,' this does not mean that no effort should be made. 'The man who says, "Everything is predestined, therefore I will make no effort" is intruding the false assumption "and I know what is predestined" '.[19] In other words, because we do not know what's coming next, we go on doing what we think we ought to do. It's like a cricket ball: you hit and you think youv'e made a sixer, but the man on the boundary-line catches it, and you're out. Therefore this is what I believe:

Life is like a journey on a horse–driven chariot. The horses are necessary to pull it and the chariot for the rider to sit. Life is like the sun and sunlight. So the soul and the body are both inseparable from birth to death and both have their own values. A dead man can't see even though the mechanism of his eyes is intact, as before, because his soul has gone, and a blind man can't see either even though his soul is in him, but the organ of sight, his eyes, are defective. Those who deprecate the body should ponder over the blind man and those who deny the soul, over the man with eyes, butts who's dead. Body and soul are like the seed and the plant; there can be no plant without the seed, nor seed without the plant. As Browning puts it:

'Let us not always say'
"Spite of this flesh today
I strove, made head, gained ground upon the whole!"
As the bird wings and sings
Let us cry "All good things
Are ours, nor soul helps flesh more, now than flesh helps soul".'[20]

There are lands like Alaska near the pole where the sun can't be seen for six months, but could the people there say 'There is no sun for this period?' So too the soul's invisibility cannot be taken to be proof of its non-existence, and further as we have said, it can see as well as be seen in Out-of-the-Body experiences. It seems to me (though sometimes it also doesn't) that there are various states of consciousness because, although man is endowed with only five senses there can be lives in other planets where there are beings with senses more than five, and that even with human beings on earth there is the possibility of going beyond these five senses as for example disappearing from sight seeing through closed doors, knowing the past and the future and the instant of a man's death. These powers [called *siddhis*], says Patanjali, the writer of the *Yoga Sutras*, can be got by the practice of Yoga[23] Even otherwise all human beings live through varying states of consciousness wakefulness, dream and dreamless sleep. One can also go beyond these three states to a fourth one which is the merging of all these three.

It appears that soul is light, ethereal, without limitations, invisible but knowable, the Knower of everything and though not God, of the nature of God. This soul is attached by an invisible cord stretching out from the heart's cavity and is like a skein which can unwind itself and go wherever it may choose to–a skein of infinite, length but with the end so firmly attached to the heart that it can never be severed except by the command of the Supreme Being. The soul actually travels to places real or of its own making and during the course of such travels it is beyond human control. These dream-journeys of the soul, unconnected with any of its lives, past, present of future refresh and invigorate it, as a man fond of travelling and visiting places feels fresh after an outing. That is why even after having dreamt all through the night one still wakes up refreshed, and that's why if one who is fast asleep and dreaming, is suddenly woken, he feels acute discomfort, for the journeying soul has to rush from wherever it is, back into the heart. It seems to me, though I have no evidence for it, that the introverts dream more than others and their dreams are far more vivid, and though there is scientific proof to believe that dreamless sleep is more invigorating than sleep with dreams, I do no thinks it is so. All sleep seems equally restful– so long as we are unconscious of the external world.

Human beings have no control over the events of their lives which are pre-destined at birth according to the law of karma; the only freedom human beings have is in their attitude to others and in the way they make use of the gift of human existence. For example one may be kind, helpful, charitable gentle and sympathetic to those whom he comes across, family, friends, relations or persons unconnected: or he can be selfish, rough, unkind, violent envious and unhelpful. The wider the circle of his goodness the better he has done, the order of excellence from good to best varying respectively with family, relations and friends, and the completely unacquainted. The freedom in using his life well or badly means whether he spends it in making money beyond his needs, lascivicious pursuits, perpetual amusements and so forth, or usefully in gathering knowledge which is spiritual in nature. Since these two–the freedom to do good or bad to others and to waste the gift of life or usefully spend it – are the only things in man's control, karma is restricted to judgment on these two points only.

Lastly there apparently is rebirth and life after life, till one is perfected, the state of perfection being that in which one sees everything as God. When one has reached this state his soul no longer needs a body for working towards the goal and being no more in need of rebirth remains a disembodied soul which is then merged with the World Soul.

3

EARLY YEARS

With virtue and quietness one may conquer the world.

LAO-TSE

My mother was a very saintly woman, with unswerving devotion to God and always ready to willingly give away in charity whatever she had. She would never send away anyone empty-handed from her door whoever the person was. About this my father wrote in his Memoirs, 'Dozens of beggars visited our place every day. Some of them were stout persons capable of earning their livelihood. "What is the use of feeding such people" we [meaning he and other members of the family] said one day, "this is misplaced charity." "It should not be our lookout" she replied, "to see who is deserving and who is not. When one has spread his hands before us, it should be our duty to satisfy his wants as far as we can." If she hadn't had her meals and a beggar came, she would forego it and give him the food. A devotee of Rama and Sita she found herself after marraige in a thoroughly Islamic atmosphere. My father wrote in his Memoirs about her, 'My sisters were trained in the old Kayastha fashion. They had read Karima, Dasturussubian from a maulvi. My father, used to recite from Sadi and other Persian poets for his prayers. When your mother entered such a home she must naturally have been bewildered. She was however, of firm resolve. Amidst jeers and taunts she sat down to adore her Sita-Rama ... she was scolded for wasting her time but continued in her resolve.' The bond between her and the Divine was very strong indeed and because of this she had a magnetic personality which had an overpowering effect on people. My father recorded some of these incidents in his Memoirs [which he wrote for me and my brother] which are reproduced here:

> 'Your mother had a magnetic influence; those who came into contact with her could not help abiding by her wishes.... her presence inspired reverence for her in those who saw her. Once while going by train we entered a compartment which was jam- packed. As usual everybody wanted the greatest room for himself, but there were three passengers who were particularly selfish. They had spread their legs and covered themselves from head to foot with a coverlet, pretending to be asleep. They didn't care to give us even sitting space. After a few moment one of them peoped through his sheet and saw your mother. He got up at once, as if stung by a

scorpion. "Make yourself comfortable, mother," he said, and then motioning to me, suggested that I might move to another berth, allowing her the whole of that for herself. Once we were travelling in June [the hottest Indian month] and got down at a station where we had to change trains. The wind was searingly hot and we had water in an earthen vessel (*surahi*) but a drop of lemonade had got into it by accident and she would never drink such water. You were a child about five and your brother yet a suckling, and it seemed both of you were on for having a sunstroke. Just then an elderly woman took over, appearing as though from nowhere. She gave you milk mixed with cold water, and revived both of you, looking after you in the train too, which we boarded. When we reached our destination, I asked, your mother to get that kind woman's address. On inquiring she said "There is no need to ask for my address. Divine will put us together for this brief time. I have done nothing except my duty". As soon as the train stopped she kissed both of you first, and then your mother, stepped down on the platform and disappeared

'Once your mother and I were going on a *palki-gari* (phaeton) to bathe in the Ganga during the Magh-mela a religious gathering). After a fixed point there was a wooden fencing with an entrance only for special VIPs, and beyond it one had to walk as no carriages were allowed. She asked me to speak to the constable on duty to let our conveyance go past as a special case. I declined to do this. She looked puzzled for a moment... and then put out her head and motioned to the constable to hear her. He came as though drawn by a magnet. "I want to take my carriage right up to the Bundh" was all she said [she feared to walk lest her foot tread inadvertently on bones or rubbish; she was very particular about maintaining purity of the body]. Strange to say the constable immediately cleared the road and allowed us to pass. I recollect many instances where her personality exhibited a magical effect but I omit them for fear of prolixity... I do not recollect any occasion when God did not listen to her prayers. Whatever she wished for always happened whether it was for herself or for others'.

Despite all this, their marriage was neither smooth nor happy, for the temporal and spiritual, like oil and water, do not mix. Hindu marriages [I say Hindu, because the Moslem ones are on a different pattern] bear the 'made in heaven' hologram, unlike the Christian ones in which the sacramental oath often lasts only till the bride and the groom are before the altar. Nonetheless the Hindu concept of heaven being a place where you can have binges with apsarases (heavenly hymphs), the heavenly warranty lasts only a couple of years. So while on the surface everything is hunky-dory and the newhyweds appear to be over the moon, soon the clouds appear, and they are under the weather. It's the Hindu bride who takes the biscuit in marital fidelty, in adapting herself to a man whom she has perhaps seen only once and that too chaperoned by elders, and to a family and household which may be as different from hers as night from day, and maintaining a suppressed calm in the face of cracks and gibes. Ironically rural weddings seem to be more westernized than the towns ones with ease in changing wives and husbands, readymade 'divorces' testified by the heads of the village assemblies and grass windows with storks dropping their babies while their husbands are busy earning in towns. The Hindu husband fits more of the stereotyped one except that his amours are comparatively secret and less daring. Anyway the Indian marriage apple-cart manages to drag along, even though when it reaches the end there are hardly any apples in it, and it's a safe bet that lovemaking in the land of the *Kama Sutra* is a rather dreary affair.

What really is the dividing line between love and sex. There are of course the Romeos (the Indian Majnus), but they are the exceptions, for as Byron says:

'Man's love is of man's life a thing apart,
'Tis woman's whole existence'.[24]

The Avon bard's concept of women concealing their love and sitting like patience on a monument seems to be a poetic flight of the imagination and Byron, the amorist who had many loves, was perhaps nearer the truth[25] The dividing line between love and last (sex, if you prefer to call it) is very thin indeed, for the two are like word and meaning, paper and the writing on it, or the two faces of the same coin. You can't have the one without the other. Swinburne pays greater homage to lust than to love[26], and Shakespeare's enigmatis observation that love does not look with the eyes but with the mind[27] are pointers to the supremacy of sex. The West associates sex with mere physical union and that too quite often of the extramarital kind. The East does not emphasize the physical aspect, though it does not ever repudiate it. Even the sages and gods of Hindu mythology keep ejaculating at the mere sight of lovely girls (called apsaras), as the two Adityas, Mitra and Varuna, did on seeing Urvashi, and they never miss ravishing lovely women. The great sage Vishvamitra had sex with Menaka who got a girl by him, Shakuntala, the heroine of Kalidasa's classic play about her and Dushyanta, Indra, the god of the firmament committed adultery with the sage Gautama's wife, Ahalya, and that too by deceit, and we find Krishna, whom Hindus believe to be Lord Vishnu's incarnation having sex with almost every lovely lass he came across, though he was steady with Radha, abducting Rukmini who was really the betrothed of Shishupala, and that too when he had a seraglio of over 16,000 wives! Shiva, one of the Hindu trinity, who is often worshipped by a representations of the *linga*-and-*yoni* ('prick-and-pus') went on a binge to the Himalayas, as we are told in the *Shiva Purana*, with his consort Sati, and he could not assuage his lust even after 36,00,000 years![28] The *Purana* says about their lovemaking, 'Shiva dallied for a long time with Sati. Then passion woke up strongly in her, she embraced him so tightly that she seemed to enter his body and his juice flowed into her'. The *Bhagavata Purana* too does not make a fetish of sex and gives a no-holds-barred account of Krishna and the *gopis* (cowherd girls): 'The *gopis* were so enamoured of him that they did not even care to tidy their dishevelled hair, or to set right their loosened dresses and brassiers. Krishna tenderly wiped their perspiration, the girls thrilling at the touch of his nails [which recalls the *Kama Sutra*!] The girls were tired after dancing with him so long, so he entered the waters of the river [Yamuna] along with the beauties, who pressed round him, 'their breasts squeezed to his limbs so that the saffron-paste on them covered his body'.[29] In the *Rasikapriya,* the poet Keshvadasa says about Krishna that he is restless for women with dark and dirty bodies, seeking to cohabit with them in the lonely places in lanes and in stuffy rooms where firewood is stored.[30] The *Upanishads*, perhaps the most sacred of Hindu scriptures, along with the *Gita* and the *Vedas*, while describing the soul which is immersed in the Supreme Being, says it is 'as a man clasping his wife limb to limb drowned completely in bliss and unaware of everything else',[31] and one of the *Upanishads* in fact gives a very vivid account of the sex act, not mincing words.[32] The attitude of a Hindu to sex therefore is of wonder, and adoration which is almost worship. To him sex is as divine as love, indeed one of the aims of a full life; and the desire to acquire wealth honestly, the impulse to have lawful sex [there are no lovers and beloveds, only husbands and wives, hail wedded love, as Milton would say]; are as essential as the practice of virtue and the quest for emancipation.

4

EDUCATION THEN AND NOW

The prosperity of a country depends, not
on the abundance of its revenues, nor on
the strength of its fortifications, nor
on the beauty of its public buildings;
but it consists in the number of its
cultivated citizens, in its men of
education, enlightenment and character.

MARTIN LUTHER

Born in British India I had to go through a thoroughly English education, and my father (who did not remarry despite pressure from everyone all round) who looked after us took care to see that I was given the best of it. He would give us (me and my brother) a rupee a month, a large sum those days, and for every word we spoke in Hindi we had to drop a pice as 'fine' in a small wooden box with a slit, and at the end of the month the box was opened and we all had eats from the cash in it. Thus the foundation of English or perhaps more correctly 'Hinglish' as its pidgin version could be labelled, was laid which was later to blossom into bloomers such as 'a stepney in my dickey' 'he is out of station', the minister on reflection said that his statement was infructuous, resiled from it', 'I put up at the Victoria hotel' and so forth as Derek Brown says, and rightly dubs a "pukka" education... with lots of Shakespeare, P.G. Wodehouse, with liberal dollops of Keats, Wordsworth...[33] One can't help being amazed to find so many whose mother tongue is not English, still winning worldwide acclaim in the West by their writings which falsifies what John Keats said long back:

'Since every man whose soul is not a clod
Hath visions and would speak, if he had loved
And been well nurtured in his mother tongue.[34]

What really is an Indian's mother tongue? In this country, more appropriately a sub-continent, the term 'Indian' comprises people of various religions speaking one of the fifteen languages specified in the eighth schedule of the Indian constitution each language being double-dutch to one who speaks another, which often results in humour, as for example the woman to whom *khokhi* meant a cough who went to a

Bengali doctor and said 'Doctor, I am getting *khokhis* all the time', on which he assured her 'Don't worry, next time you'll have a *khokha*' [in Bengali *khokhi* means a female baby and *khokha* a male one]; and another woman in whose tongue *kothi* meant the uterus who complained to the doc that her uterus fell, i.e., got displaced every time she was about to have a child, and was shocked to hear him reply 'Next time it happens, call a competent engineer! [in the doc's language *kothi* meant simply a house]. Humour apart, here the rose's perfume varies with the name by which it is called and often the rose turns into a thorn, for language like religion is the insignia of egotism and intolerance. In India cars with English number-plates are smashed bill boards pulled down and English shop-signs wrenched off and destroyed just because some vote-hungry politician has given a ban-English signal. A Tamilian will flare up if spoken to in Hindi (even if he understands it) and I recollect an occasion when I was in Madras in a hospital. A messenger was taking with him the list of names of the patients the doc would see, and I, who too was on the waiting-list, instinctively without any ill will, asked him in Hindi if my name was there too. I could see the anger in his eyes as he blurted out rudely '*I don't know HIndi*'. Of course had he really not known it, he couldn't have known that it was HIndi in which I had spoken. A Kanada speaking person will not tolerate Tamil, a Moslem will find Hindi repugnant to him and so on. The war of tongues goes on, as a Goan member of the legislative assembly put it long back 'North Goa will blow up if the Bill to make Konkoni the official language is passed, and the south it it is defeated'. So the framers of the Constitution solved this balled up problem by allowing the continuance of English as the 'associate' official language while theoretically Hindi remains the official one. But it is the other way about, and while lip-service is paid to Hindi, English remains the lingua franca.

And so I went through the school and college days frantially trying to master a language which wasn't my mother tongue and blissfully ignorant of that which was. I started at the St Mary's Convent Allahabad which was wholly managed by nuns. Education was neither so burdensome as it now is nor did it start so early. There were fewer students in a class, only around twenty or twenty-five. The discipline was remarkable and the uniform-wearing children (boys were permitted in the earlier classes from the kindergarden to class three) would form rows of three and march classwise when the school-closing bell rang. There were round metal badges with 'Good Boy' and 'Good Girl' inscribed on them, and every week the Reverend Mother would visit each class and pin the badge on the proud winner of that week. So the badges went in rotation encouraging good conduct and discipline. We were taught Browsing's *Pied Piper* and the boys joined in making a large representation of the rats following the piper on a wooden board while the girls made a doll's house. There was particular emphasis on pronunciation and good writing, but very little grammar. We would fold in our knuckles and put our hands each day on our desks while the teacher went round with a ruler seeing if our fingernails were pared and giving a light hit if anyone was found to have long nails. A few incidents stand out one rather poignant, which if childhood memories weren't so sharp, would be lost in the fog of time. Convents managed by nuns are far more efficient than the ones we now have bereft of them. One day there was a downpour followed by a drizzle which showed no sign of ending, and it was just when school was over. One of the nuns who was constantly with us till someone from home arrived, brought out her new Duckback waterproof without any hesitation and covering me snugly with it, seated me on the ekka which those days used to take me home about five kilometers away from school. Needless to say my father got it washed and dried and wrapping it carefully in a paper-packet, sent it back to that benign woman with his gratitude. Another time a boy pushed me and I fell down the three or four steps in the stairs, getting a small cut which was instantly attended to in the first aid unit of the reformatory. Such was the care given in the Convents of these days that a nun was deputed to take me home on the school bus. But then came the part of this incident which in the recollection pains me, though it was done in all childlike innocence. My father on whom the burden of looking after me fell after my mother's early death, was of very simple habits and absolutely unconcerned about dress. When the bus arrived he was standing in the veranda clad in just a cotton banian and a dhoti. Anglicization has its dark spots too, and seeing him I shouted 'He's not my father! he's not my father!' I can now, after the gulf of years, imagine the anguish he must surely have felt but I do not recollect even a shadow of it on his face, for he never once in his distressed life, lonely and spousless, let the darkness of his grief even touch me, so much so that I never even knew what death was till I saw him die.

We made patterns with plasticine on wooden slates and our teacher asked us to bring some bits of bread for rubbibng out the old patterns to make room for the new ones. But in my household the only bread was the unleavened dough for making *rotis* and so I shared some brought by an Anglo-Indian boy from his home. Shiced bread, which is now just as popular as dough *roties*, was then taboo in orthodox HIndu households for the bakers were mainly Moslems and anything touched by them was considered to be defiled. After class three, I had to shift to the allied boy's school, the St Joseph Collegiate, which was in the same compound on the other side of the central cathedral with its tall clock-tower. The principal at that time was Father Augustine a very nice, benign and jolly person with a flowing white beard. The large-sized table in his room, almost three-fourth as big as a billiard-table was cluttered with odds and ends of a staggering variety, and among them was his pride possession, a powerful telescope. When we boys went to him, he would put the eye-piece at its narrow end to our eye and say 'See, how big the tower looks'. We'd exclaim in wonderment 'Oh! it's very big. father and seems to be very near'. He would then reverse the telescope so that the broad and was toward us and ask 'And now?' 'Oh! Father it seems so very far off and so tiny' we'd say in amazement. He detested corporal punishment and never used the rod or cane, but when after him Father Hogan took over, the flogging started. There sure was method in this school and even scraps were regulated. When two boys ached for thrashing each other they had to go to the head, I forget his name, but he too was a padre, and tell him about it. Word then went round that there would be a scrap that day. The head-padre made meticulous arrangements, there was a regular boxing-ring upstairs. In the lunch-break the two were given boxing-gloves, the headmaster acting as referee and those who wished to see the fight stood by in the hall where the ring was, quite an enthusiastic audience, but it was all done quietly, no shouts of encouragement and cheers, and when it ended the winner shook hands with the loser; the steam was out and they were friends again.

The school library was my favourite haunt and I never missed the library-day. G.A. Henty's books were the rage those days just as Enid Blyton's are now, and I waded through all of them and others too. But the small library couldn't cater to my avidity for books and observing this my father would take me to a bookshop-cum-lending library. I would choose my book depositing a few annas, they were surprisingly cheap then, and after reading it return and take another, the shopman charging a small lending fee as his profit. The arrangement worked very well and I devoured the fairy tales, *Chandra Bai and Ratna Bai,* Grim, Anderson and a host of others. Although the majority of people in India are HIndus, the second language taught in Anglo-Indian schools was Urdu. A *maulvi* (Urdu teacher) used to take classes in that language while the class-teacher, whom we had nicknamed 'Fandu', a rather stern disciplinarian, would stand by, cane in hand. The *maulvi* would write an Urdu letter on the blackboard and one by one we would be called to read it. The teacher, who did not know Urdu, would ask the *maulvi* 'Right or wrong', and if the letter had been incorrectly read it would instantly be followed by a whack from Fandu's cane, and thus it went on, 'right or wrong', with no sound heart other than the boys reading the *maulvi's* letters punctuated by the swish of Fandu's cane. For some reason a Hindu, whose mother tongue wasn't Urdu, was expecated to pick up the language more quickly than an Anglo-Indian, perhaps because as far as the English were concerned they believed that Hindi and Urdu had and affinity with each other. They haven't. Hindi is as different from Urdu as Latin from Greek, if not more. Hindi, like English, is written from left to right while Urdu is written from right to left, and the scripts are entirely different. It is universally believed that simple Hindi sounds much like Urdu, about which I recollect the person who was completely floored when I politely asked him *ap ka kya ishma shareef hai aur kahan daulat khana*? 'What's your name and where do you live?' A Moslem would hardly make any sense out of *griha-pravesh* a common Hindi word for housewarming. The Nehru Committee Report recommended that Hindustani should be the lingua franca and official language of India under Swaraj while according to M.K. Gandhi 'Hindi or Hindustani alone can be the national language'.[35] The allusion to Hindustani in the Nehru Committee Report shows confusion in thought. 'Hindustani' is a chimera, for every language has two essential constitutuents, the spoken word and the script, and what is the script of Hindustani? However, much as I tried, I couldn't make it in Urdu, and when I got an 'F' against it Fundu called me and said 'you are an Indian, yet you've failed in Urdu. You should go and drown yourself in the Ganges'. The English rulers appeared to have a partiality for Moslems and Moslem culture right from after the Mutiny of 1857 and this continues ever after independence. The Oxford Dictionary, for example, which is considered to be one of the standard ones of the English language has 'Allah' in it but not 'Ishvara'. The UNESCO prints its greetings on New Year's cards in Arabic but not in Sanskrit even though one of the earliest of the British governor generals of India, Warren Hastings got distinguished English scholars to translate Sanskrit classics into English!

From *gurukuls* to *madarass*, from *madarsas* to Convents-education has been continually somersaulting in India. In the Vedic period about 2000 B.C. teaching was oral and the object was to develop character and sharpen the intellect. Even in the age of the Brahmanas which followed immediately after, though there were no books, students learnt the scriptures in the *asharamas* of gurus and there were a kind of mobile schools teachers going round giving lessons at the homes of their pupils. Thus education was taken to the doorstep. The Upanishadic age was one of wisdom with the system remaining more or less the same, but a new element added was that education was also extended to women like Maitreyi and Gangi Vachaknavi. The art of writing came in the age of the Guptas and Mauryas and the Brahmi was used by Ashoka in his records, the Aramaic was introduced in Punjab by the Achaemenian conquaors, from which the Kharoshthi alphabet written from right to left was evolved, but still written manuscripts did not make their debut. By about A.D. 500 to A.D. 1000 education became systematized and famous universities like Nalanda in Magadha and Valabhi in Kathiawar, were established, to which students from abroad too sought admission. Emphasis was given to military education also.

The Moslem conquest gave a setback and the Hindu centres of learning such as Taxila, Nalanda and Vikramshila were destroyed, the teachers fleeing to the existing HIndu kingdoms to escape persecution. It took some time for education to be put back on the rails in *patshalas* and *tols* of the Hindus and the *makhtabs* (usually attached to mosques) for Moslems. Women's education gained some ground, but only among the higher classes. Paper had not yet taken modern shape but there was silk parchment long before the coming of the Moghuls which was manufacted at Sialkot and Shahzudpur. Manuscrips were handwritten, for printing was done for the first time in India only in the mid-sixteenth century by Jesuit missionaries at Goa and Rachol. However libraries of handwritten books were maintained though on a very restricted scale and under royal patronage.

When the British East India Company suceeded the Moslems, education was in a disorganized state The Asiatic Society was founded by Sir William Jones and the Calcutta Madarasa by Warren Hastings the governor general in 1781. Macaulay's famous Minute on Education which led to Bentinck's resolution of 7 March 1835, doubtless gave a great impetus to English, but Indians were perhaps more enthusiastic to imbibe the new rulers' language and culture, as Reverend Alexander Duff observed: 'The excitement for western education continued unabated. They pursued us along the streets; they threw open the doors of our palankeens; they poured their supplications with a pitiful earnestness of countenance which might have softened a heart of stone', and persons like Raja Rammohun Roy decried Sanskrit, Roy saying 'the Sanskrit system of education would be the best calculated to keep the country in darkness...' The schools and universities kept coming, but apparently they could cater only to a few, and the census of 1901 disclosed that only 98 men and 7 women out of a thousand people could read and write. Numerous commissions were appointed, as they always are in every thing in India, their reports museum pieces for archives, for committees, commissions and investigations invariably coming after the horse has bolted from the stable, have but two objects, firstly to sweep the dust under the carpet and secondly to efface the faults and corrupt practices of governments from the public mind. The ponderous sluggish machinery moves after the catastrophy – fire, famine, flood epidemic, accidents, poison gas leack, earthquakes, whatever – never before. 'Preavention' is a word not found in the dictionary of India's politicians and administrators who never fail to visit places and victims that have suffered, to have themselves photographed by eager newsmen so that the people may admire their solicitude for the nation. Thus the outcome of various measures and schemes to advance education in India before and after partition (I would really call it negotiated freedom) was that in 1951, just after four years of Swaraj, there were 167 literate persons out of every 1000, thirty years after the number was just a little more than double, i.e., 362, the increase being a bare 0.65 per cent per year on the average, and with 64 per cent of the people illiterate, education cannot be said to have made any appreciable headway[36] The provisional figures of the census of 1991 proudly proclaimed that the literacy rate showed an impressure growth from 43.56 per cent in 1981 to 52.11 per cent.[37] That leaves about half of India's population illiterate, i.e., they can't even sign their names and only put thumb-impresions on papers which are Greek to them and even among the other half who are literates, a tiny segment only can reach the higher stage of education. In the present times there has hardly been any advance even after forty-seven years of Swaraj, on the contrary education has become more complicated by various new factors. The *gurukuls* and *tols* of old had only the single aim of teaching with dedication while now exploitation has replaced it. English remains the craze and the three or four year old child with his lisp and earliest words, is taught to call his dad 'papa', get going with the English alphabet and proudly come home and say 'ma'm has given me 'very good; rattle off. 'Johnny Johnny yes papa', press the button to turn on the movie cassette on his TV and be puzzled if someone called it 'doordarshan', greet people with 'good morning' and 'good night' and see off with 'bye', There is this two year old grand daughter of mine who meets a repimand with 'sorry *dadi*' (that's her grandmother)! A girl of two or three learns to say 'bye' or 'ta-ta' instead of *namastey* and my grandson who is a little past five will acknowledge a ta or thanks with the very Americanized 'welcome'. To quote Derek Brown again 'New schools are springing out everywhere, Tutors tout their names on signs fixed to treetrunks. Cheap text-book abound in every bazaar. The English most of them offer is at best a rudimentary variation of "*babu*" office language... The preposterous public schools, on the other hand with their blazered uniforms their Latin mottoes, their play-the-game standards, continue to process the offspring of the governing classes, without concession to India, let alone America. Innovation, as we say here, is eschewed, in favour of the quaint but moribund language of another land, when God was in his heaven and there was a stepney in every dickey'[38]

A feature of the Indian educational system which is swiftly eroding efficiency is the crazy race for reservation on various bases like caste, religion and so forth. These reservations, which apart from applying to government jobs–the most coveted employment in this country– have also come to admission in schools and colleges in some provinces. The extent is anything between fifty to eighty per cent, condemning India to eternal mediocrity. Courts keep on ruling such reservations as unconstitution and politicians keep on making them. Democracy in India seems to be a kind seasaw played by the courts and the parliaments, and no sooner a court rules what is unpalatable to palitical parties in power, the parties circumvent it by legislation. Thus the seesaw keeps going up and down, rulings and enactments, enactments and rulings, and it is those who have kept the game on who suffer, the citizens, half of them blissfully unaware of what it's all about, as an American poet and critic says: 'It [democracy] is supposed to reduce all mankind to a dead level of mediocrity in character and culture, to vulgarize men's conceptions of life, and therefore their code of morals, manners and conduct - to endanger the rights of property and possession'.[39] Nothing can be truer of Indian democracy than this. There is a bright side to reservation too. As Gandhi said long back 'The parents take the lead in giving the wrong direction [to students]. they feel that their children should be educated only in order that they may earn wealth and position.... our students are weighed down with cares and worries.'[40] This is as true today as it was then, but reservation has weaned bright students, particularly those with technical education, from prestigious government jobs to careers in prominent business firms which the ogre of reservation has not yet gulped down, and of these a lucky lot are able to get assignments abroad in developed countries whose governments are more interested in merit than in mediocrity. The schoolboy's bag today slung on his back, has become frightfully heavy with subjects like computers and advanced learning at comparitively much earlier stages. No longer is he: 'A laughing school-boy, without grief or care',[41] there is sleepiness in his eyes and weariness on his face. Knowledge has certainly increased but its soul which is morality and character is a clod. The blazered-uniformed and Latin-mottoed 'public' schools could more appropriately be to called 'privileged' schools, there is hardly anything public about them for they are beyond the reach of the middle class, but not of the Indian politican who denounces English education and breathes fire and brimstone against such schools yet sends his boys there, while more than ninety per cent of India's people can't even dream of meeting the cost of education in them.

Another aspect of Indian education is the absence of good text-books and also their spiralling prices. Indeed instead of easing book-publication, our governments believe in putting education on the back-burner, and one province has even levied a trade tax of two per cent on books! With literacy going down the drain in India and governments still looking on education with disdain it seems our politicians are keen to keep Indians illiterate and poorly educated, for obviously it is then easier to misgovern and yet get the votes. Village schools, some of which I have myself seen a few years back, are hardly organized centres of education. There is a school master who's usually absent and when he is there, the boys (rarely girls) sit on the floor on strips of coarse cloth (*tat patties*), intoning their lessons in a sonorous singsong tone, the teacher sitting some way off engrossed in his own work. The school-building, it there is one at all (if there isn't it's just a school under a tree) is often in various stages of dilapidation, so that it hardly gives any protection for the children from wind and rain.

Indian book-publishing is greatly handicapped because of the high cost of paper, poor binding and the lackadaisical attitude of bodies like the University Grants Commission in releasing funds to libraries. The latest move in this field is that leading international publishers are separating from their Indian counterparts and thinking of having their own branches in India. A report says: 'John Wiley and Sons (under the banner of Wiley International) and Longman UK; both among the world's higher academic publishers, have taken advantage of the new regulations [which allow foreign companies having a majority shareholding to float a new company] to break away from their Indian subsidiaries'.[42] It is anybody's guess though, whether this would turn out to be a boom or a regression, for the Indian reader of English is perhaps more at ease with rhyme and metre in verse and the 'moribund language of another land' with its verbiage and cliches, than the 'heavily colloquial and deliberately idiosyncratic' one in vogue.

The high prices of books places them beyond the reach of book-lovers, for even a paperback can't be got for less than a hundred rupees or so, and the days for hardcovers are over for a print order of less than 2000 would be downright uneconomical and with their prices soaring to between three or four hundred, only libraries could be the buyers. Those who have money, the businessmen and men in the professions, are not interested in books and have no time for them and those who are book-lovers have no money. Besides tastes are fast changing and now in the land of the Vedanta and *Gita*, porno reigns supreme. With the Indian readers' newborn insatiable appetite for sex, the publisher who wants to keep on, has to switch over from the serious to the tittilating and the books change their outergarments from wind breakers to flimsy gowns. Then there is the writer who after getting half a dozen or so of the 'Editor's Compliments and Regrets' neatly printed in various forms of courteous innuendoes, finally gets an offer dubious or without strings, and the MOA is executed to the satisfaction of both. But often, as I have found that does not mean a thing, and I have been sent back at least two of my own manuscripts years after. Even when that's not so, the Indian author is much like the Pied Piper when the question of royalty arises:

'When suddenly, up the face
Of the Piper perked in the market-place,
With a "First, if you please, my thousand guilders!"...
So, friend we're not the folks to shrink
From the duty of giving you something for drink,
And a matter of money to put in your poke;
But as for the guilders, what we spoke
Of them, as you very well know, was in joke.
Besides our losses have made us thirfty.
A thousand guilders! Come, take fifty!'[43]

Despite all this Indian publishing marches along turning out hundreds of books in colourful jackets, close competitors of their British and American counterparts except in the binding which survives just a couple of bounces, with neverending sentences sprawling across the pages in defiance of Fewler and Gowers.

My father, who was working then in the Civil Secretariat as a clerk, had saved a little money from his meagre earning and thought of buying a second-hand car. He was on the way to get one which he had seen, when he was told that an Englishman who was about to leave India wanted a buyer for his car. So he went to him with about fifteen hundred rupees in his pocket. 'Oh, that's too little' the man said 'my car is spit and polish, I'm an owner-driver, don't let anyone else touch it' My father said, 'Well then I'll have to forego it, fifteen hundred is all I have'. The Englishman's passage was booked and he had to leave that same day to get his ship from Bombay (there weren't any planes then) so he reluctantly took the cash and my father, who had brought a driver with him got into the car. It was a Ford 29 model with a collapsible hood, a sturdy car made to last, a real bargain. The Secretariat was then in part of the building which housed the Accountant-General's office in Allahabad. The car replaced the ekka in taking me to school and when it came to fetch me home I went to my father's office first which closed about half-an-hour or so after, so that he could also come back by the Ford. The Secretariat was rather cramped, for space was very short for two such prominent offices of the government (it was British rule then, the year 1931). The paper slips having the letters of the alphabet placed neatly in a wooden case on the office-rack, delighted me. These was then used for flagging references. There were also blue and red slips with 'IMMEDIATE' and 'URGENT' printed on them. These are still used in the offices of today but they have no significance any more.

In school in class four and five we had two very different classmasters. Good old Fandu was a well-meaning man but so much of a disciplinarian that we dubbed the class as 'hell'. De Souza who taught us in class five was a kind man, soft-spoken and forgiving most of our failings, and so we called his class 'heaven'. It was a quick transition from hell to heaven, save for those who had the misfortune of staying behind, for there was no purgatory in between. Alas! my stay in 'heaven' was soon cut short, for the British Indian governemnt decided to shift the Secretariat from Allahabad to Lucknow, and it was mid-session. Allahabad was an important town with the High Courts the Accountant-General's office and the Secretariat, and a host of other government offices, and really the de facto capital of the United Provinces but a rather gloomy place, a kind of Sleepy-Hollow, while Lucknow was pulsating with activity. My father took me there once or twice to see my sister who was a babe when my mother died and was being taken care of by my mother's sister, and the glitter of the town fascinated me. So I was happy when I learnt this, but of course my father wasn't, for it meant leaving behind the house which had been his home for almost forty years, so the whole family along with its partaiarch, my grandfather who had retired after meritoriously serving the British Indian government as deputy collector, the highest assignment a native was entitled to; moved over to Lucknow after selling off the old ancestral house. Its memories still linger in a corner of my mind, for the brain, one of the many miracles of our God-given human bodies, forgets nothing and keeps storing away all odds and ends like an old *kabariwallah* putting things in his sack.[44] There was the varanda with the corrugated iron-sheet roof, the *saur* (for lying-ins) where the pregnant women would rest segregated from everyone, till the period of confinement. Here were born all babies with just a widwife to carry out the childbirth. There were no obstetricians, no caesareans and no nursing-homes. The reason for the lying-in isolation was that there were no antibiotics and the only way to prevent infection of the baby and the mother was by a self-imposed segregation with as few attendants as possible. The nursing mother was given a special diet of *harila* and *sithaura*, the constituents being gum, dried-fruits, molasses and other nutriments. Maybe there was a proportion of infant mortality too, but the children who survived were strong and healthy despite not getting the large package of vaccines and drugs that are doled out to babies now. Mangoes were my grandfather's weakness, as indeed they are for many others, so much so that he would count their number on the trees, of which there were many excellent varieties, while they were yet unripe! But we youngsters, braving the scorching summer wind would upset his calculations by stealing out as soon as we heard his siesta-snores, wrenching off the low-hanging green fruit from the twigs and secretly savouring their sour tang with pinches of salt. When I was about ten I fell ill with pneunonia, considered to be a serious and often fatal disease in those pre-antibiotic days, and it took me more than a month to recover. My grandfather, who was adept in Urdu and Persian, but knew no Hindi, bought a book from a pavement-seller, *Tota-Maina, Athon Bhaga* (*The Parroat and the Starling*) by Pandit Rangilal, apparently a happy-go-lucky jovial writer (*rangi* meaning 'gay' or 'passionate'). The book had a jacket with the picture of two birds sitting on the branches of a tree, though doubtless if it had been published these days it would have a smasling young beauty with peep-through-the bra-breasts, and it would surely have been discarded, but the birds were innocent enough. My grandfather gave it to a young brahmin servant to read out to me the stories of illicit amours and lovely young girls which featured within its inncuous covers. The servant who had a nodding acquaintance with Hindi must have got a kick out of it for the invocation by the author on the inside said, 'for the entertainment of amorous people', but as for me the only purpose it served was that the sonorous voice of the brahmin boy put me to sleep[45]

So we arrived at Lucknow in 1935 and took a house on rent. There are more officials today in one department out of hundreds in the Secretariat than the entire lot then right from a peon to the chief secretary, just about 200-250 odd. The British government in India too cared for its servants, of whatever rank, much more than our Indian government now, and each person was allotted a decent-sized plot in a posh locality for building his house, at a subsidized rate on lease, later made freehold after paying a nominal sum. Our rented house was in a lonely spot in the city, so we engaged a watchmen for the night, but he turned out to be a queer, like other servants. After half-a-term in St Francis I got into La Martiniere, the most prestigious college in the city then.

5

SLAVERY AND INDEPENDENCE

Excess of liberty, whether in states or
individuals, seems only to pass into excess of slavery.

PLATO

After Partition, the Indian administrative machine remained practically the same except for the change in names, for which we seem to have a craze. A country which takes pride in preserving its monuments pulled down the lovely white marble statues of queen Victoria and on their pedestals came up uncouth black ones of various Indian leaders, the great and the insignificant, politically and personally motivated, inaugurated with fanfare and flourish and garlanded by *netas*, out to flaunt themselves. It would have made Megasthenes, the Greek ambassador of Selucus Nicator turn in his grave. He came to India in the Mauryan period (early fourth century B.C.) and recorded, the 'Indians do not rear monuments to the dead, but consider the virtues which men have displayed in life, and the songs in which their praises are celebrated sufficient to preserve memory after death'.[46] What a comedown from the time India (Bharat) was free twenty-four centuries before to when it became free again in the twentieth! The names of the roads were changed, the Hindus and Moslems fighting to have them named after leaders of their own respective communities. For example the name of the road on which I live created a furore the Hindus wanting a Hindu name, the Moslems a Moslem one, till the problem was solved by the British who were packing up, by giving it the innocuous name of South Avenue Road; all to no purpose for as soon as the Anglo-Indians had gone away to Australia, where for some unaccountable reason they felt they would be better off, and the Englishmen sailed for home South Avenue Road, on Shastri's death became Lal Bahadur Shastri Marg, 'Windsor Place' being perhaps retained out of consideration to independent India's first governor general. The Anglo-Indians who precipitately migrated to Australia did not appear to get a good deal there. My brother, who went to Australia for a year to study construction projects met one who bemoaned his lot. He was a deputy secretary in India, quite an exalted position. When he went over he was asked to fill a form giving details of the kind of work he was doing in India. He proudly wrote, 'I would get files from my department on which I gave orders and signed' They concluded he would be suitable for making inventories and gave him the job of a storekeeper!

The Indian Civil Service (the ICS) called a covenanted service because the employer was the Secretary of State for India, had nothing Indian about it except the name. Initially the examination for entry into it was held in Britain and very few Indians could afford the expenses of going abroad and face the social stigma which followed on their return. Most of the ICS men were Britishers. Indians could reach only a low level in the administration or the judiciary which was also manned by a section of the ICS. For example an Indian could rise utmost to the position of a deputy collector in the administrative line, a munsif in the judicial and an assistant secretary in the Secretariat. As Attlee remarked:

> '... India was protected by an Indian Army–Indians officered by British in all the higher ranks–and by British units. It was absolutely essential in the conditions of the world at that time that we should have a certain number of British forces there and Indianisation of the officers could only be done very slowly. Earlier there had been viceroy-commissioned Indian officers- almost glorified sergeant–majors–and although there were some young ones coming on there wasn't at that time, I think a single officer of the field rank.... More than half the British in the Indian Civil Service had gone [on the eve of Mountbatten's assignment in India]. The ICS Indians worked extremely loyally, *but it was idle to suppose that they weren't just as patriotic as everybody else and just as enthusiastic for Indian nationalism.*[49]

As regards the army, the British had lost trust in Indian officers right from the Mutiny, and even before that it was almost wholly under British supervision, but it was strange that even the Indian ICS, were suspect. It was the policy of the British to humiliate and distrust Indians, and of Indians, the Hindus more. It was there long before Attlee. In 1883 the Ilbert Bill proposed that all district magistrates and sessions judges (a handful of whom were Indians) would be designated ex-officio Justice of the Peace, and so would be able to try all Europeans and Englishmen. As a reaction the editor of the prestigious *Spectator* wrote:

> 'Would you like to live in a country where at any moment your wife would be liable to be sentenced on a false charge of slapping an ayah, to three day's imprisonment, the magistrate being a copper coloured pagan who probably worships the *linga*, and certainly

exalts any opportunity of showing that he can insult the white person with impunity'.

The Eurasian and Anglo-Indian association presented a memorial to the governor general in council saying that the natives of India 'are not peers and equals of Englishmen. The trial of an Englishman by one who is not his peer, is an infringement of a great constitutional right'[48]

A deputy collector or a lower Indian official, would have to take off his shoes before entering an English officer's room and put off his cap. Of course the Indian enjoyed much greater dignity, izzat as he would call it, than his counterpart in free India. When my grandfather, while in service as a *hakim pargana* (the sub-divisional magistrate of today), went touring in the villages, it was on horseback then, or in a phaeton where the road would allow it passage, the villagers would line up on each side, bow, and present gold *asharfis* to him, not to pocket but just so that the *hakim pargana* sahib would touch it with his hand, and that they considered a signal honour. There *was* corruption but only up to a certain level. An official up to the tahsildar was game, but when he went higher, he eschewed money and exchanged grease for integrity. It was not as we have it today when the sky's the limit. The British, despite Clive's *jagir* and Hastings's Begams of Oudh – only a few among many – prized hard work and honesty. When repairs were being carried out sometime back in independent India in a government treasury, some gold coins of the Raj were discovered the inscription on which said that they were for 'rewarding honest officials'.

The British ICS officers were whimsical and some of their Indian counterparts were no less so. There was one of them, Nethersole, who called his head-babu and told him. 'I am Nethersole, but if you don't see that I get my salary on the first of each month I will become "Leathersole" '. There was another who had a unique way of meeting visitors by which he ultimately succeeded in getting rid of all of them. He would call his orderly and ask him, *kitna log hai*? ('How many visitors are there?') Sahib *atha das hai* ('There are eight or ten, sahib'). *Theek hai*, *theek hai* ('All right') the sahib would mutter. After some time he'd ask him again how many had come and was told the number. So it went on till there were about thirty or forty persons waiting. He would get up and going to them say *tum log hamse milne aya hai?* ('You have come *to meet me?*') and on their nodding their heads, *accha, aj ka tamasha ho gaya, kal phir hoga* ('All right today's show is over, tomorrow we'll have it again'). The visitors stood it for a few days, thinking the sahib might be busy with other important matters, but soon the truth dawned on them and they faded away. Another ICS man, who hated touring, would sit at his table for a few days, then one morning he would shift his chair on the other side of it, call his orderly and say *dekho, hum daura par chala gaya* ('See, I've gone on tour!').

There was no money-under-the-table (new it is passed over it without compunction) there was only baksheesh and *dalis* (a basket of dried fruits and other delicacies made as an offering). With things dirt cheap this wasn't any drain on the pocket. Baksheesh was the regular thing, just as a tip in a restaurant. There was this sahib who was having a bath and outside a kind of haggling for baksheesh was going on. It was a *seth* (businessman) rather miserly. 'It'll be ten rupees', the orderly said, for youv'e come on a Sunday'. 'Ten! come on, take six', 'All right seven, not seven either, then eight'. The sahib who was listening and had done, put his towel round and peeping out of the side-door said *Are le le, le le, bara kanjus hai, is se jyada nahin dega* ('Oh, take it, he's a hunks and won't give more!').

There was the British district magistrate who was faced with a communal problem – which still keeps coming up – the Moslems wanted to take out a *tazia* procession on a route to which the Hindus objected. The British ICS officer tried to effect a compromise, but all in vain. In desperation, he told the two leaders, the Hindu and the Moslem to come with him and talk it over. He went to a depression a little distance away. There catching hold of their heads (he was a tall and stalwart man) he kept banging them saying each time, *tazia idhar se jaye ga ki udhar se* ('will the *tazia* go this way or that?') After a few such bashings, the two exclaimed *huzoor jidhar se ap kahenge udhar se jayega* ('Sahib, it will take the route you decide on') And so the problem was solved in a few moments! So effective is Kautilya's *danda* [punishment].

It was difficult to meet an ICS officer at his home an the man to be tackled for it was his orderly who knew his sahib out and out. There was this man who got on the wrong side of him, but insisted that the sahib should get his visiting-card. As he was a prominent man of the town, the orderly couldn't refuse but as there was no baksheesh, he also whispered to the sahib that it seemed the visitor had the itch for he was scratching himself all over. It was one of diseases the sahibs dreaded, so he told his orderly to have him out instantly. The man had learnt his lesson so next time when he came after a few days he was generous and the orderly was quick to announce him. 'But isn't this the man who had an itch?' The sahib said. 'It is, *huzur*, but he has been treating it and it's gone now'. 'All right then call him in'. The 'itch-man' would never know about how the orderly managed it, but he never again forgot the baksheesh. My father told me how he had managed to make it. This particular Englishman was strict. No *dallies*. That was the problem. The orderly thought it over and said 'All right you bring one and I'll try' When the *dali* came, the orderly opened the packets of dried-fruits on the top and placed the basket in the room. The sahib was busy doing some work and his children (the *baba-log*) were playing in the room. The orderly beckoned to the open packets and the *baba-log* were at them taking out fistfuls. Meanwhile the sahib had finished what he was doing and walked in. Seeing the baskets he asked the orderly how it had come there. *Ek admi huzur se milne aya hai* the orderly said, *dali laya hai.* ('A man has come to meet you, he has brought it'). The sahib frowned *Dali* he said, *dali nahin cahiye le jayo use lauta do* ('I don't want any *dali*, take it away and return it ti him'). The orderly pointed to the children and said they had eaten some of the dried-fruits and would it be nice to return it now. That did it. 'All right' he said 'tell him to come'. My father had some reasonable request to make, and the work was done. It was difficult to meet the British ICS officer, but once with him it was easy to have the work done for their 'yes' really meant yes. It's the other was round now, you may meet the his Indian counterpart in independent India (after cooling your heels for sometime in his personal assistant's room) but all you'll get out of him will be some sort of non-committal answer like 'I'll see' or 'I'll have it examined', every time you go.

The Indian ICS were almost as hard to approach as the British ones, and some were just as capricious. One of them was a commissioner of whom various stories were current about his kinks. It was said he wouldn't ever deign to speak to his servant. His wife had gone away for sometime so his cook would serve him food. He started with one *chappati* then, two and three. When he served four, the commissioner rang his wife 'Come at once, the cook is overfeeding me'! He wouldn't speak to his chauffeur either, but the man knew the commissioner's office and drove him there every morning. One day he just sat on the car and when it reached his office, he shook his head, meaning 'no'. The other places he used to go to were the government house and the district club, so the chauffeur drove him to these places and seeing him vigorously wag his head each time, took the car home and opened its door for him to step out. This ICS man was scared stiff of infection, so much that once when his car had a breakdown on the highway and a tonga was brought for him to continue the journey, he insisted on having it disinfected throughly before sitting on it! These are hearsay accounts, but related by people who could not possibly fake them and they have the ring of truth for at least his crazy bacteriophobia was seen by me once. The commissioners of those days (the first decade of Swaraj when there were a scattering of ICS officers yet) paid just one visit to each district in their change each fall, not as now, almost every month. This ICS man camped in an inspection-house almost seven kilometres away from our district. A high ICS officer whether Indian or English, indeed more so the Indian, was a Raj to himself and except for the howdahed-elephants and the royal retinue, his durbars on occasions such as the commissioner's winter-visit, or the New Year's Day which was then more relevant than Holi, Diwali or Idd, were the same as the Moghul *jharoka-i-darshan*, except that instead of the *jharoka* there was just a chair. After this durbar at the inspection-house the commissioner paid his flying visit to the district which then had a young bachelor ICS as its district magistrate. The DM had cautioned us about the commissioner's fad, so we placed our chairs almost eight or ten feet away from his table. As soon as he entered and saw us he furiously waved us off exclaiming *door door* ('more away further'!). So we all took our chairs and shifted further away. Giving us all a close look, we happened to freshers as it was a small first-posting district, he said [to the collector] 'have you told the government that all your officers are young and inexperienced *including yourself*?'!

Despite their freakishness, the decisions and orders of the ICS officers had a quickness and finality that those of our present civil servants lack. In the Raj even a day's delay in disposal of a letter (which we euphemistically now call a 'reference') had to be explained. Now an official may sit over a paper a month, a year or till Doomsday. There are numerous reasons for this, but if we were to group them under heads, one would be 'the system' and the other pure and simple idleness and stalling, I had the occasion of seeing some of the old files of the Secretariat of the Raj. The job of the office, and that meant the clerks, was only to put up the paper and the precedent, in other words look up what previous orders existed in the matter, along with the letter received (the abbreviation being 'w/r'). That was all. The entire noting on the file the notes being brief and to the point was done by the officers, of whom there were few and mostly, at least till 1947, of the British ICS. The administrative ladder had just two rungs, the deputy secretary and the secretary. The chief secretary of those times was just secretary of the appointment department and he had no jurisdiction over other departments nor any authority to interfere with their working. There were no mammoth conferences with teas and packed lunches resembling more political gatherings than administrative meetings, no 'please speak' on files which has now become a frequent device to evade a decision. My father used to say that he learnt about the change in the secretary of his department – from Langford to Gwynne, from Gwynne to Mudie and so forth – only when the signatures on the files changed. If a senior officer wished to consult has junior colleague, he would just walk across to his room and do so. At four-o-clock in the evening the British ICS officer, clearing his table, would pick up his tennis racquet, change shoes and be off. No late evening meetings on official discussions. He distinguished work from play, which we do not. Quite a few files went to the governor who usually was the final authority. When the concluding order was passed [there was often disagreement], the file came back marked to the office ('o'), for putting up the draft for conveying the decision ('dfa') which the superintendent (now termed 'section officers') did, writing it out [in English] by hand. It was here that the bloomers and gaffes came. There was the governor of the North-West Frontier Province who ordered for a more aggressive policy and wrote 'we have so long been barking, but now we should bite'. The flummoxed *babu*, quite reasonably associating a bark and a bite with a dog but understandably reluctant to associate the governor with one, wrote in his draft 'His Excellency has been so far barking, but now he is going to bite'! Then there was the secretary of a department an IAS officer, who had the audacity of sending a reminder by name [a 'DO'] to an ICS member of the board of revenue in which I was then serving as an assistant commissioner. The piqued member wrote on it 'What cheek', and sent the letter to the office. The *babu* to whom the letter came wondered what draft reply he ought to put up for being familiar with the human anatomy he was puzzled why one cheek had been mentioned instead of two, and sought my help. I told him that it meant that he should forget about the whole thing and no reply was required.

The secretariats and indeed all other government offices and important places like government houses where the governors lived were quite different then. English officers hated being enclosed by walls and armed sentries at their gates, nor did they have any need for such trappings. Their houses had no boundary-walls, only hedges, and so too the offices. The Secretariat at Lucknow, capital of the United Provinces, had no wall surrounding it, just a hedge and barbed wire stretched on steel angle-pillars. Sten guns were only for the army and the British ICS officers were content with their orderlies. Governors like Hallet and others played golf in a government house with only a waist-high boundary wall, and running outside it was a narrow mud-strewn pathway on which the British sahibs along with their memsahibs would go horseriding and gallop along, the mud preventing the horses' slipping. The Lucknow Secretariat was planned by an English architect, Mortimer, whose name still figures on a marble slab inside, but that and the bright brass knobs on the solid doors in the rooms of the old building, is about all that remains of that magnificently conceived and beautifully executed building, airy, with spacious rooms and corridors covered by thick carpets on which officials and visitors treaded softly with muted steps careful lest they cause disturbance to the officers inside. Forty-seven years of independence have reduced the lovely building to a maze shorn of light and air, where hundreds of coolers (for the *babus*) and air-conditioners (for the IAS folk, the successors of the British ICS.) buzz, making the whole place look like a factory rather than an office, every inch of space used up for the ever-expanding bureaucracy the secretaries – joint, special, additional and principal. It is amazing how we have systematically ruined the gifts of the Raj or made them mark time. The grand hospitals with names changed from George or Victoria to Gandhi or the Nehrus, have become fillhy with the johns overflowing with shit, the cracked plasters, sweepresses with soiled rags fixed to wooden staves moving them too and fro to sweep the agelong wornout floors and rude nurses and indifferent doctors. I once had the misfortune of staying in one of these general-wards of the 'GMH' (in India there is always in everything the general and the special) and the four days in it were real torture. There was one bedpan for three wards each with about forty beds, which meant one between 120 patients all of whom were confined to the bed with fractures. The poor, who could not afford to buy a bedpan would start shouting from four or five a.m. 'Ghasitey'– the sweeper, in plaintive voices, *are bhai Ghasitey ab to a jao* ('O brother, Ghasitey, come, delay no longer') for the urge to relieve their bowels was getting stronger with each passing moment, but brother Ghasitey was busy attending on those who could tip him a couple of rupees for each use of the bedpan. In the evening a hospital orderly came and took away all the iron stools on which the attendants sat for there would be a class of freshers held in the ward and the stools were needed for them. There was a boy of about 12 or 14 years, his leg in plaster, and something fixed inside it kept pressing the leg, so from about midnight he would start screaming in agony, *hai mar gaye* ('O, I'm dying') but the doctors came and went, usually so swiftly as though they had to catch a train, just glancing at the bed-tickets, and no one bothered about the boy, till one day a relation of his arrived from the village and seeing the distress of the child got hold of a sharp knife and cut away the plaster – perhaps what the doctors ought to have done long back.

And as against that, I had to stay once in the days of the Raj at the 'B' – hospital, to prepare for which event, a special silk nightclothes were made for me. The Raj always distinguished between Englishmen and natives – the BMH (British Military Hospital and the IMH (Indian Military Hospital) the clubs exclusively for Englishmen and so forth. An Indian was unwanted in his own country. Of course he isn't any better off now as a citizen, for freedom has brought with it through the years, what may be called the tyranny of government departments with which he is often concerned – the electricity (power or 'Hydel'), banks, insurance, post and telegraphs telecommunication (telephone) food (supply) and the innumerable other sections of the government. But of that later. This hospital the 'B' had two distinct divisions. One outside a gate was for Indians, that inside, where I went, was for Anglo-Indians; they had made an exception in my case. There wasn't really much wrong with me, just some fever, perhaps induced by a cold, and I was well again soon, but the few days I was there were delightful. No attendant was allowed and I was all by myself. The room I was in was spotlessly clean, with lovely curtains and fixtures. There was a bell push hanging by my bedside and I could, I was told, have a nurse instantly to attend on me. I was about fourteen then, and one night at about 1 a.m. when I was awake I thought of testing it, so I pressed the button. A few moments after the nurse was standing before me. These were all Anglo-Indian nurses there. To make up for it I asked her for a glass for water After the fever had gone a nurse gave me a rub with a wet towel. She got all my clothes off and covering my loins with another towel got busy talking all the time. Her hands were all over me and I don't know if she got a kick out of it, but I was too young to be aroused and I was feeling rather embarrassed. The hospital was spotlessly clean, a neat well-maintained toilet attached and not a sound heard except the soft steps of doctors and nurses in the corridor. The food was very good, served with testeful imported cutlery.

For everything that fails with us, it is the 'system; which is blamed, whether it is a serious railway accident, a plane crash, a scandal, scam or fraud, a power failure, an epidemic, corruption, anything. There are inquiries and reports. If anyone too high up is found guilty he is let off, and if he is lower down he may be punished. But usually the finding is that it is a 'system-failure', though what this means remains a mystery, for behind most 'system-failures' there is someone who has bungled, either in the manufacture of the part which has caused the mishap, or in the working. The former is a combination of corruption and carelessness, the latter of inefficiency and indolence. Quality control is not maintained, and the items which make the machine are passed because the person concerned wishes to favour a particular firm. The slipshod working is perhaps because of imperfect knowledge of what the man is handling, but more often because of lack of interest in what he's doing or he doesn't want the new sophisticated device as it offers less scope for corruption. So we have hydraulic jacks which fail to completely close various parts of the plane so that the engine has to work under strain which may exhaust the fuel before time, wheels that fail to slide out, causing belly landings, railway signals that don't always function so that trains ran into one another, electric transformers which fail causing prolonged power breakdowns, buses which have outlived their life and being still pressed into service cause accidents and so forth. You ask for a new power connection and after a great deal of rigmarole and perhaps soap, you get a overhead cable with a few joints from where it may burst when it rains hard, circuit breakers which burn up, meters whose points get out of function soon after they are installed. The result is that you have to replace the sub-standard parts supplied by the power department and fixed by them and charged to your account, by genuine ones. This is not the end of one's troubles. There are wrong bills to be righted and those received with an 'NR' on them which means 'your metre has not been read'. The electricity department does not have the capacity to get metres read, so they hand out the metre-reading to 'contractors' on a fixed payment. The contractor pockets the money and just gets NR entered on all the bills (the VIPs are an exception, as they are in everything). The consumers crowd round to get bills corrected in serpentine queues and after the *palm-oil* they may be successful or else hear some brash stuff and go back in a huff. There was a private company in the Raj known as Martin Burn which departed with it, leaving happy reminiscences of its efficiency and ever since Indira Gandhi put the bulldozer to private enterprise and the government bit off more than it could chew, we have to put up with fluctuating voltage, power-cuts and power failures terribly long waits for repairing pole-fuses and so on. Surgeons have to leave patients lying on operation tables in the middle and the harried attendants rush to fetch gaslamps; I recollect once in a prestigious hospital in a district town the power went off just after they took my daughter to the operation theatre for her appendix operation leaving us all plunged in anxiety and we learnt later that the surgeon, who luckily was expert at the job, had operated in torchlight! India can never have trouble-free steady-voltage and continuous electricity for the transmission wires almost everywhere run overhead on iron poles and since streets have huge trees lining them, the authorities responsible for felling the ones with dangerously protuding branches and rotting trunks, passing up their presence; the power goes off as soon as a strong wind blows. The power-stations have now even started putting it off themselves when this happens! The expenditure to replace these miles and miles of overhead wires will be impossible to bear for a country so poor as India.

This of course is only one of those countless things in which we have hit the skids. Take sanitation. There's a lane running alongside our house which was made in the Raj for conservancy purposes when the Secretariat moved to Lucknow in 1935 and the colonies for its employees came into existence. While the British government ruled, there was a tall man the head-*jamadar* (the man supervising the sweepers) with a stentorian voice who would stand every morning outside the lane and shout at the sweepers to keep working whenever he found them lax. Then he would call my father ad say 'See sahib, the lane is spotlessly clean, not a leaf anywhere.' And so it was. The women of the houses skirting the lane would use it for visiting one another. On prominent festivals such as Holi and Diwali, he would come and salaam and be content with a couple of rupees as baksheesh. Ever since independence came the man with his sweepers disappeared, garbage piled up often waist-deep the manhole covers were no longer in place, the sewer wasn't cleaned, the muck overflowed and squealing fifth-eating pigs made the lane their dwelling place. It couldn't have been worse, but it was, to our dismay. The place became an ideal meeting ground for peddlers and drug addicts. Periodically the rotting corpse of a dead dog wrapped in a gunny bag would be there and when it began smelling awful, frantic appeals sometimes heeded often unheeded, had to be made to the corporation to have it removed, and once instead of dogs it was a man decomposed and stinking till the body got removed. Corruption, inefficiency, lack of funds and political interference have made our corporations and village panchayats nonperforming and often oppressive, much like the one of Hamelin town in need of the Pied Piper whom they can't pay. Whether in or out of government control the story remains the same, garbage-piled unlit bumpy roads with gaping coverless manholes littered with banana skins and peanut peels, contaminated drinking water, when it comes at all and arbitrary inflated tax bills which make you miss a heartbeat and be resigned to grease.

In our crazy planning, decisions are hasty, resulting in taking steps from which we have soon to back out. For example the Indian constitution framed in a hurry by copycats, has had seventy-eight amendments in forty-seven years, while statutes like the Indian Telegraph Act and those governing the post offices and railways.have hardly been touched when they really needed to be made customer-friendly. The amendments of the constitution have opened the floodgates of repression by giving the right to the Indian parliament of amending it (the 24th amendment) and while the seven freedoms remain protected the protection is just a cocoon which tyrranical governments can get rid of any moment.[49] It is here that we have marked time by pulling down what we have built and in not building where we should have, thus putting the kibosh on democracy and preserving colonialism.

About forty years back there was a flash flood in Lucknow with about two-third of the town under water. I was working as a deputy secretary then in the Secretariat and since it was an emergency, along with other officers. I was put on flood duty, the district magistrate still being the supervisory authority, but working under the direction of the chief secretary. We were given two hundred rupees for sundries. I was told that I was to be in charge of camp number so and so for flood affected people who had fled home because of the flooded waters. The roads being sunk in water with boats plying over them, the place I was allotted was approachable only by rail from the city station to Dalibagh just a distance of three or four miles, but the rush of people moving about was so great that the train went jam-packed and every time it started to move someone or other pulled the alarm signal and it stopped. So it took almost five hours for the train to cover those four miles! When, after this torturous journey I reached the place where the camp was to be, along with just one helper, a clerk in an office, there was no camp, only people sitting of lying on the ground or on cots they were able to procure. No one could enlighten me about the 'camp'. Meanwhile it was nearing sunset and I thought if I could not get back, I would be another homeless refugee at that forsaken place. Luckily a railway engine was going to the city station so I persuaded the driver to let the two of us get inside and while he stoked the fire in the steam-engine's furnace we had a quick return for there was no question of chain-pulling and all that. Next day we were instructed to issue ration-cards on plain paper under our signatures and that the government had decided to distribute flour, rice, sugar and other essential commodities on them. So I took a battery-operated mike and loudspeaker on hire from a firm for a day and the next morning kept announcing that rations would be distributed. By the time of my departure hundreds of such temporary ration-cards were made and given to the flood-victims. But on reaching home, tired after this task, lo! a government message was there telling me that the policy had changed and there would be no rations! I feared to return there for they would recognize me as the man who came with a cloth bag and mike and handed out those signed slips – there was no distinctive proof of my being an agent of the government, not even a cop; and I would be treated as an imposter and perhaps given a sound thrashing. So I went, but made no mention of the sudden reversal in the government 'policy'. Thus it went on and finally the people who sat in the committee-room of the secretariat blissfully unaware of what was happening on the spot, suddenly realized that there couldn't be any camps without *shamianas* (large tents) or *ballies* (wooden poles). So an officer was deputed to carry these by the crawling train and he arrived one day while I was on the camp-site and sullenly dumped the *ballies* and *shamiana.* Anyway a good four or five days after there was, for the first time, something to do, and I got busy getting the *shamianas* pitched with the assistance of the local labour available. By this time the government realized what should have stuck out a mile right from the start that the stranded people out there had no arrangement for cooking and so cooked food was the need not foodgrains; something the social workers, but for whom many would have starved, knew long before for during my train journeys often in open bogies of a goods train, I would find myself surrounded by voluntary organizations carrying basketful of *puries* to feed the flood affected people. And so almost a week or ten days after we got instructions for opening government-kitchens. By that time the flood waters had largely receded and those stranded had returned home to clean up and salvage what the flood had left usable, so the 'camp' had practically no flood sufferers, only those poor houseless people who would like free meals at public expense! While I was returning one evening a khaddar-clad youth stopped me and asked what was going on. I told him all we had been doing and after listening patiently, he said *ap log kuch jaldi aa gaya* ('you government guys seem to have arrived rather early!'). And that I think summed up the whole flood-relief operation better than an editorial could have done.

Thus the Indian system while dealing with times normal as well as abnormal, keeps hip-hopping like a grasshopper with much noise but little action. In calamities it moves up and down like the needle in a sick man's electrocardiograph, getting at solutions long after the need for them is no more and relapsing into laxity a soon as they have passed. For example recently there was a plague epidemic. Age-old garbage heaps began to claim attention and futile half-hearted efforts made to remove them, and that too in areas where the VIPs lived, so much so that from such VIP places rats reported dead from any cause were whisked away on ambulances which normally weren't available even for people having heart-attacks!; and as soon as the epidemic faded out the garbage-heaps were forgotten awating another epidemic. The 'system' passes up the ordinary citizen and caters specifically to those who matter, who constitute a handful. While we call our institutions democratic they are in truth feudal in their essence.

I was admitted to class five of an Anglo-Indian college a very ancient institution founded by a Frenchman, who it was said won the sprawling and majestic monument which housed it in a cook-fight. It was a lovely building, semicircular, with a very high plinth and a tall rectangular structure in its middle having crisscross steps by which one could reach the balcony at the top. There was also an underground passage beneath the building. Toward the front a number of stone steps led to the drive and across it was a T-shaped lake with tall ornamental lat in the middle. On the plinth there was an ancient canon and the steps were copiously covered by Martinians who had neatly recorded their names by cutting the stones. The lake provided opportunity for fishing when the water rose in it in the rains, and after class at lunch-time there would be a line of enthusiastic anglers with improvised line and hook down the slope for there were plenty of earthworms for bait. Down the drive was the tuck shop managed by the College boys themselves where patties were the favourite. The chapel and library were housed in the middle and beyond was the passage skirting the principal's office which was studiously avoided by the boys for fear of disturbing him – such was discipline those days. Adjoining this old building was a passage with wooden lockers where one could keep what he wished to leave behind before going to class, and which served as a place to put our hats (topees) too. This led to the new wing with the grand Spence Hall, having a wooden floor, a commodious and grand place with a stage and verandas on three sides and balconies all round its upper storey with classrooms alongside the veranda on one side. The hall served admirably for holding examinations, plays, functions like the annual Founder's day and prize-distribution and also as a dance-hall. Behind, in the old building there was the swimming pool, One could get on to the high plinth by the steps or by a pathway up one side and down the other. The dormitories were towards the entrance lining the drive, the whole college having a huge area of land several hundred acres belonging to it, but gradually quite a bit taken over by the government after independence for housing its ever-expanding ministers' residences.

Those were the days before the rot in the Indian educational system had set in. The universities had distinguished professors to teach and students eager to learn, and whatever politics had infiltrated the campuses was linked with the spirit of Swaraj and net with destructive agitation. The schools and colleges followed suit and were to a large extent disciplined. There were of course, the schools and colleges with Latin mottoes, universities too, like *Laboret Constantia, Semper Sersem*, and (for the university of Allahabad *Quot rami tot arbores* ['as many branches so many trees']. But admission wasn't so tough as it is now. For example, in one of the prestigious present day colleges a man seeking admission for his daughter was asked if he could foot the bill, which they said would come to about twenty-five thousand rupees, for educating an orphaned child! The man couldn't, so his daughter didn't get in. Most such schools which are at the top and therefore the most sought after, interview the child's parents instead of the child! Besides there is the donation and a tall sum alone does it. Maybe it's the population explosion that's responsible, or perhaps it's just greed, however, as in many other spheres, dedication has given way to exploitation. Anyway the schools with 'blazered uniforms and Latin mottoes', spread all over India are still the most coveted ones for those who can dish out the dough.

The Anglo-Indian schools insisted on uniforms and lining up and marching to the classrooms. We went so till the hat-locker where we kept our topees. The uniform has been adopted for almost all schools now, the ones for the common people as well as for the privileged, but the disciplined entry into classrooms was exclusive for the Anglo-Indian ones. I was to learn this much later when I had done my senior school certificate. At that time in class eight we had to appear for the junior certificate and in class ten for the school certificate. These examinations were conducted by the Cambridge University at the recognized overseas centres and the sealed packet of papers, coming by sea from England, was ceremoniously opened by the local bishop, the answer-books too going there for marks. One year the ship carrying them met with disaster and ever since then we had to make carbon-copies so that one could be retained and the other sent. Our teachers, the principal and the vice-principal were mostly Englishmen but there were a few Anglo-Indians too and only a sprinkling of Indians. Those were still the days of small classes, just about thirty or thirty-five students to a class and of those only four or five would be Indians. Reservation for any caste or community was quite unknown but being basically Christian insitutions there were concessions in fees and admission for deserving Christians. The system was in any case far better than the idiosyncratic caste and religion oriented one in the India of today.

British rectitude and *true bluism* are no longer what they were in the post-Victorian era, having yielded to the fleshly and the soft-shell. British princesses and heir-apparents go caterwauling and get involved in affairs and scandals played up by ambitious journalists and the highfaulting royalty seems to be in the doghouse. But in those times British character was on the upcome and impartiality was their national characteristic. We had a taste of that in the college, so much so that during one prize-distribution (held annually on the Founder's day celebrations) a British governor and patron of the college noticing that most of the winners were Indian boys expressed his dismay in the speech he gave later at the poor achievement of the non-Indians. That was of course the spirit of pax Britannica working in the minds of British imperialists who could not understand why if Britain could rule the waves it could not rule minds. The English teachers were, however, scruplously fair and they recognized and prized merit wherever they found it. My very first week in college proved that. The English teacher, an Englishman, had a novel way of encouraging studious boys. He contributed to a boy's magazine *The Champion* which was popular then–he probably got it for his own children, and he would set an essay and give away the back number to the boy who wrote the best one. He asked us to write our views about the lat in front of the school building. Next day he announced 'This week's *Champion* goes to a new boy' and he named me and added 'I did not want any long account of the lat's history, all I wanted was your own view about it, the impression it creates in you'; and I was all over myself as I went up to take it from him.

Another incident is firmly etched in my mind and it again shows the nobility of English character. This time it was another Britisher, a Scot perhaps. He was very particular about homework, And woe betide the boy who neglected doing it. He would ask us to open our copy-books and put them on the desk and go round with a cane giving a whack on the open palm of any boy who had not done it. I was very conscientious about it and never missed doing it, but one day for some reason I couldn't. When the teacher came to my desk I told him so. He paused, a moment's hesitation, and then went past without raising his cane. As he went back after his round all the boys began to shout 'Partiality! partiality!' The Englishman's face became red, with embarrassment I suppose, for indeed he had been partial in ignoring my slip. When the cries subsided he said aloud 'No, its not that. This boy never misses doing his homework and it's just today that he hasn't done it'. It wasn't a good enough excuse and he knew it and so did I. But those were the days of discipline and after that no boy said a word. The point of relating this incident is to show that the British had no racial hatred, at least the enlightened among them hadn't, and it was confined to the restricted ambit of administration and a few misguided individuals who like Macaulay felt that everything British was superior to everything Indian.

Although the Moslems ruled quite a large portion of India for about seven centuries and a half and tried their best to Islamize it, imposing their religion and culture on its people, but unless the people of a country willingly accept what is so inflicted, it does not work. Therefore even though when partition came which was meant to give the Moslems a separate homeland, but which curiously left more Moslems in India than in Pakistan; neither the Moslem religion could make a dent on Hinduism even though it was propagated by the sword, nor did Persian catch on. Though politicians keep playing piped music to placate Moslems, print government publications in Urdu – a certain chief minister even got out electoral-rolls in that language, and the Indian government has prescribed the *achkan* and tight pyjamas as India's national dress, the Moslem language religion and culture remains confined to Moslems alone. But just two hundred years of British rule has firmly and irretrievably anglicized India in almost all spheres. We have adopted the English language, the English calendar, pop, jazz and discotheques, lighting candles, cutting, birthday-cakes with 'Happy birthday to you dear so and so', etc., the English dress sporting the latest fashion; we take out our marriage processions men, women, and children doing the twist on roads, our kiddies grow up watching WW cassettes and American movies on the TV, we quote Shakespeare rather than Kalidasa and Keats and Shelley instead of Tulsi and though we haven't adopted the Christian religion we observe the Sabbath almost as meticulously as a Roman Cathelic would with our offices, shops and schools closed. All this because the British culture was gracefully given and willingly taken. Even after forty-seven years of freedom schools run on the Anglo-Indian system with English as the medium of instruction are preferred for the children of even those who decry them, because of their better education and discipline. An American ambassador, Chester Bowles, leaving America for India writes, 'both Indians and Americans had advised us that there was no suitable school in New Delhi, and warned that "The *best* Indian and all the Westerners" sent their children away to Westernized schools in the mountains.'[50] Bowles didn't take that advice but what his Indian friends in America told him is indisputably true. And I experienced the difference between these two classes of schools–the Indian and the Anglo–Indian – when I had done my school certificate and had to take up then the Intermediate Board examination as the Cambridge system sponsored certificated ended there. There was no biology in my college at that time and as I wanted to be a doctor, the study of this subject was essential before one could take up his course in the medical line. So I thought of leaving the old college where I had studied so long to join one which had that subject. It had to be an Indian college and I chose the best one available and as admission in that was hard to get I had to make special efforts I could sit for the Intermediate Board examination a year and a half after leaving the Martiniere as the sessions of Indian schools started from July and of the Anglo-Indian ones from January, and even to this the principal of the new college agreed only on condition that I passed a test at the end of the year in December. The very first day at that Indian school–the most prestigious one in town–filled me with dismay and I was completely disillusioned. Instead of the orderly entry into the classroom, the boys ran ramble-scramble, as the bell sounded, some holding up their slipping dhoti-hems, barging through the door, pushing one another .Inside the teacher's voice was drowned in the loud talk, jeers and catcalls as he tried to teach the subject on which he was lecturing. It was a vain attempt and he soon gave up and sat down morosely on his chair behind the table. The government had some kind of distribution-of-nutritive-food scheme going, and what could be really distributed after money had gone down the pockets of those charged with its execution was just gram soaked in water! So during lunch-time a bucketful of gram was placed in the quadrangle and the boys pounced on it taking out handfuls as though a famine was on ! Enough. I decided that I just couldn't stand it. If I faced this kind of rowdiness day in and day out I would be having kittens. So I went back to my old school told them of my plight and entreated them to take me back I would forego biology and take up science instead. The very next year the biology section was started, but I had missed the bus. Such are the quirks of fate, but the Intelligence that shapes our ends works for the best and I believe I could have never been a successful doctor for it is not in me. Anyway, I mention this here to show what a chasm exists between the English-medium schools and the Indian ones. No wonder despite the many hurdles parents still make a beeline for getting their childrens' admission in Anglo-Indian schools and convents – the 'Westernized schools in the mountains'.

The annual Founder's day was a treat we looked forward to. After the governor's speech and the prize distribution there was the Founder's feast and in the evening the spacious Spence Hall was cleared for the dance. In the topmost ultramodern Indian society the ball has found a niche, and as in many other cultural fields our five star hotels have turned toward Westernism with pop, tap, tango, cancan, Go Go, Hip Hop and cabarets. Old and popular movies having decorous songs and themes have given way to salacious tunes and caigy dances, the girls with bared bosoms and swinging hips. TV screens revel in warnographic cassettes. But at that time even a ball was exciting for us, particularly the Indian boys in the college, and watching the Founder's day ball I felt that some of the couples were so closely glued together that the contact must have aroused their libido. True enough after the show was over, the toilets would have used condoms hastily discarded, tucked under washbasins. There were also prankish boys who took vicarious pleasure in putting off the main-switch and plunging the dance-hall in darkness which was doubtless welcomed by the gyrating couples, giving them the opportunity for a more intinate fusion of the bodies. The dictionary calls a kiss 'a touch with the lips to show affection or as a greeting'[51] But to us Indians it means something more and that's why the Indian screen has movies with girls and boys in all kinds of provocative poses, but, except in stray offbeat scenes, the boy's lips may stray all over the places - cheeks, bosoms, brows, eyes and so on- but never press on the lips of his girl! In the Orient the kiss is the first step in lovemaking and is invariably in bed or at any rate in private. It is certainly not a mere greeting or 'a salute with the lips'.[52] The Hindu how-to classic, the *Kama Sutra* devotes a whole chapter on kissing as a prelude to making love.[53] And when

Vatsyayana goes on to narrate later in that book how the girl ought to be induced to it, he says that the first thing to do after embracing her is to 'kiss her mouth gracefully and softly without making a sound'![54] Not the smacking kind but that which draws the whole soul',[55] the type Helen would give

'Sweet Helen make me immortal with a kiss!
Her lips suck forth my soul'[56]

The kisses which marked the blackouts, while the dancing went on weren't of this soul-sucking kind, for one could hear the sighs and the sounds while the darkness lasted. Then there was the underground dimly lit passage down the centre of the building, leading perhaps to the founder's grave–though I never went down – which was open for entry that day, and it must have provided an opportunity for much necking and spooning.

Sex, which is the rage of Western civilization where virginity is not considered an asset and most teenagers get rid of it at the earliest opportunity, is now the latest scream in India too. The English *Madam* has been eclipsed by flashy magazines with nude or semi-nude girls on the covers and indeed one person who started such a mag is facing a charge of having lured a girl by deceit and then forcing her to strip, photographing her and putting her nude picture on the cover! Everything seems to be dominated by sex, fiction in literature, exhibitionism in society, the off colour in mags, the lewd in songs and the obscene in films. The youth of India have made a cheap copy of the risque' western culture and forgotten their own. That is the tragedy with India. The visiting foreigner is too courteous to decry this particularly when he's in a host country, but the truth is that what we pride on–the Western balls, discos, cabarets, dress, bars (the refined pubs), the handshakes and byes instead of the graceful *namastey* and even the Hinglish which would leave Fowler shocked – are just those things which are affected hypocricy and over the left. The Westerner is not impressed by what is done much better in his part of the world; and incidentally we haven't adopted from the West what was really worthy of imitation, things like punctuality, hard work and ingenuity. India makes watches of the international standard, yet they remain only showpieces. Clocks hang on office walls and most peoples' wrists are adorned with a watch, but Gandhi's Ingersol is unremembered. Invitations to lunch mean really that the lunch will be at tea time, to tea that it will be at dinner-time and as far as dinners go if the invite is for nine the first invities might arrive at ten and the last ones around midnight. When I began service in 1947 (The year of Partition) the premier (as they called the chief-minister of the United Provinces then) was a very nice and competent person, unlike our self-seeking power-hungry politicians of today, but he was distressingly unpunctual, arriving even ten to twenty hours after the given time. And that goes for most things and persons, from the humble office goers to governors and ministers and prime ministers and from buses and trains to planes. People who have apparently no work to do crowd round roadside snake charmers and even a person with roots, potions and poisonous reptiles advertising their cures, roadside palmists or whoever can catch his attention.

During the years of the Raj I had two experiences of our police. the occasion was the Holi festival when children and grow-ups sprinkle colours and coloured water on others. There was another boy with me, both of us with coloured water in our syringes, when two persons passed by. There was also a cop in uniform going on his bicycle, so I refrained from sprinkling the water lest some of it fall on him. The boy with me, a neighbour's son, however, let go a jet and some of it fell on the cop. The boy ran away for fear of the cop's rage, but as I had done nothing I just walked on The cop came to me and catching hold of my arm and pulling me roughly said 'You rascal, I'll take you to the *thana* (police station)' and began to force me to sit on his bike. 'Does your law say' I said 'that you can catch a person even if he has done no wrong? I didn't squirt the water on you it was that boy who ran away' It would have made no dent on the cop were it not for a man, a welldressed and respectable person, who stopped to see what went on. He saw the logic of what I said and exclaimed angrily to the cop. 'If you take this boy, I will go to your police station and speak to your officer about this'. That did it. The cop let me go and meanwhile my father, whom my campanion had told about this was also coming near. The other episode is more illustrative of the ways of the police. We used to sleep out in the compound of the house with a Marelli table-fan (made in England, foreign goods were easily got then). One morning the fan was missing, obviously stolen sometime in the night. A few days after a cop came with a long-haired man and asked us if a fan had been missing. My father said, yes, but he hadn't reported the matter to the police, and rightly so, for getting involved with them meant, as it does even now, more trouble and no relief. Hardly any thefts are ever worked out in India and chasing the police for them is fraught with trouble, just trouble. Anyway, in this case the man seemed to be a little deranged and he had himself pointed out the place where he stole the fan from. The cop asked my father to write to the superintendent of police about the theft, and went away. Soon after a head-constable came to investigate. 'Have you got the receipt for the fan?' he asked. My father who kept his papers very carefully, said he had it and went to another room to fetch it. The head-cop gave it a lookover and went away. When he reached the gate, my father's gaze fell on the table and he was shocked to find his Westend Swiss pocket watch missing! The H.C. had put it in his pocket and gone. We got the fan back in a bashed-up condition long after when the case in court finished, but we had the watch stolen by the cop and so it was kind of quits. As they say 'set a thief to catch a thief'! One of our teachers who was an Englishman had a pedigreed dog of a very good breed, round his neck an expensive collar. One day the dog was collarless for someone had removed it. So he bought another collar and this time he put a tiny lock on it for safety. It was no good, the collar was again pilfered, along with the lock. So he put a stronger collar-and-lock round the dog's neck and this time someone made away with the dog too! leaving the poor Englishman completely bewildered.

Crime and corruption are rampant in India and indeed the world over, but the variety differs. The main reason for this variance seems to be the country's object poverty. Professor Ajit Kumar Singh of Giri Institute of Development Studies Lucknow made a study the farmers of ten districts of Uttar Pradesh. His finding were 'over three-fourths of the marginal and small farm households were found living below the poverty line of Rs 1,500 per capita. About one-third of the households were found to be indebted'. These poor farmers of whom half of them were illiterate, had to take recourse to their own sources of irrigation like wells, tanks and water-lifting devices (*rahats*) because of the poor performance of the government run irrigation channels. Professor Singh found that these poor and marginal farmers had to take loans from private moneylenders at a rate of interest as high as 62.5 per cent per annum, and 'In the majority of cases these loans were taken as "compensation loans" which the farmers generally failed to repay resulting in confiscation of their lands by the moneylenders'. They could get loans from banks and government agencies of course at a much lower interest-rate but being illiterate they could not fill in the forms etc., required and besides they were unable to give the security asked for, while moneylenders gave loans without any such guarantees.[57]

The main problem in regard to our villages is the tiny bits into which most of the farmers lands are divided. An Indian writer says:

'India has a rural system in which the top ten per cent cultivators own 50 per cent of the total cultivated area, the bottom 50 per cent less than 3 per cent, in which 72 per cent of the 55 million holdings are below the average size of about 5 1/2 acres, in which about 20 per cent of the rural population is either actually or virtually landless and therefore unable to benefit much from development'.[58] Chester Bowles, onetime American ambassador of India has the same story to tell:

> 'But what is happening among the 80 percent of the people living on the land? When anyone looks at the Indian scene the villages are everywhere in the background. Unlike a sprawled-out American rural community with a house in the middle of each farm, the Indian village is a crowded cluster of perhaps a hundred mud and thatched huts, with perhaps one thousand acres of farm plots, usually divided into hundreds or more tiny holdings all lying within a short radius. Every day the peasants walk to their fields over ridges which dam up the water in the wet rice and paddy fields. From an aeroplane at night these dim lit villages often look like endless army camps encircling cities and towns. 'These 500,000 villages are still centres of feudalism and poverty. Most of the villagers... rent their land at exhorbitant rates or work as labourers for a large landlord. Most of them are heavily in debt to the village moneylender'.[59]

An attempt was made long back in Uttar Pradesh, in one way the heartland of India, to do away with these small holdings by consolidating the land into large bits by exchanging farflung plots. with one another. It did not work and in truth resulted in much corruption and even dissatisfaction for quite a few cultivators got inferior land in exchange of theirs. The quite some courts which were created to dispose objections burdened the litigating cultivators with a great deal of graft and grease, and in the long run everything done was undone because the law of inheritance again fragmented the consolidated holdings (*chaks*), there being no right of primogeniture in the Indian legal system.

It wouldn't be quite right to say that the villages have not progressed. Long back when I was a sub-divisional magistrate, my work had to be mostly in the villages. What actually could be accomplished by the new schemes introduced by the government of independent India will be narrated later. Here I only give my impression of what the villages were like at that time (about 1944 to 1953). Most of the villages had no roads and were approachable by a muddy bridle path (called a *leek*) on which only bullock-carts could go. This was an open cart to which two oxen were yoked, the refined one (called a *shikaran*) having a kind of canopy to shelter the persons who sat in it. I was camping in a faraway village in the interior and having taken a few day's leave, was eager to catch the train from Ait station which passed it early morning. The local village zamindar considered it a great honour to have the *shikaran* got ready for me with a cosy quilt to keep me warm as it was winter and bitter cold. It was rather difficult to sleep on the cart going along the bumpy dirt road and I could have just forty winks on the five miles to the station, which took the greater part of the night, reaching it in the early hours of the morning. The platform had a small shed which could cover just about a bus and it was a noisy place. So I spread out my bedding on the ground away from it wrapping myself as closely as I could in my quilt making it a kind of sleeping bag, but the cold couldn't be kept off and I caught a chill. Of about eighty per cent villages that had no roads there were at least sixty per cent that hadn't even a bridle path and one could reach them only on foot or doing acrobaties on the uneven ridges of the fields. The villages bore a distinct demarcation by caste, there would be a thakur *bustee,* (locality) a brahmin *bustee*, etc., and set apart from the rest in isolated seclusion a Harijan *bustee*. the mud-built thatched huts had a solid wooden outer door, the size denoting the status of the owner, a narrow parlour and inside under the low-roofed veranda huge cylindrical earthen vessels full of the little wheat which the small land yielded, sealed with a mudpack to prevent it rotting. It used to be a distressing scene with half-clad children squatting on the floor and perhaps an old man no longer strong enough to work on the field, puffing at his hookah and ruminating without bitterness on the misery of existence. In India it is the healing touch of the Divine which whisks off all sorrows conferring the gift of acceptance, but at the same time taking away all initiative that makes for progress, for we seem to pat ourselves on the back for all our successes but for the failures – poverty, malnutrition, illiteracy, unemployment epidemics, floods and the errors and rapacity of our surgeons which leave many dead, deformed, crippled or blinded – we do not denounce those who are responsible and find our satisfaction in the working of fate and the will of God. The pathways between the rows of houses were uncomfortably narrow, with an open pothole for each hut (called a *nabdan*) into which the dirty water flowed. There would be a drain of sorts which instead of draining away the dirty water would fill up with rainwater itself, with the drains and the *nabdans* making a continuous stretch of slush an ideal breeding place for mosquitoes. There weren't any latrines and the villagers would sit outside the habitation in open field-space to relieve themselves, something which still continues even in towns.

The women of the villages had the worst of it, for in the rains the pathways were often in knee-deep water and they had to wade through to reach the place in which they could empty their bowels. I took the opportunity while visiting the villages to see a Harijan *bustee*. The huts here were so close together on either side of the dirt road that it would be difficult for four abreast to pass through. Pig, goats and sheep (few could afford cows) mingled with the half-clad children. It was so bad that I sickened halfway and had to turn back. That was how the villages were about thirty years ago, and indeed they were the legacy of centuries of slavery and colonialism, for neither the Moslem rulers nor the British bothered about villages except for extracting revenue, sometimes at exorbitant rates. It should be added however the we have done hardly much to improve their lot. A report of 1994 says:

'Nearly 97 percent of the rural population is denied power and sanitation facility even today. The Seventh Plan allocated Rs. 93.02 crore for rural sanitation of which only Rs. 4.58 crore was utilized. The English Plan outlay for it was Rs. 380 crore and Rs. 294-23 crore for the state sector. But by the end of 1993 only 2.5 per cent of the people had sanitary facilities. Obviously it was a dismal failure in achievement due partly to laze but largely because the money went down the pockets of those who were responsible for the execution of the work. and even where latrines were built they remained unused, serving in some cases as storage sheds!'[60]

The Moghuls confined their decadent culture (which for most rulers and their henchmen was confined to wine women and song) to the cities, and Englishmen found pleasure in their Indian *bibies* (concubines), and the royal messengers of the nabobs went round the villages carrying away be force young and lovely virgins for sex-hungy potentates. When independence came, there was some progress inas much as various schemes for the uplift of villages were devised. There was the 'green revolution' which made a good headstart by bringing food production to the 150 million tonne mark, but then it came to a standstill and as is the fashion with our government agencies whenever there were failures, there were denials and various fatuous excuses like droughts and floods. The cultivator still eagerly scans the sky for the first monsoon clouds. The irrigation system, a gift of the Raj, has marked time and the sources of water-supply remain unexploited, most of the water of India's mighty rivers simply flowing down to the sea. So is the case with ground water. In places the use of it is so great that tubewells fail, and elsewhere there is plenty which isn't made use of. In our villages and among the poor of the towns wood is still the fuel for cooking. That, along with the ever-expanding population needing more and more living space has denuded the land of trees and forests. There are no forests worth the name below 9,000 feet – and the tree-line ends at 12,000 feet. At least ten million acres of forest land has been lost between 1951 and 1981. The food-grain remains stored yet people starve because there aren't enough waggons and trucks to move it. Rice has the same story and the much-needed potatoes rot because there aren't enough cold storages. The production of fertilizers is too inadequate to meet the demand, and against the estimated demand of 179 lakh tonnes by 1995 the present capacity has only a projected 35.48 tonnes. Power is another constraint and just as there is darkness in towns there is no electricity to keep the village tubewells going. According to the studies of Holland's Waganingan Agricultural University Indian's existing resource of soil, sunshine and water can produce ten times as much as India produces today. The failure is in human effort and endeavour. As one of the dailies puts it 'Our experts make the plans, our politicians decide they want so much of the cake, even before the cake has been baked'[62] In truth very little of what is supposed to go as relief to the cultivator really reaches him. Most of it goes down the pockets of the various officers and officials who are given the work of its distribution. An American sociologist who had made a study of the trends in one village in Uttar Pradesh, wrote 'After living six months in Indian villages I've come to the conclusion that the problems are insurmountable... but I have developed an immense faith in Indians and believe that somehow a people as basically decent and intelligent are going to find a way to oavercome their insurmountable problems?[63] Perhaps we should live on that hope, though the solutions have not yet come.

A study made by an American writer lists the gifts of British rule as 1. Improvement in law and order and decline in wars and banditry 2. Reduction in famines 3. The laying down of railways 3. Control of epidemics.[64] While it can't be denied that the British rule in India was far more beneficial in many respects than the Moslem, and certainly more tolerant, it wasn't such a great boon as the writer makes it out to be. First, the famines. In the Moghul times the first famine (1555-6) in Delhi was so hideous that Badauni the chronicler wrote 'Men ate their own kind' and the 'whole country was a desert'[65] Between 1573 and 1595 there were five famines affecting Gujarat, North-west India, Lahore and Kashmir. In 1630 there was again a severe famine in Gujarat in which women sold themselves as slaves, mothers sold their children and whole families drowned themselves to escape the pangs of hunger and people cut up corpses and ate their entrails. Famines kept on occurring in 1683, 1686 and other years. So much for the Moghuls. The British did no better. In 1770 a terrible famine in Bengal carried away a third of the population. Instead of helping the sufferers the British forced them to sell their rice to Europeans who held a monopoly and even to sell the seed they needed for the next harvest! The land revenue was collected with greater severity. Some of the severest famines occurred in the latter half of the nineteenth century and in the early decades of the twentieth. The famine of 1860-61 in which over two lakh people died in the North-Western Provinces was largely because raving Englishmen burnt up whole villages and plundered grain stores. In 1866-7 one third of Orissa's population died while grain lay plentifully in neighbouring areas. What was the British transport system then doing? The governor general, a candid man, himself wrote 'there was want of foresight, perception and precaution regarding the impending calamity'.[66] About 4,50,000 people died the same year in a famine in Bellary, Salem, South Arcot, Coimbatore and Madura due to government mismanagement. In 1868-69 there was a severe formine in Marwar (Rajputana) and a third of the population perished. In 1873-74 Bengal and Bihar were affected and in 1876-87 Southern India. Mysore, Hyderabad, Madras and Bombay. In 1888-89 there was a serious famine in Bihar, Orissa, Madras, Bombay, Ajmer and Marwar. Between 1908 and 1910 famine conditions were created in different parts of India and in 1943 the severe Bengal famine was the last one and most devastating:

> 'The whole life of the people was disrupted. Parents were forced to throw their children and babies on the roadside in the hope that somebody might pick them up and feed them. Husbands were forced to leave their wives and the whole family at the mercy of events. Women were forced to sell themselves and enter brothels. Out of 1,25,000 destitutes who came to Calcutta it is estimated that quite about 30,000 young women joined brothels to contine their breathing.[67]

The British tried to tackle these famines by appointing Famine Commissions (1866, 1878, 1898 and 1900, but the fact that famines continued inspite of them is evidence enough of their inadequacy. In fact the Famine Commission Report of 1880 said:

> 'no remedy for present evils can be complete which does not include the introduction of a diversity of occupations, through which the surplus population may be drawn from agricultural pursuits and led to find the means of subsistence in manufactures or some such employment'[68]

But the British never promoted village industries leaving cultivation as the only source of livelihood for farmers. Food-grains sorely needed in India itself were exported creating artificial shortages, which ironically they made up by importing them again from outside![69] This is the undistinguished record of 'reduction of famines' which V.M. Dean claims to be the measures 'to reduce the famines due to the unpredictable monsoon rains and compounded by inadequate means of transportation, which left some parts of the subcontinent to starve while others had ample sources of food'.[70]

What have we done after 1947, when after years of foreign rule we were somehow given the gift of freedom? It can't be denied that the villages have progressed. They have. Many are now connected by road and one can take a car or at any rate a jeep right into them. Soon after I started service jeeps 'land-rovers', their more sophisticated form, had started making their appearance, and their special gear engaging all the four wheels could take them through slushy and uneven paths where cars would get stuck. Pucca houses of brick and mortar are speedily replacing the mud-huts. The radio transistor and TV are now common in quite a few village homes. Yet it is just as vain to change the face of the villages as to get rid of the winding lanes of cities like Varanasi or replan urban monstrosities. Nero wasn't really a sadistic tyrant fiddling away while Rome burnt. He wanted to redesign that hotchpotch city and bring some order into it, but he could hardly have that mishmash of houses and buildings pulled down to do it, so when 'divine help' came in the great fire that engulfed Rome he expressed his delight by fiddling, for on its ruins a new well-planned city could come up. But one can't wait for a fire to refashion what has already mushroomed into ugly towns or disorderly villages. And so the villages go on, a mixture of medievalism and modernity, some with the same rutty mudtracks which have existed for centuries where the sight of a car would cause excitement, others with city-like amenities and urbanized dwellings, Gandhi was a stickler for cottage industries but his thinking was rather antediluvian, centred, as it was, round the spinning-wheel (*carkha*) which he said 'is the sun of the solar system of our activities'[71] In his Wardha education scheme which he wrote of in his paper. The *Harijan* (1937) he tried to link education with vocational training. The goods the students produced would be bought by the state at a fixed price and sold. But the products were not good enough to stand market competition and the scheme flopped. Cottage industry in India is not like what it is in developed countries, as for example in Japan where small mechanical parts (which are later assembled) are all made in village homes. India's village industries are largely handlooms and handicrafts and employ only about a thirtieth of the idle people in villages[72] So the influx to the cities in search of occupation continues unabated and we haven't really done much in these forty-seen years of freedom and whatever little is done is being ever undone, like the web of Penelope, because of the steady bursts of population the impact of which is most in the villages. According to the government version (which usually makes the picture rosier than it actually is) the conditions existing in both rural and urban areas in India are as follows:

> 'The per capita availability of land in the country is declining at a very high rate because of the population explosion. According to official sources with the population growth it would decline to 0.33 hectares by the turn of the century as against 0.89 hectares in 1950.
>
> 'Estimated per capita availability of land for animal population would go down from 0.51 hectares in 1950 to 0.24 hectares by the year 2000.
>
> 'At present rural and urban settlements, roads, railways, water supply, mines, defence and industrial installations use an estimated 21 million hectares. An additional area of two to three million hectares would be required for these diverse purposes by 2000 A.D.
>
> 'The total geographical area of India at 329 million hectares constitued 2.4 per cent of the world's area, but India supports 16 per cent of the world population.
>
> 'Out of an estimated arable land of 166 million hectares in the country, at present 141 million hectares is used for cultivation. the sources noted that the vast increase in population along with widespread poverty in India leads to the degradation of environment in many ways by putting pressure on scarce resources like land, water and energy.
>
> 'They noted that environmental protection and ecological

balance were essential to ensure that development is sustainable in the long run. Land abuse, water and air pollution, soil erosion, deforestation, situation of rivers and loss of biological diversity over a period of time pose a threat to ecological security and human health. The growing demand for food, fuelwood and fodder is leading to an unsustainable use of forest resources. Loss of valuable top soils due to reckless deforestation is affecting soil productivity and thereby the standard of living of millions of small and marginal farmers. The sources said the result is growing deterioration in the quality of air and water, proliferation of slums, illegal construction and undesirable change in the use of land, all of which contribute to urban poverty.

'Transport is a major source of land, water, air and noise pollution. Land abuse is due mostly to the railways and road transport which need a vast dedicated corridor and occupy 3.1 per cent of India's total area and 4.6 per cent of urban land. Sixty per cent of air pollution in India is due to emissions of vehicles moving on the roads. Although traffic density and petroleum, oils and lubricants (POL) consumption are not high as compared to those in developed countries. The rate of pollutant emission per vehicle in India is 35 per cent higher than that in the United States for various reasons such as poor maintenance of vehicles and roads, lack of traffic planning, high proportion of overaged vehicles, crowded highways and a large proportion of two and three wheelers'.[73]

The American ambassador whom I have already quoted, had the same impression about the snags and sawyers in the development of Indian villages due to population growth: 'Each year these villages produce new millions of Indians and then see millions die. One-fourth of all babies die before their first birthday and half the children never reach the age of twelve'.[74] Another report says: that though there may not be the usual type of famines, the ones in the independence era may be man made because food production has not kept pace with population growth. At present food production is 182 million tonnes. By the year 2050 this will have to be doubled to feed almost 1.5 million people, which will be an impossibility. Evaen today with grain stocks of 30 million tonnes abotu 300 million people go hungry. A UNICEF study says that more than 5,000 children die each year due to malnutrition, and a Washington based World Watch Institute that by the turn of the century India will start importing food grains and continue to import them for at least the next 50 years. 175 million hectares of land is affected by erosion and the subsequent loss of top soil that sustains crops is about 5,333 million tonnes per year.[75]

So what has been done to stem the evaer-rising population? The British never bothered about schemes of public welfare, for they had the twin aims of governing which necessitated colonialism, and economic exploitation. Besides, the population exploision hadn't become so formidable as after freedom. Mahatma Gandhi was against birth control by the use of contracceptives and believed that sex was meant 'only for the act of creation', and 'any other use of it is a sin against God and humanity'.[76] The view is of course outmoded, but is nonetheless shared by many Catholics even today and even by their head, the Pope. It is true that birth and death are in the hands of God, but birth control cannot be said to be a transgression of the divine will for there are many failures too. One may practise any conventional method and yet there could be births. True there are vasectomy, medical termination of pregnancy and so forth, but in quite a few cases the outcome of these may be unexpected. I know of a couple who after two children, went in for an irreversable method and thereafter both the children died, leaving them childless. But then we can by no means leave population control to nature and thereby leave people exposed to the misery which such an ultimate check involves. Sex can never to taken by those who make love to be just for procreation, a hypocrisy which is advocated by idealists, for the rapture of lovemaking drives out any other thought except that of its sheer pleasure from the mind. If sex wasn't meant for pleasure in all its multifarious aspects there would be no reason for writing the *Kama Sutra,* the *Perfumed Garden* or Ovid's *Art of Love* Nor can contraceptives be condemned, for the pretentious moralists who are against them ought to realize the ills of overpopulation. So presuming that continence and the rhythm method advocated by some, are no answer to family planning, we revert to the question what can be done to check India's population burst and what has been done about it. Nothing much. Indira Gandhi put the screw to family planning which did more harm to it than good. Firstly, she confused between its private domain and that of the state. It is the right of states to demand that its citizens do not burden it with more than it can bear, but *how* the citizens discharge this obligation is not its concern. A couple may limit their family to the desired norm of two or three children by any of the means they adopt, even Gandhi's old-fogyish continence, for if they have not put an extra burden on the state they are on the right side of it. Indira Gandhi forced vasectomy on the men and what is more, fixed targets which perpetrated horrors either out of fear or to win favour. As a paper reported:

> 'A Harijan youth paid the tailor Rs 50 for stitching him a wedding dress. The marriage procession left, but then news went round that the bridegroom had been vasectomized. Unawares he was made to undergo the operation, when he hadn't the faintest idea what vasectomy was. He was promised Rs 5000 and two *bighas* of land, and those who vasectomized him knew he was unmarried. The marriage was off, leaving the bridegroom bitterly weeping. People were repeatedly sterilized to make up the target. Many over seventy, some unmarried, widowers, and in some cases both husband and wife were made to undergo the operation. No wonder the achievement was 121 per cent , but also left behind an ace record of misery'.[77]

According to latest reports family planning has failed to make any impact in the most densely populated province of India (U.P.) and in its villages, where it is needed most. The Nirodh indigenous condom was rejected as its inferior kind made of sub-standard material was distributed. It was so unreliable that the villagers weren't even prepared to take it free of cost, the deluxe superior variety being reserved for the rich elite who could pay for it. Besides, the villagers said they were short of living space and so could not keep the condoms away from the prying eyes of children, nor did they know where to stuff the used ones. The other methods too failed, IUD (Intra-uterine-devices) and sterilization because of lack of trained medical persons, leading to complications and fear of these, and pills because the village folk could not keep count of them. There were other reasons for failure too like caste, social stigma and lack of education. The result was that each couple in the state had more than five children (the TFR or total fertility rate.) This was the highest in the country, the all-India average being 8.8. The crude birth rate per thousand persons was 35.7 and couple protection rate 33.7 per cent against the all-India average of 29.5 and 43.5 per cent respectively.[78]

Meanwhile the government sleeps the sleep of the Sleeping Beauty and we have't yet completed the hundred years of independence, so the Prince hasn't arrived. Some politican has a sudden gush of affection for Mother India and deplores the misery being caused by rising population. Somewhere some committee is appointed (with us they usually are to accommodate some favoured person) which keeps collecting statistics ('damned lies' as one called them) and after many extensions of the term of the committee a huge report is made, cyclostyled and forgotten. But of course the storks do not know anything about these and keep dropping the babies. The ones which last are the boys, for as the World Bank discusison paper 'Violence against Women - The Hidden Health Burden' says:

> 'In a prospesctive study of all births within a 12-village region of Tamil Nadu, it was found that 58 per cent of deaths (19 out of 33) among female infants were due to infanticide. The girls were most often killed within seen days of birth. The two most common methods were to feed them the poisonous sap of a plant and to choke them by lodging rice balls soaked in milk in their throats. There were no male infanticides during the two-and-half-year study'.

'The paper also drew special attention to widespread foeticide in China, India and the rupublic of Korea if tests showed the baby in the womb was a girl'.[79]

Coming to the railways, and the telegraph and its allied mode of communication, the telephone, these were doubtless introduced by the British, but their objective was facility in administration and not the public good. The telegraph was of priceless assistance to the British rulers in crushing the Mutiny of 1957. When the sepoys massacred Christians in Delhi, two Anglo-Indian lads in the telegraph office managed to send off a message to Ambala, Lahore, Rawalpindi and Peshawar: 'The sepoys have come in from Meerut, and are burning everything. Mr Todd is dead, and we hear several Europeans; we must shut up'. Thus did the introduction of the telegraph pay off. Punjab was warned in time. The railways were mainly meant to carry troops, and civilians to Nainital and Simla, the hill stations to which the government ICS officers moved in summers, and from where they carried on their official work (the *babus* of course stayed behind). When freedom came these services, the Indian Railways and the Telecommunications ought to have been made customer-friendly and user-friendly. The Indian mind, with exceptions of course, is largely imitative not innovative, and so the laws governing the railways, postal and telegraph services remained unchanged with their imperialist and colonial slant. These departments of the government remain user-hostile and user-unfriendly even though they are no longer monopolies of the government but are largely for the convenience of the citizens. The Indian railways claim that they are immune from paying compensation and never bother about accidents caused by the carelessness of their staff in which hundreds of lives are lost. The ministers in charge just put in a word of regret in the papers and that's all. Every important politician regrets and forgets. We are back to the medieval age and to the days of the East India Company when 'the king [and that implied his servants too] could do no wrong! The law of torts not being applicable to the Indian laws even though they are an indifferent imitation of the British ones, compensation for loss and injury is a distant dream, an endles legal corridor leading up and up and one may start a civil suit for it when he is a youth which ends when he is dead and cremated. In his inaugural address to the national convention held on 24 January 1994 Justice VB Eradi president of the National Commission (a body formed only in 1986 after about forty of the forty-seven years of freedom), said:

> 'The Indian Post Ofice Act. 1898 and the Indian Railways Act 1890, are two very ancient statutes enacted during the British colonial period, but they are on our statute book as existing laws in force. It is expressly laid down in section 6 of the Post Office Act and in a similar provision contained in the Railways Act, that the postal authority and the railway administration shall not be made liable to pay any compensation in the event of delay in delivery or loss of any letter or other articles sent through post or of any goods consigned by rail. These provisions were enacted at that time to protect the interest of the imperialist British government and they are totally out of tune with the altered state of things presently existing in modern independent India'.[80]

The same is the case with the laws governing electricity (The Indian Electricity Act 1910) and the telephone which is curiously governed by the same Act as the telegraphs are, namely the Indian Telegraph Act 1885. The result is that these departments still preserve the colonial attitude and, while having the ills of inefficiency and lack of straight dealing, in addition adopt the attitude of you-be-damnedness. The cover story of a prominent magazine sums up the dismal apathy of the telecommunications department thus: 'What the authorities are aware but will never admit in public is that there is rampant indiscipline in the lower cadre of the staff, *corruption at all levels*, poor supervision, slow execution of the work on hand and a general apathy towards work.... Not surprisingly, there are complaints galore – of frequent irregularities of billings, of blatant malpractices that unscuplous subscribers in collusion with linesmen and other technical staff indulge in, such as tampering with lines to ensure that the subscriber trunk dialling system (STD) calls are registered on another number'.[81] A doctor who had no one abroad to ring, almost had a heart attack when he received a phone bill over a lakh for calls to foreign countries which he had never made! Deciding a case about excess billing and other matters a Justicc of a High Court was constrained to observe: 'The telephone service in India is run as a State monopoly. The officers concerned, on that account, should not take it that they are doing a favour to the citizens by providing this service. It is not left to their sweet-will to grant telephone service, to continue or discontinue it or to deal with the citizens as subjects of a colonial regime. They are bound by the rules and principles of natural justice and fair play. There is no scope for arbitrariness, unreasonableness or discrimination. They do not have absolute power which they can exercise at their whims'.[82]

The postal service, which too was introduced by the Raj, has doubtless expanded immensely after Swaraj but again that's all that can be said for it. It has been more and more mismanaged during the years and is not only user-unfriendly, it has gone haywire. Letters are lost in the mail, and often bundles of them are dumped by jittery postmen in ditches! It was reported in the papers that one such bundle was seen lying in a nullah by a passerby as its tip (with a few envelopes floating in the water) was visible. He informed the postal authorities, but they did not care, so with the help of his neighbours he salvaged the bundle and dumped it on the postmaster's table. It was found to contain dozens of undelivered letters, some even with cheques in them, a good few so greatly damaged by the water that nothing could be done except to forget about them. Deliveries which used to take two or four days now may take weeks and even months. Registered letters and parcels which by virtue of being given a receipt bear a kind of guaranteed delivery, are lost in the post and you may complain till Doomsday but no one bothers. As is the inevitable fate of all complaints they are all gulped by the Indian paper-hungry monster into oblivion. and, as we have said, the postal authorities can fling section 6 at the complainant and say, go hang. Telegrams intimating arrivals reach long after the person has arrived, those informing relations about serious illness come after the person has died and those being informed about deaths arrive long after the cremation! It is not mere inefficiency alone that has let down the postal service, corruption too, as in about all government departments, is the villain. One person who sent a bank draft of a lakh rupees to his relation by registered post found to his dismay that it had been intercepted and cashed. Dividend warrants sent by post disappear. It is a strange contrariety that on the one hand we are delivering money orders by satellites to reach the payee in minutes and on the other hand we have postmen cycling miles and having to climb up three floors to deliver letters in the scorching winds of June and the bitter cold of Indian winters. But then in everything there remains two Indias as Dadabhai Naoroji, one of the earliest critics of the Raj said:

> 'In reality there are two Indias–one the prosperous, the other poverty-stricken. The prosperous India is the India of the British and the other foreigners. They exploit India as officials, capitalists in a variety of ways, and carry away enormous wealth to their countries. To them, India is, or course, rich and prosperous. The more they can carry away, the richer and more prosperous India is. The second India is the India of the Indians – the poverty-stricken India'.[83]

Things are much the same today except that it is our grabby politicians with an insatiable appetite for weath and power who have filled the shoes of the 'British and other rulers' and the money is not carried away anywhere but lies in foreign banks in dollars and pounds or whatever the currency there is There are scandals and scams, loan-*melas*, election-funding and partisan awards with the result that our solicitous leaders make their piles and the India of the poor becomes poorer, of the rich, richer. There are indquiries of course, even by parliamentary committees, and the guilt is established, but then everyone is given 'a clean chit' and there is happiness all round. No politician even thinks of propriety or feels bad about pilfering the country's weath. Everyone who is in disgrace cries himself hoarse that he'll resign, but no one does, for as one writer says, 'In India resignations are never voluntary. People enjoy being cremated in office'.[84] I will speak of the Indian brand of corruption later, here I only wish to say that our mega-cities and villages are evidence enough to show that we haven't gone a step further from the two Indias conceived by Dadabhai. There are the mega-millionaires afflicted with affluenza and there are the underclass, palaces for the one, pavements for the other, as the American ambassador who has been quoted before, tells us in his first impressions as he and his family drove from the airport to downtown Bombay:

> 'This ride is a disheartening introduction to the new Indian Republic especially on a dark and sultry night.
>
> 'The strange new smells, the grim miles through one of the world's worst slums, the sidewalks covered with tens of thousands of sleeping people, some on cots but most of them lying on the hard

pavement, the ever-present poverty, misery and squalor, were impressions which we each absorbed silently and apprehensively

'No more reassuring was the fantastic old hotel named after the Victorian age. Its enormously high ceilings, the many turbaned servants, its air of elegance and luxury were in shocking contrast to the streets through which we had just passed. As we were led along the great halls to the Viceroy Suite, five large echoing rooms with incredible large bathrooms, we were all awed, and the children uniquely subdued'.[85]

The rich and the poor exist in all countries of the world. Just as there is inequality in the hours of days and nights, in the seasons and the heat the sun gives to our earth, that is to say in nature, so too the fortunes of human beings vary. But poverty in the prosperous developed countries is quite different from poverty in the Third World with 'teeming squatter shanty towns rife with malnutrition disease and poverty'.[86] For example in America a person earning about a thousand dollars a month would perhaps be poor enough to qualify for a government dole. In our country he would be considered to be stinking rich. There is the man who comes to our house to milk the buffalo, for here unless the cow or buffalo is milked before your eyes, the milk is certain to have water mixed in it in varying proportions, so much so that even the poet of India's most sacred and literary epic, the *Ramayana* uses this as a simile to illustrate the virtue of friendship: 'See the love and nobility of friendship, water [when mixed with milk] sells at the price of milk, but when the sourness of guile enters, the two separate'.[87] This man is employed by the owner of the buffaloes on a salary of eight hundred rupees a month (about six dollars a week) and he works the man to death from seven in the morning to eleven in the night so that he is at home only for about six or seven hours. His young wife died leaving behind four children, all youngsters, and a relation of his who lives in the lower flat hardly a flat, just a room, has the goodness to look after his kids. There is an old woman past sixty-five who comes to do our odd jobs in the morning who has to go through the scorching summers and is always wanting but never able to buy a table-fan costing about thirty dollars. And just a short way off there is a huge palatial mansion belonging to a rich industrialist with a colour TV in each of over two dozen halls, the floors covered with carpet so thick that it makes treading on the floors an ordeal. There's a man at the wicket gate with a phone and visitors, whoeaver they are, may go in only after he has got the let-him-come signal from inside. Such is the India of today where the glamour mingles with the squalor of poverty, the warp and woof of our social fabric, an India which from after the glorious eras of Asoka Harsha and Chandragupta remains the same through the centuries of the Moslem conquest, the British rule and the fading glimmer of independence, for as Phaedrus says:

> 'When states new rulers seek
> The poor change nothing but their master's name'.[88]

What the Raj took away from India was more valuable than what it gave. Macaulay's minutes and Bentinck's policy of anglicization tolled the bell for the ancient Hindu philosophy of the Vedas, the Upanishads and the *Gita* which had elicited the admiration of intellectuals like Max Muller, Schopenheur, Paul Deussen, Aldous Huxley and others. It was on 7 March 1837 that Bentinck passed the historic resolution 'all the funds at the disposal of the government will henceforth be spent in imparting Indians a knowledge of English literature and science'. The vanity of mankind is such that each race while extolling its own religion and culture, gives short shrift to that of others. Macaulay's prodigious memory could go back to Chaucer, Spenser and Shakespeare but no further and so without knowing either Sanskrit or Arabic or Persian he averred that 'a single shelf of a good European library was worth the whole native literature of India and Arabia'. Nonetheless it was not the Raj alone which was averse to Indian learning, many Indians too spoke in their masters' voice, for example Rammohan Roy and Ishwar Chandra Vidyasagar, so much so indeed that when a boy went out with his father to pay obeisance to the goddess Kali in a temple, he greeted her by saying, 'Good morning, Madam'![89] This trend has continued unabated right through independence, with the adoption of English as the medium of official correspondence in the government of India and the ever-growing popularity of English medium schools, and while even developed nations of the West, Germany, France, Japan and so on and even the Asian ones like China, pride in speaking and learning their own language and priding in thier literature, they are amused to find Indian politicians, administrators and ambassadors flaunting their English in various forms and accents, to follow which must doubtless strain the nerves of those whose mother tongue it is. All our prime ministers, with the lone exception of Shastri and perhaps the prercent one, have been through educaton in foreign countries and were more or less products of an alien culture. Following their lead, bureaucrats, business tycoons and most of our only too westernized youth, have exchanged the traditions of the East for those of the West. Very few of them have any knowledge of the Hindu scriptures and many may not even have heard of the *Rig Veda,* the *Puranas* and the *Brahma Sutra.* I recollect one politician who was completely mystified when I mentioned the *Upanishads.* thus the Raj left us cheap imitators of everything Western and we lost that one thing of which we could be proud.

After doing my Intermediate U.P. Board examination in science, I decided to change over to arts for my taste was primarily for literature. The craving for a government job, particularly of the administrative kind, prevailed through the centuries of foreign domination, the faujdar and kotwal in Moghul India, the tahsildar and qanungo under the British, and when we got our freedom we retained feudalism along with democracy and the Provincial Civil Service, the Indian Administrative Service and the Indian Police Service became the most coveted jobs. While western nations have evolved citizen-friendly governmetns, we maintain one in which the ordinary citizen is a persecuted guy. In the India of independence one's status stands out as prominently as a tiepin. Take the signal-beacon which our VIPs started using when Swaraj came. It started with a simple red light (or a flag in the day) on the front of the car's bonnet exclusively for commissioners. Gradually it started flashing on almost every administrator's car even that of a sub-divisional officer, the lowest of those in the district; and it assumed different colours and varieties, red for ministers, blue for bureaucrats, some right on the top of the car with intermittent flashes, some revolving, each one loudly proclaiming the VIP-ness of the man inside. It's feudalism on the rampage, and not content with that our influence pedlars must have carbine-toting cops to demonstrate their importance. A survey says:

> 'A policeman on the left, a gun toter on the right and a car full of them trailing behind seem to have become the latest status symbols of the bureaucratic and political meatgrinder in the capital. If you are "someone" in Delhi [an official or unofficial VIP], a cavalcade of khaki-coloured uniforms is an essential appendage....'

The British I C S did not need to flaunt themselves this way, their colour was a sign of their superiority, and even now, though we are downright censorious of apartheid and the colour bar, a *fuck-off* invites special interest. These being the special privileges of our bureaucrats, every young person who has gone through the grind aspires for the

Indian Administrataive Service, the successor to the ICS. for it promises security and a cut above the rest, and incidentally a six-figure dowry. A change is in the air though, firstly because caste reservation in government jobs acts as a brake on merit and the high-caste aspirant's chances of success are limited, and secondly because of the comparitively large pay-bill of persons employed in private firms (often twelve or thirteen times as much as the highest a bureaucrat gets).

So when I had done my Intermediate and was to enter the university for graduation, I chose the one at Allahabad which was those days considered to be the ideal training ground for those who aspired to get through the competitive examinations for the administrative services. It was then, too, that I discovered the potency of 'putting in a word' in free India, where having a pull has various labels like '*paua*', 'kilo' [from the weights they represent], apart from the more refined ones like 'ZOR' (strength) and this was the first step in the ladder of our variety of corruption, the lowest rung – we'll speak of the others later. There was a particular hostel in that university which had the distinction of having its warden the vice-chancellor himself, and which was specially reputed for turning out stuffed shirts, and so this was the one I wanted to get into. But it was a hard row of stumps, as I learnt later for the qualifications for getting into it were either very high merit or the get-through-pull, or as some gossiped, a handsome face! I had none of these, so I got a brief curt reply to my application, sorry, no go. However I was spoiling for it, and I recollected that an uncle of mine, an ICS of old, who was occupying a very influential post, might do th trick. I did not know him from Adam but I took a chance and wrote him a post card for his *shifarish.* I didn't get a reply but my father did, something, to the effect that a letter had been received by him 'which purports to be that of your son. There are many other hostels [implying that if possible I might be persuaded not to insist on this one], however I would like to know your views in the matter'. My father wrote back saying that yes it was indeed his son's letter and he wanted this particular hostel, but he [my uncle] needn't bother about it. It seemed that despite that my uncle for once allowed the bond of relationship to override the vanity of power, for I got another intimation from the hostel saying that I should appear for an interview on such and such a date. I was over the moon, but now when I write these recollections it strikes me as rather queer that it should require an interview to get into a hostel. Yet when one sees what's happening today, after forty-seven years of freedom, about a simple thing as admission of a child in a prestigious school, it isn't a wonder at all that in 1941, when I joined the Allahabad University I had to be interviewed. We find now that even the parents of the child seeking admission are called for an interview with the principal and whoever else there is, and it's not just formal (as mine was). They are asked searching questions some of them aimed at the amount of money which can be extracted from them, which they euphemistically term subscriptions.

I went nattily dressed, but there was no interview. I was just given an admit card and was in. There was no room for new entrants so the hostel organization had set aside one of the university staff's houses for us calling it the 'hostel annexe'. We were two to a room but it was a nice homely plae. The house next to the annexe was occupied by a very literary person who was said to be a homosexual and it was a joke among us 'Look, so and so is calling you'! On the very first day at the university I was down on my luck. It was hot and sultry so I had put on a *kurta* (a long loose muslin garment) and pyjamas and had gone to the library to deposit the prescribed money for membership. I had a hundred rupee bank note in my *kurta* pocket, but when I put my hand in it alas! the bill wasn't there. That upset me a great deal for at that time it meant a lot of money and my poor father whom I sent a telegram about it must have felt even worse for it was almost half of his monthly pay. Anyway there was no help, for Faggin's academy has a wide net and it's difficult to escape from it. In the locals in Bombay, for example one is a sure victim of nimble fingersmiths, particularly if he's a non-Bombayite. By the time you miss your dough and catch hold of him the swag has passed through many hands and is lying in the pocket of an innocent looking member of the gang.

Indian universities have good libraries to start with, but soon in many of them, as indeed in libraries in general, quite a few of the books are mutilated by unscriplous readers, and just those pages that you are looking for, are missing. The weakness of books published in this country is their binding and one or two drops on the ground wreck them, so they are soon on the racks rebound in black, title-less and ready for another bounce. In some libraries one can go through the rows of bookshelves and pick out his book. But then there are many who do not put it back in its place and after a time they get so mixed up that it becomes quite impossible to trace out a book by its number on the index-card. In universities and some public libraries the system is that you can't enter but have to hand over a slip with the number of the book you want to a chaprasee. It's a nerve-wracking and troublesome process for the chaprasese tries his best to dodge and if you finally hand him the slip, he just goes in and ocmes out empty-handed without having really looked for it.

The Indian universities have their problems and, as in almost all other educational institutions, these problems have grown with the years. The academic atmosphere too has deteriorated. The greatest disservice has perhaps been done by our governments and politicians. Mahatma Gandhi's view in this matter is atavistic. He says, 'The students cannot be away from politics. Politics is as essential to them as religion. Politics cannot be divorced from religion.'[91] The Congress governments which have ruled India for practically the entire period after Partition, seem to think otherwise. Their leaders have been shouting from the housetops that religion must not be mixed with politics, the main object of their insistence on this being to create a Moslem vote-bank for themselves. Our universities have become the haunt of goondas, hoods and hooligans, some even having illegal arms, like country-made pistols. There are tiffs and scraps in which blood is shed. Instead of becoming portals of learning, they have turned into political arenas exploited by political parties and *netas* (politicians). The unions of the universities are the root cause of their ruin. When elections are held for electing office-bearers the walls are disfigured by posters. Tempers rise and heads are smashed. Not content with polluting civic life our politicians make a moekery of education. One chief minister took the bold step of dissolving the unions, consequent to which there was marked improvement in the academic atmosphere but after him the degradation set in again. Our governments turn a Nelson eye to all this for they have little interest in improving the campuses. In appointment of the staff, admissions, examinations in which copying goes on unchecked and in almost all affairs, it is nepotism that reigns supreme. Teachers have lost interest in teaching and students in learning, so that our universities turn out third grade lads who are lapped up by the various government services. A report says 'In one of the universities over half a dozen students were awarded their Ph Ds without doing a spot of work. The students engaged a man who wrote the theses on getting an agreed sum. A section of teachers in the Hindi department and some members of the staff are alleged to be involved in this racket'[92] Another report gives the distressing information that admissions to universities were made on fake mark-sheets. '... fake certificates and mark-sheets were distributed and even sold by the so-called student leaders who used to move on the campus with writing pads of ministers and their seals.... The students who took admission by submitting fake mark-sheets include sons and daughteres of a Medical College professor and a top-businessman of the state capital'[93] The apathy of students to learning was seen by me when after leaving the Allabahad University I took up a combined course in research in English literature and law (LLB) in 1945 in another university. The ornate doos of te leture-room for law, a gift of the Raj, had lovely panels of mils-white grooved glass. As soon as the class began some students would go out and keep scratching the glass with a coin which would get the goat of the lecturer and kept putting him off. Some students would sit near the doors and the windowsills and disappear after the roll-call. Others got their names called out by their chums so that most of the hall had empty seats. However when I entered the Allahabad university in 1941 things weren't at all so bad. There were the unions of course and the politics too was there - I remember a bearded colleague who would keep making speeches outsie the union office he became a chief minister later, handsome recompense for his orations! – but they were disciplined and affected only a small section of the pupils, for most came there for an education which would get then through a first-grade govern;ment job.

The universities suffered too from the lackadaisical attitude of the government to education in general. A report says,.'India spends on education much less (3.6 per cent) of its gross national produce (GNP) compared to other countries. There are only a few countries who spend less than India [Burma, Pakistan, Afghanistan and Nepal]. The education commission has recommended that India should spend at least 6 per cent of its GNP on education. Even of the money spent, salary payments and administrative costs take up almost the entire amount [30 per cent] with just a tiny bit of it left for eductional benefits of students'.[94] The Universities Grant Commission which finances libraries and higher education has become increasingly tardy in releasing these grants, with the result that libraries do not have money to buy books. This has also an adverse effect on book publishing and in order to survive more and more publishers are bringing out cheap paperbacks, mainly faste-selling books of utility which the readers can afford. Lack of government's interest in literary activity, paucity of funds and the politicizing of education leading to indiscipline and disorder on the campuses are mainly responsible for the decline in educational standards. There are other reasons too, like corruption overpopulation and inertia, but these are general ills which assail almost all facets of development, not education alone.

6

THE QUIT INDIA MOVEMENT

Here is a *mantra*, a short one, that I give you. You may imprint it on your hearts and let every breath of yours give expression to it. The *mantra* is – Do or die.

MAHATMA GANDHI

In 1942 I had moved from the Annexe to the hostel. I was their in the second year of my graduate course in English, History and Politics. We had the advantage of having the university doctor just adjacent to the hostel compound. He was of the firm view that all diseases had their root in an upset stomach and as soon as the ailment was mentioned he would write out a prescription for an evil tasting laxative, mag sulph. So whenever we went to him we would tell him that we had already taken mag sulph!

1942 is graphically etched in my mind for it was the year when Gandhi launched has Quit India movement. The Mahatma was a great man commanding influence which perhaps no man ever had. The Indian nation responded to him as they never had before to anyone mourning when he was arrested, rejoicing when he was triumphant and even rioters and insurgents laid down their arms when he fasted as he did at Noakhali, earning the sobriquet of a 'One man boundary force' by Mountbatten. Nonetheless he remains a riddle. In 1942 when he launched the Quit India movement he said 'Japan's quarrel is not with India She is warring against the British Empire.... If India was freed her first step would probably be to negotiate with Japan', and in July 1944 just two years after he was not only offering to withdraw civil disobedience, but was also prepared to give full cooperation to the war effort! He undertook a fast – which incidentally was his favourite way of wresting from the people what he wanted. When Patel was reluctant to pay Pakistan the unpaid cash balances he forced Patel and Nehru to pay them and yet did not say a word to prevent partition, even though he prophesied 'it will be an orgy of blood'.[95] He hurried off to save Moslems at Noakhali when the post-partition massacres took place, but when he got a telegram on 17 August 1947 that a terrible massacre of Hindus was taking place in Punjab and 'Your presence in Lahore is necessary', he just passed on the telegram to Patel for 'full information', knowing that by the time full information came hundreds of Hindus would have been massacred for in Punjab the Moslem police were machine-gunning Hindus and as Robert Turnbull of the *New York Times* wrote 'blood flows oftner than the rain falls',[96] While upholding the cause of the untouchables, Gandhi put his trust on the *varna* system,[97] Though highly sexed himself, he wrote 'whatever over-indulgence there was with me, it was strictly restricted to my wife...', he advocated continence for others.[98] Gandhi halted the civil disobedience movement when a minor incident of violence at Chauri Chaura took place, on which Nehru wrote 'we [C.R. Das, Motilal Nehru, C. Rajagopalachari, Lala Lajpat Rai, Sampurnanand and himself] were angry when we learnt of his stoppage of our struggle at a time we seemed to be consolidating our position'. C.R. Das was even more critical: 'the Mahatma opens a campaign in brilliant fashion, he works it up with unerring skills, he moves from success till he reaches the zenith of his campaign, but after that he loses his nerve and begins to falter'. After reacting to Chauri Chaura so strongly, Gandhi completely repudiated his campaign of non-violent civil disobedience in 1942, making a mockery of the hundreds who perished in various movements like the Dandi march and so forth. The two great principles he fought for and tried to achieve were Hindu–Moslem unity and civil disobedience by peaceful means. He failed in both, and the Quit India movement shortlived, ill-planed and badly executed, epitomized these failures. 'I will not cry halt to the movement' he wrote 'even if there be an outbreak of violence, rioting bloodshed etc;.' He called it a 'fight to the finish', and wrote that India may be entrusted to God or in modern parlance, to anarchy',[99] as though he did not see any difference between orderliness and the holy mess of anarchy! He thought that thereby 'all the parties will fight one another like dogs, or will, when real responsibility faces them, come to a reasonable agreement. I shall expect non-violence to arise out of that chaos' Thus 'a true India would arise from the false one'. All this was only a frustrated man's pipe dream and the only thing which has come out to be true but much after, in our times not in 1942, is perhaps the part about the parties fighting one another like dogs. Nothing arises out of chaos, everything dissolves into it, and the new India he spoke of did arise, but it was a truncated India, for the movement of 1942 convinced Jinnah that a Hindu Raj was in the offing, and it made stronger his determination to get Pakistan. The irony of it was that even the Hindus under Savarkar dissociated from it and the Sikhs openly condemned it. So in a way Gandhi and the Congress were alone, or perhaps it might be more correct to say that the movement was yet another attempt by the self-effacing saint-politician to impose his will on a doting Congress of which he had virtually become a dictator. Attlee said about Mahatma Gandhi 'A combination of saint and astute politician Gladstone must have been a little like him - but with ideas difficult to reconcile with modern views of progress, difficult for the west to appreciate anyway. But a tremendous force. .... On the whole the saint [in him] was uppermost. It didn't make it any easier. Saints do not fit awfully well in a democracy any more than do sinners. and the dictatorial saint can be quite as bad as the dictatorial sinner, you know, especially if he thinks you're a sinner' [100]

We had heard that the Mahatma had given a call for the overthrow of British rule, but beyond that we knew nothing. Yet there was an air of excitement and expentancy as though something vital for us was about to happen. We wandered though the empty streets our hearts surging with indignation, our hands itching to do something but no one knew what was to be done and how, for the leaders were behind the bars and at least one of the features of the movement was becoming quite evident, namely every man on his own as Yusuf Mehar Ali said 'Every man a Congressman; every house a Congress house, and Asaf Ali wrote to Maulana Abul Kalam Azad, 'There will be no restriction on the movement which Gandhi has contemplated. There will not be any rule...' So we went about in groups along the lonely roads with brickbats littered about at places, evidence of disorder of some sort, hoping that something would happen to force the British to announce the end of the Raj. We did not quite know what it was all about, and having had discipline instilled into us, for the ogre of politics had not swallowed it by then, we could not bring ourselves to demolish, dismantle or destroy, even though these were the avowed objects of this Congress-sponsored agitation. Students who got embroiled in it were mostly those who got caught in the general disorder by chance. There was, for example a lad who was on his way home in an eastern district of the United Provinces and before he could reach the train stopped, for the agitators had uprooted the railway line and dismantled the track. Though he had nothing at all to do with all this he got involved in it, for when the hooligans hold sway it is the innocent who suffer. Anyway, my friend got his reward when the Raj was wound up five years later by being declared a 'political sufferer' and getting concessions in government service. My route homeward, when the authorities got the hostels vacated, was safe and I arrived home without any trouble on the way. But then I wrote a letter to a friend who was to come later, to bring some books I had left behind. They never reached me and my friend said hadn't got any letter. Apparently, like other letters which the British authorities censored, mine too get into their files, for in a burst of enthusiasm I had ended the letter with the sentence 'Let us hope we will now meet in a free India'. A free India wasn't on the cards then, and in fact the British were in a miff for Gandhi had planned his Quit India just when the Allies were having reverses on all fronts in the World War with Rommel proceeding towards Cairo and the Suez, the position grim on the Russian and Chinese fronts and the Japanese in complete control of the whole of South-east Asia. This letter lay on the police files and came to light much later, when I had sat for the competition and qualified for the provincial civil service in 1946 [the ICS had gone by then and the IAS had not started]. A deputy inspector general of the criminal investigation branch who was also a family friend kept harping on it, pleading his helplessness in giving a clean chit in the face of so 'damaging' an observation, but by the time my appointment came, the Raj had packed up and gone and so had the deputy inspector general. However the letter seems to have had another offshoot, for at about nine in the morning a police vehicle stopped at our gate and a police officer along with a couple of cops came in. My father who was dressing up to go to the Secretariat where he was an assistant secretary came out wearing just a dhoti and banian, and also the sacred thread on which the bunch of his keys were knotted. The police officer said 'We have received information that your son has proscribed books, we would like a search'. My father kept cool and taking out the key to my room said 'Go ahead, I never enter my son's room and I can't tell you about his books. You may go in and see for yourself'. Meanwhile my father's orderly who had come to take the files, was standing there and watching Those days the Secretariat orderlies used to be dressed in ornate uniforms with a glittering band almost a foot wide wound round their waists and brass badges. The inspector went up to him and surprised at his presence said 'Why are you here?' The orderly, a tall man in his turban said scornfully pulling himself to his full height 'I'm here because I'm sahib's orderly' (pointing to my father). 'And who is the sahib?' 'He is an assistant secretary in the Secretariat'. The officer did not stop a moment, and placing the key on my father's palm and muttering 'Maybe our information was wrong' hotfooted it down the drive. Such was the dignity which an officer of the assistant secretary's rank had in the Raj. Now in our era of independence I know of two secretaries who have been roughed up by elected members of the assembly and even by their own staff. Had the police officer searched my room perhaps he might have found a couple of banned books – even Mahatma Gandhi's and Nehru's were prohibited – but he did not dare.

The British Indian government used ruthless force in crushing the 1942 movement, 'Leonine violence' Gandhi called it, – machine-gunning mobs from the air, firing, lathi-charges, tear-gassing arrests and so forth 4,000 to 10,000 killed according to Jawaharlal Nehru's *Discovery of India.* Processions were of course disallowed, and I recollect how once we lined up in the arts faculty of the university campus prior to taking out a procession. A tall Englishman, perhaps a magistrate arrived along with an armed police force. He held out his hand with the wristwatch on it and shouted 'I give you five minutes to disperse. After that we'll open fire'. We stood fast for the first there minutes – he kept announcing them as the hands of the watch moved – then there was a little dithering, a few broke away and ran, then some more and before the five minutes were over, the grounds were clear of all students. That evening, however, they collected again [I wasn't there then] and marched out. A short way off the police stopped them and started firing, the students lying low on the ground to avoid the lethal bullets, One of them somehow couldn't manage it, perhaps suffocated by the tear-gas which had preceded the firing, and stood up for a second. 'Shoot him' the officer shouted 'he is alone' Just then another lad stood up too and shouted back 'No, he is not alone' He was promptly shot through the breast. His statue was put up before the university union. Quite possibly it is still there–the name as far as I can recollect, Lal Padmaker Singh, It was all so tragic and sad, but then the stubbom *netas* of free India are not behind in their brutality which indeed is much more of a rough spin, and less pardonable because while the British fury was against an alien race and to preserve the Raj, the ruthlessness of our politicians stems from nothing but their own personal aggrandizement. People are shot in the India of today merely to make the voting-bank of politicians secure. For example, hundreds of unarmed Hindus were massacred at a Hindu place of pilgrimage in an action which one Congress leader after making an on-the-spot assessment termed as 'more horrible than Jallianwala'.

Although the professors and lecturers of our university could not actively participate in the movement their sympathies were with it. They would be secretly pleased if their students boycotted classes in protest. Indeed one of our professors wrote out on the blackboard the lines of a Shakesperean sonnet:

'They that have power to hurt and will do none,
That do not do the thing they most do show
Who, moving others, are themselves as stone
Unmoved, cold, and to temptation slow;
They rightly do inherit Heaven;s graces;
And husband nature's riches from expense;
They are the lords and owners of their faces,
Others but stewards of their excellence'..

'Who do you think that reminds you of?' our professor asked us. When we were silent, he said with unmistakable pride, 'Mahatma Gandhi, of course'. Then he wrote out the concluding part:

'For sweetest things turn sourest by their deeds
Lilies that fester smell far worse than weeds!

'That' he explained 'is what the British administration is'.

With the hostels vacated and the university closed, the students were at peace, except those few who get caught unawares in agitating mobs. Mismanaged, disorganized, sporadic, ill-planned and badly executed the movement however did accomplish two things – firstly it made the British realize that Indians were as much determined and indeed more, to get rid of the foreign yoke as they were in 1857, and secondly, it paved the way to Pakistan which was a gift given to the Moslems to reward them for their loyalty, and foolishly conceded by the Hindus.

7

THE TRAINING CORP AND MINIATURE DURBARS

Trust me, false praise has charms, false blame
has pains
But the vain hearts, long ears and
addled brains.

HORACE

I joined the University Training Corps (UTC) which was believed to be an asset in competitions, though I knew it wasn't my cup of tea, for I was wholly a studious type more at home with books than with marching-boots. We were given a pair of uniforms socks and *puttees* etc., and told to try on the many pairs of boots lying in the stores to select the ones which fitted the most. They were sturdy but rather rough on the feet particularly on long marches, as once when a cranky officer decided that we should march from Allahabad to Pura Mufti, a village about twelve miles off for our annual camp. Quite a few of us had to line up for getting the sores on our heels treated by the camp doctor, when with our haversacks and water-bottles, we finally arrived. I was a flop, and the most exacting were the yearly camps with ten or twelve of us huddled up in a tent through which the cold seeped in which could only be dissipated by the morning sun. The lights-out would be observed early and an officer would come round to check that the lanterns had been extinguished, but the chatting went on late nights and I had difficulty going to sleep. The whole organization was managed by the university and the officers were our own lecturers and teachers but when in camp we were under military regulations, and there was the same discrimination between Indians and Englishmen as in every other department in the Raj. For example, once I fell ill with slight fever and wanted to go home but according to the rules that wasn't possible and I was put in a Indian military hospital. (IMH). This one was for natives while the *up-to-dick* British one, the BMH with swell Anglo-Indian nurses and yummy food was for the ruling race. The toilets were smelly and while I had just slight fever most of the beds were occupied by army jawans with all kinds of serious and infective diseases. A man came every morning with a whole bucketful of milk and I was rather intrigued to notice that he would pour out as many glasses as a patient wanted. So when he came to me I asked him what the proportion of milk was in the bucket. 'Oh its about one to six' he said 'want any more?' He was a truthful guy anyway. The *chapatees* we got were thick and half-baked, no sick man's meal those dumped down our *thali* (dish) with the finality of a 'take-it-or leave-it', and if it wasn't for a thoughtful officer of ours who brought us cadets of the UTC some oranges. I would have starved. I don't know if the interview boards before whom I appeared in the competitions added on an extra marks for the UTC< and I'm certain the U.P. one didn't, but the strict routine was good in many ways. We got enough exercise marching up and down, though our sarge had often to yell out my name when I was out of step, we learnt to be disciplined and got arms-training of sorts with dummy 303 rifles, feeling the kick of the real ones at the firing-range. I didn't actually end up as a crackajack for I could become only a corp with just one stripe and to be truthful, despite its good points I wasn't sorry to leave the UTC either. My sarge couldn't stifle a snicker when it was my turn at the bayonet -training, with me running up to the dummy with a 'charge!' that might sound like a greeting to a real enemy, and a thrust which would never touch any internal vital organ. Maybe, however, I did better than the over-enthusiasts who hit so hard that the 'dummy' unused to such exuberance just toppled!

In 1943 I started my two year's course for the post-graduate degree in English. There was a rush for the tutorials of the top-hole dons. There was particularly one who was not only adept in teaching us correct English but also in getting us to learn right pronunciation. Besides his way of teaching was very methodical. I managed to get into his tutorial. Another don, master of several languages, gave us pedantic lectures, wonderful in their erudition, but the grapevine said that if one depended solely on his lecture-notes he was sure to scrap out. Nonetheless he was a professor who commanded respect and admiration and had no equal in learning. Our Shakespeare class was taken by the vice-chancellor himself and when he entered the room you could hear a pin drop. He wouid lecture so dramatically that it was almost as though the performance of the play was being held on the stage, and the closing sentence of his lecture on *Julius Caesar 'Help, ho! They murder Caesar!'* would almost recreate Calphurnia's cry in her sleep! There were the indifferent ones too, but they were rare. For example there was one who would sum up the Romantics thus 'Keats is Keats and Shelley is Shelley, and what to say of Wordsworth, he is above all'! The fact that the warden of our hostel was the vice-chancellor gave it a cut above the others, it also gave us a kind of training in bootlicking, which, I found later, acclimatized me to the nerve-racking bureaucratic durbars when I entered the administrative service. It was customary for us hostellers to pay periodic visits to the vice-chancellor, neatly dressed, awaiting his pleasure. Hours passed while we sat patiently all for a short interview of less than a minute. I remember the wearisome wait in the great man's veranda, each one expectantly hoping to be called in next, and when I had chomped at the bit and was face to face with him, it was an awkward moment, with me having very little to say - I recollect some clear as mud remarks like 'you have a very good library, sir' [he was proud of it and liked it being praised. I heard he even lent a book or two to his favourites, not me by any chance']. 'Do grape grow wild in Kashmir, sir?' [However they grew, it was obviously no concern of mine]. Thus when I had filled the minute with idle talk, both of us were mutually relieved to part and I went back with light steps, glad to have done the month's quota of these obligatory visits. Another curious convention was for the hostellers to send a basket of choice managoes to him when he was holidaying in Musoorie and in return to get a typewritten post card of thanks. That was considered a privilege by the sender. I recollect with a twinge of conscience that, not wanting to be left behind in the *tufthunting* I prevailed on my poor father to send the big man a basket of *dusheri* mangoes the best in the market. Now I realize it must have been hard on him for they were costly and a substantial drain on his thin purse. But he's dead and gone. The stereotyped thanks came, a poor recompense for the penalty my poor father paid to keep me in line with the upper crust

When Milton wrote 'They also serve who only stand and wait',[101] he was of course speaking of God. God is very much connected with India, though. We have already spoken about Gandhi's urging the British to entrust India to God or to anarchy. He was perhaps right about the two being the same, and in fact, when the British went we were left to God anyway, for everywhere we see people right from independence till today standing and waiting. It seems we have all the time in the world. The Moghul *jharoka-i-darshans* have given way to the ministers' durbars and umpteen people keep cooling their heels just to 'pay their respects' and win the VIPs' favours. As I said my training in the formal visits to our hostel-warden prepared me for what was to come, and I have had to spend dreary hours just to wish some stuck-up bureaucrat a happy new year, or waiting for some VIP politician who arrives eight or ten hours late. Waiting, which in other words means spending time without doing anything, seems to have become our guidepost–waiting at railway crossings, waiting for trains or planes to arrive or go, waiting in offices, banks and almost everywhere the citizen gets involved with the ponderous and dillydallying government machinery. Once I had to go to a certain bank for some work. The girl who looked after it would go away as soon as I began to tell her about it, and when she was there the power would go off plunging the bank in darkness. This went on for more then half and hour before I could find her in her seat and the lights on too. So Gandhi wasn't in the wrong for seeing things as they are, India is already in the hands of God, and maybe anarchy is round the corner.

8

A HOMELAND FOR THE MOSLEMS

Let me tell you that Moslem India will not rest content until we have established full, complete and sovereign Pakistan.

JINNAH'S SPEECH ON 5 JUNE 1946 AT NEW DELHI

It is curious that the British at that time should have taken no action against Jinnah for openly inciting the Calcutta. killings.... Nehru or Patel would have received short shrift. Did the government fail to move because Jinnah's Direct Action was aimed at the Hindus and not against the British? There can be no other explanation.

FRANK MORES. WITNESS TO AN ERA

I took my MA degree in English in 1945 and started preparing for the competitions, as everybody does. Government services, particularly the administrative ones, remain the most coveted jobs even now, though we seem to be in the midst of a change inasmuch as the ones in top firms are one up them because of the comparatively much larger pay-packets. Against a four figure salary of about eight thousand rupees in the month for a top IAS officer, that of an executive in a decent firm would be about seven times that much. Much depends, however, on the kind of posting a government officer gets. We will speak of corruption in detail later, here it would be enough to say that with its tentacles spreading out further and further, an administrative officer on a lucrative post, in collaboration with his political mentor, can easily outstrip the highest paid executive in emoluments, by going in for doodle. That's why there's such a rush for 'prize-postings'. It's only the vanishing honest lot who have no share in the cake, who are the sufferers.

All this came later. In my time a decent government post drew respect but not pelf. I thought it would be best to take as my main subject in the optional ones, that with which I was most familiar, namely English. So out of the 500 marks reserved by these, I proposed taking 400 in English and just a hundred in British history (which I hadn't studied in my graduate classes). I sought the help of my erstwhile English professor to whom I went and requested to be told what books I should go through. The reply he gave me put me off somewhat 'Tell your father' he said 'not to waste your time and his money, for no one succeeds in the provincial civil service competition with English as his subject'. Nonetheless I recollected Kipling's line 'If you can trust yourself when all men doubt you' and pressed him to tell me.[102] I soon got over the damper my prof had put on me and went ahead with my preparation.

During my university days I had learnt that a certain brahmin was the chairman of the U.P.. Public Service Commission, the body which interviewed those who sat for the competitive examinations. I had already been primed in apple-polishing by the monthly durbars of the vice-chancellor, and so thought it a good idea to get round this chairman, and would join him in the evening walks he had every day after being introduced to him by a common friend. I imagined it would work, but I did not know how mistaken I was. After the interview my father went to see him and he said 'well, your son has had some experience now, let him try next year'. That left my poor dad crestfallen. Obviously that man had given me so low marks in the interview [104 out of 200, as I learnt later when I got their breakup], that he was sure I wouldn't hit it. It wasn't that I was that bad, but something of which my young mind was unaware then though now it's plain as a pikestaff. That is the bane of our caste-system. We'll say more about this later too. This business of caste is peculiar to the Hindus. At that time the division wasn't only between the upper caste and the lower but also among persons of the two classes in between them. The brahmins claimed superiority as they always have and so they were set against the others, particularly the one to which I belonged. So he had studiously excluded me. It was my first experience of this *godawful hoodoo*. Anyway this 'twiceborn' could not do much beyond flinging me a little low in the list of the successful candidates, for the history examiner had, in some fit of generosity given me eighty-five per cent and that too when the map question [solid marks for that] was answered wrongly. Was it generosity, or was it my own achievement? I think, as I look back, it was neither. That higher power that sits in our hearts and souls, that guides hands helplessly to accomplish his designs; it is he that pulls that strings to make us dance about, and I have a feeling that from what I have learnt about my mother, she too must have had a hand in it, for God may be the master of the universe, but he is a slave to his devotees. My prof too must have been delighted, for even with English [in which I had over seventy per cent, I did not waste either my time or my father's money. The ICS had gone with the British and the IAS had not taken its place. It took two years just to change the name of the service and the service conditions – the kick off of the vaoillation that was to dominate the years of freedom when a decision became a *sixty-four dollar question*. So the same year I also sat for the competitive examination for the combined All-India services, taking English too among other subjects. This time there were five persons on the interview board and the chairman was a South Indian, Needless to say it was the first time I had seen them. The questions asked were trifling ones: 'How do your move about in Delhi?' 'I take a tonga, sir' 'Why don't you take the city bus?' 'Sir, I do not know the bus-routes, for I'm not familiar with Delhi. Besides, I would have to wait for catching a bus and then walk from wherever it leaves me, while with the tonga I do not have to waste time'. Then came the favourite question of interviewers, and the chairman asked me 'What's your hobby?' That one flummoxed me for I was one of those rare birds who lack a hobby. So I told him 'Sir, I don't have any hobby, but whenever I have time to spare I compose some verses? 'Oh, really, can you recite any of them?' I recited one which had appeared in the university magazine. It was my own with perhaps a likeness to W.B, Yeats' sonnet 'When you are old any grey and full of sleep', [103] and it seemed to have hit the mark, for he asked me 'That's yours?' 'Yes sir, it was in the university magazine.' That did it, and when another member asked me how many marks I had got in firing in the university training corps and I said I had forgotten, the chairman silenced him by saying 'Oh, he could easily forget such a small detail. Has anyone any more questions?' They took the hint and I was told I could go, much to my relief, for I had been having sleepless nights in the noisy hotel my father and I had unwisely chosen. In this case I had gained by alphabetism instead of losing for with my name beginning with a 'B' I was the first to be called and I was glad to get rid of the interview early. Later I learnt I had been given 180 marks out of the 200 allotted for this, a smashing ninety per cent compared to the measly fifty per cent or so the provincial commission caste-ridden chairman had given just three or four months before! Thus the unreasoned and narrow segregation of caste which has created races within a race in Hindu society left me disgusted early in youth.

I got through the central competition also and was offered a job as a Finance Officer, but because by this time partition had come with the decision by the British to give Jinnah Pakistan, a clause was added in the appointment letter 'temporary for the present, likely to become permanent'. Of course it didn't mean a thing for a candidate selected through the Union Public Service Commission would hardly be thrown out, but it did make me think. My brother and I decided to go to Delhi to find out more about it and we went to catch the train to the capital from

Jhansi [my first posting as a probationary deputy collector], but just as we reached the station the train steamed off. It was the only train I ever missed in my life, and the normal thing would have been to catch the next one, but when we returned we began to doubt if our inquiries in Delhi would reveal anything and giving up the idea of taking the government of India offer, I wrote a polite letter refusing it. Later, I learnt that when the IAS. was instituted two years later, most of the Finance Officers were absorbed into it. I had missed the bus, and the postman never knocks twice:

> 'There is a tide in the affairs of men,
> Which, taken at the flood, leads on to fortune....
> On such a full sea are we now afloat
> And we must take the current when it serves
> Or lose our ventures'.[104]

The worldly wisdom of that cannot be disputed, but in the 'affairs of men' it is not men who are the arbiters. The *Gita* says that all actions of whatever kind, are comprised of five factors, namely the body which is the seat of action, i.e., the stage on which the drama of life is played; the agent or in other words the incentive to works; the instruments of action, that is the hands, feet, mind etc., the gross and subtle senses; the different individual efforts made; and, finally the fifth factor, providence or the divine will.[105] Now of these, the fifth is obviously not in our hands, and so it is the Moving Finger which writes the holograph. Did I ever regret my choice to stay on the provincial job and decline the central? Frankly speaking I did, but now gazing into the mirror of past memories I think perhaps it was all for my good. I was able to look after my aged father and be with him when he died, something more valuable than all the advantage in pay and status I might have gained in changing over to the other service. Regret is always the outcome of ignorance, for a man can never 'grasp the scheme of things' nor can he ever shatter it or remould it for when fate, or the divine will, makes him take one particular road at a crossing, he does not know what dangers lie on the others, and if he has missed the tide at the flood maybe had he taken it, he would have been drowned. It is only God to whom time is three-dimensional, for whom there is nothing like the past, the present on the future, who can know how events will turn out, whose hands change the tracks for life's train either for its smooth passage or for its destruction, for the good or for evil, and we helpless mortals can only hope that 'somehow good will be the final goal of ill'.[106]

From after the Mutiny the British have always been more inclined to the Moslems than to the Hindus. One reason for it appears to be that even though the Christian ethos is more akin to the Hindus in respect of non-violence, the religion itself is more matched to Islam than to Hinduism. The Moslem, like the Christian, has a fixed place and time for prayers, detests idol-worship, asserts the supremacy of his religion ['I the LORD thy God am a jealous God...'][107] does not believe in rebirth but in instantaneous divine judgement–the *Yaumul fat-h* of the Holy Quran and the Day of Judgement of Christians - believes in resurrection, the *as-sa'ah* of Islam, and finally the Holy Quran mentions some of the Prophets of the Holy Bible. Another reason for the affinity of the British with the Moslems is that largely the Moslems kept out of the national movement and Gandhi's non-cooperation. This nearness of the two is evident in many ways. Despite isolated admirers of the Sanskrit literature (most of whom were Germans not Englishmen) Urdu was always given preference to Hindi under the British rule. The Anglo-Indian schools, like my own, the Martiniere, even employed *maulvis* to teach Urdu as a second language and Persianized Urdu was the language of the offices and courts under the Raj. So it is easy to see why when Gandhi launched the Quit India movement in 1942 by initiating direct action, the British crushed it ruthlessly but when Jinnah decided on Direct Action to achieve Pakistan on 16 August 1946, which was nothing short of a *jihad* against the Hindus or a *qatl-i-am* of the Timur type, the British government did not lift a finger. Partition again demonstrated that same affinity. Attlec, the architect of Pakistan, and Mountbatten the mesmerist, his emissary, realized that India would be plunged into an ethnic holocaust in which the knife-wielding and violent Moslems would be at an advantage, yet the two of them, one an eminent statesman who was fully aware of what he was doing and the other a distinguished naval commander who knew what would happen, put into action this Utopian scheme. The whole thing was like the witches' cauldron: 'Double, double, toil and trouble; fire burn and cauldron bubble'.[108] The fire did burn but there was a difference, for while the cauldron of Macbeth's witches had dead animals in it, the fires ignited by frenzied mobs in 1947 had the fetid stench of burning human flesh, as a historian records: 'They [the women] knew they would be captured and raped. Some of them had babies in their arms. They fed their babies their breast milk, orying of the fate overtaking them. Then they threw the babies in the fire and jumped in after them'.[109] Mountbatten must have known the merciless and horrible nature of Oriental savagery, yet he forced it on India. Partition was a strange concoction of ambition, haste, obduracy helplessness, handshake and even romance. Mountbatten kept the Radcliffe award which delineated the boundaries of what was to be Pakistan and that which would be the truncated India, locked in his drawer for two days [to let the Indians enjoy their newly acquired freedom!] and so from the 15th to the 17th August crowds wandered aimlessly not knowing what would be their future home. Radcliffe himself, who had never seen India before, was given just one instruction; to divide India with SPEED. So with a map which wasn't accurate he sat through the gruelling Indian summer with frenzied mobs outside his camp screaming 'Allah -O-Akbar', 'Har-Har-Mahadeva' and 'Shat-Shri-Akal'. And as he drew the boundary line on the map he said to himself 'I am going through this terrible job as fast, as well as I çan, and it makes no difference because in the end, when I finish they are all going to start killing each other anyway!'[110] Mountbatten had hung his calendar pointing out each day 'so many days to independence.' That was the haste. Then there was ambition, overvaulting ambitions of the Shakespearean kind. There was of course Jinnah who was determined to be the head of the new Pakistan, and Nehru who was eager to become the prime minister of the biggest democracy in the world. Gandhi remarked 'Prospect of power has demoralized us'.[111] He was speaking in that about the dramatis personae of the drama of Partition. The obduracy was Jinnah's who to every question had only one answer 'I want Pakistan'. Mauntbatten had to admit 'The others could be persuaded [to have a united India] but not Jinnah...'[112] The handshake was also Nehru's who had the most prominent role in Partition. It wasn't only Mountbatten who charmed him into accepting it, even more, perhaps a great deal more, it was Edwina (Lady Mountbatten), 'the most sought after girl in London'. Mountbatten himself wrote to Patricia 'Please keep this to yourself but she and Jawahalal [sic] are so sweet together, they really dote on each other in the nicest way...' And while at Simla when Nehru was the viceroy's guest he [Nehru] realized how close he and Edwina had become:

> 'Suddenly I realized (and perhaps you did also)' he wrote nearly ten years after to her, 'that there was a deeper attachment between us, that some uncontrollable force, of which I was only dimly aware, drew us to one another. I was overwhelmed and at the same time exhilarated by this new discovery. We talked more intimately, as if some veil had been removed, and we could look into each other's eyes without fear or embarrassment'[113]

In 1952 Edwina sent her husband a bundle of letters Nehru had written to her. She wrote about them 'Some of them have no "personal" remarks at all. Others are love letters in a sense.... J. has obviously meant a very great deal in my life in these last years, and I think I in his too?'[114] Thus it was a kind of love bond between them, maybe platonio love 'spiritual' as Edwina called it, nonetheless love; and love is a powerful force which as Terence says 'so changes men, that one can hardly swear, they are the same'[115] Lastly, as we have said there was the helplessness, and that was enshrined in the great man who lived to see all that he stood for, undone. Never was there so great a contradiction in the apostle of truth, never so much weakness in one who could shake empires 'tremendous force' as Attlee admitted. Partition 'over my dead body' he had told Maulana Abul Kalam Azad,[116] and yet Pilate-like Gandhi washed his hands of united India and handed it over to the vivisectionists. He did not matter, and no force however powerful can stem the flood of overpowering ambition. Mournfully he said to Manu his great-niece, 'Even Patel and Nehru think I am wrong and peace is sure to return if Partition is agreed upon', and when asked why he had caved in he said 'Everybody is eager to garland my photo and statues. But nobody wants to follow my advice', words which ring truer today in 1995 than when they were uttered.[117] Whatever may have been the case, Gandhi never spoke out and that really was his weakness. One word from him might have made even the ambitious Nehru and Patel ponder, it may have even changed the history of India, but that word was never spoken, and the man who fasted for all kinds of things big as well as paltry (as for example over the unpaid cash balance to Pakistan) did not think this moment to undertake even a day's fast to protest against Partition. Euripides says 'Your very silence shows that you agree'.[118] That's what Mountbatten could have said about Gandhi.

I started service as a magistrate in Jhansi in 1947. My first know about the horror of Partition came when my district magistrate directed me to search the trains arriving at the station to ensure that no unwanted people came into the town. I went to carry it out on a train just arrived. I entered a compartment which I found strangely quiet. No noise and bustle of people hurrying to get out. It was somewhat dim inside, and suddenly I smelt something I had never dreamt – blood, yes blood, and something more, the putrid stench of rotting flesh, and I recoiled with horror as I saw in the dim light the blotches of red on the floor and all over the walls of the compartment, the headless bodies and the bodiless heads, the severed arms and legs and the disemboweled bodies – all that remained of that bloodbath these poor innocent people had undergone. These persons were only coming home from an old one where suddenly fire destruction and pillage were raging, to the new one where they hoped to settle down in peace, and here lay their dismembered bodies, a bloody offering to the love and ambitions of the great. Revulsion and rage surged in me as I stepped out of the compartment to join the cop outside who perhaps already knew what I would find, for he must have been seeing dozens of such trains from which no one would ever alight – *Aceldamas* on wheels, ever moving too and fro, monuments to Oriental bloodthirsty sadism. My district magistrate whom I reported about it was taken aback and indeed the frenzied communal orgy took most people by surprise except those whose acts caused it and who knew fully well what would happen: But not all trains were trains of the dead. A good few came with the living also, and I was switched on to searching the luggage of those who got down at Jhansi. It was a simple job but turned out a nightlong vigil, for all rains came awfully late and the delays would be announced hour after hour so that I was forced to stay put by the station till early dawn sharing innumerable cups of tea with the railway night duty staff. One particular man whose luggage I routinely searched told me he was a very special person and known to the district magistrate, but I was too full of that enthusiastic euphoria that stays on for a few years of an administrator's career, to bother, and searched it all the same. I got a mild drubbing for it, for in those days VIP-ness did not have the rancour it has today. Nonetheless it left me a little down in the mouth, for my boss had said 'everyone', and I had yet to learn that an administrator should take that to mean everyone except people of importance. The gilt is taken off the gingerbread pretty early and the eager beaver bureaucrat is soon disenchanted.

I was married while I was at Jhansi and neither I nor my wife had seen each other before, but the stranger girl I wed was very lovely and affectionate and with forty-nine years of our bond we are on the fringe of our golden jubilee. The Indian marriages were then, as even now, arranged ones. There is no courtship as in the West and the duty of marrying girls and boys devolves on the parents. The so-called 'love-marriage' means only that the two have seen and liked each other, and almost all Indian girls are virgins till they marry, in contrast to the West again: Of whatever kind they are, Hindu marriages are honest-to-God sacraments. In the majority of cases they last livelong, and in this as also in many other ways Hindu society is much more stable than in the developed countries The joint family still lingers on, though it is gradually doing a fade-out, mainly because of diminishing moral values, the go-getterism of modern living with its higher aspirations and a change in the system of living. When we were young our entire house was enough for about five or six families and now when we are old it is not enough for two. The old pattern was a common bath-and-toilet for the men in the house and one for the women. Now each bedroom must have a bathroom attached. Much has been made of the generation gap and many of our present day evils have been ascribed to it. But that has always existed and will ever exist. As T.E. Lawrence says: 'We lived many lives in those whirling campaigns, never sparing ourselves any good or evil, yet when we achieved, and the new world dawned, the old men came out again and took from us our victory and remade it in the likeness of the former world they knew Youth could win, but had not learnt to keep and was pitiably weak against age. We stammered that we had worked for a new heaven and a new earth, and they thanked us kindly and made their peace. When we are their age, no doubt we shall serve our children so'.

Newlyweds have now the privilege of a Western type honeymoon. But there was no such thing in our times. All the sweet-talk had to take place somewhere in the hubby's house bursting with wedding guests, generally on the roof, so in a way the Indian marriage (or at least its consummation) is nearer the heavens than most! Our domestic lives are really one up their Western counterparts and in this respect the developed countries are certainly inferior to the developing ones.

9

LEARNING LESSONS

> The Indian Administrative Service, in effect, does not administer.... In fact it would be better to call them 'ICS' – Indian Clerical Service – instead of IAS.
>
> *VASANT SATHE*

As an extra magistrate I had my lighter as well as my exacting moments. There is no end to the training an administrative officer has to undergo now, at some stages indeed, when he does not really need it. But all the training I ever got was a fifteen days' one with a city magistrate of the old type with greying eyebrows and a stern face. The first tough job was to get inside the old man's court [those were the days before the separation of the executive and the judiciary], for a harsh *bullet-head* who was the city magistrate's peon would motion me away every time I tried to enter. After a few attempts, once I found him dozing on his bench, and I quickly walked up to the dais and handed in the boss's order attaching me to him for training. I sat there through the two weeks, and observed that whenever the lawyers began cross-examination, even the senior ones, and exceeded three or four questions, he would raise his bushy grey eyebrows and the counsel would say 'Huzoor, this is the last question'! Whenever the court clerk (*ahalmad*) wanted to have the city magistrate's signature on the order-sheet of the court file, he would utter a string of the filthiest abuses and ask him to sit down. But the signature was mandatory and after this went on a few times he would reluctantly sign. At the end of my-fortnight's 'training period' during which I just sat, watched and wondered, he asked me whether I'd like to see a movie and on my nodding my head he called the entertainment tax inspector and asked him to take me to one [meaning a free entry]. There was little else. I watched court proceedings and wrote out a sample judgment, more or less adapting one the judge gave and sat for some months with the treasury officer, mostly chatting. It was all window dressing, and when once Pandit Govind Ballabh Pant, the premier at that time, came, I drew a blank when he asked me what the revenue papers were. He was a jovial man open-hearted and sympathetic to us beginners. 'What's your age?' he asked me [I was rather thin and appeared deceptively underage].

I told him. 'And your weight?' I told him that too, at which he was somewhat puzzled. 'That seems all right according to your age. Okay, where do you belong to?' 'Lucknow' *Achchha ab samaj me aya*, he said, *lakhnau ke log nazuk rehna pasand hi karte hain* ['Ah! now I get it, those who belong to Lucknow prefer to stay slim'!].[119] He went on to say that he would soon be starting the qanungo training school for giving revenue training to officers, but by the time that came up I had finished my probationary period. In fact most of the training given to bureaucrats is practically useless for there is a wide gap between it and actual experience in which commonsense and presence of mind are far more valuable than any theoretical knowledge. Pant was a great man. He would keep on talking while his barber was giving him a shave with a long-bladed razor; the safety razor wasn't for him. His barber was a very dexterous one for he had to time his stops and ons with Pant's talk, pausing when he talked and getting on with it while he listened to others.

There was this superintendent of police in Jhansi who thoroughly bugged me by his craze for raids (*davish*). Those days it was mandatory for a magistrate to accompany police officers in raids, for the evidence of a magistrate had far more value in a court of law than that of the police [later the court struck down this provision]. Since I was an extra magistrate, I was like a spare wheel in the boot, and the district magistrate invariably put me on to it. So just as I would be about to bed my newlywed wife, there would be the dreaded honk. Most of it was wasted time and endeavour but this man was a kind of raid-maniac. There was shortage of cloth so government had put an embargo on it, which however couldn't apply to the many Hindu states with which the district was fringed, and there was a lot of smuggling. The smugglers would bring the stuff by goods train [the railway staff conniving] and stop the train so that the waggon carrying the cloth was alongside a railroad crossing. From there the cloth would be quickly and quietly unloaded put on waiting trucks and whisked off to be sold in the black market. I was off on the SP's van and had my Webly in my trouser pocket, best to carry it he had said, we might have to face resistance. There were, of course, plenty of cops with carbines and all. We reached late night, the train was timed to arrive at four according to the police's information, and we lay flat or crouching uncomfortably on a stinking filthy bit of lowlying land. Absolutely still, no talk, no movement, the SP had said. The hours crawled painfully on, one, two, three, three-fifty-fifty five fiftyeight-two minutes to zero hour, but no train. Maybe it was late, they always are. A few minutes after the train came rattling along and –

nothing. It just clattered, clattered clattered till the noise died down and there were no waiting trucks, no stopping at the gate. The dawn was breaking when I arrived home fagged out and sleepy and for the sweet-talk there had to be another night, provided the SP greying about the brows with no amorous desires possessing him, would not honk again. There was success too just in a while, but the catch was small and not worth all that labour and nightly vigils.

Jhansi was a picturesque town with a good few dams and small stretches of forests, ideal for picnicking and shoots. The British had built very nice inspection-houses on the dam-sites with miniature libraries of books contributed by visitors. But when the white sahibs left, things became Indianized and it was only the silver fish who were interested any more in the books (mostly novels) and the only sign of the Raj which lingered was the gun-racks sans the guns, Jhansi has a rocky soil and in the house I got, there were a few small rocks on which poisonous utas reposed. My peon, who belonged to the hills, was quite adopt in handling these reptiles, playing with them as though they were ordinary creatures, catching hold of them, opening their mouths with a small stick and twiddling their forked tongues with it. There were snakes too, cobras and other venemous ones, but he took care of them all, killing them with just a thin bamboo.

Mahatma Gandhi was assassinated on 30 January 1948 at his prayer meeting by an RSS man. Nathuram V. Godse, shot at close range by a Beretta pistol. The plot had been brewing for long, and showing queer lack of insight the government failed to provide any security to the 'Father of the Nation', when ironically all kinds of securities (the Z kind etc.,) are being given now to persons who matter little. Gandhi failed to achieve Hindu-Moslem unity, but his constant attempts to placate the Moslems [which indeed has been a feature continued by politicians right through independence] had incensed the RSS, a pro-Hindu body, against him. For example at his prayer meeting at Poona he had said that should all the Hindus and Sikhs in Pakistan be killed 'the life of even a puny Moslem child in this country must be protected'.[120] Winston Churchill who had always condemned Gandhi, and Field-Marshal Smuts sent their messages of condolence, the latter [with whom he had clashed] saying 'A prince among us has passed away'. But Jinnah was prepared to say just that he was a great Hindu and did not have any wider dimension.[121] It was quite consistent in one who could not move beyond the narrow pale of Islam, for he had once said 'However pure Gandhi's character may be, he must appear to me from the point of view of religion inferior to any Mussalman even though he be without character' According to him 'even an adulterous and fallen Mussalman' was any day better than Gandhi.'[122]

I was entrusted the task of establishing the village *panchayats* and I was away with my staff in a distant village when I heard about the Mahatma's assassination on the cumbersome radio I carried with me wherever I camped. Just then some officer had come there to oversee the work, and he was getting worked up about something. I told him about the news, which left him stunned. The inspection was over and so was my work. We went back to the district headquarters and the dawn was just breaking. A *hash house* was yet open and we had some eats on the way. Gloom has fallen on the city for everyone was shocked at the dastardly assassination, and it was ironic that a violent end should come to the great disciple of non-violence.

I suddenly decided to attend the wedding of a cousin of mine and hurriedly took the day train to Lucknow. I hadn't thought of the hot summer breeze (the *looh*) to which I would be exposed daylong. The train was blistering hot and I was travelling third class. soon I felt I was about to get a sunstroke and began to feel uneasy. A uniformed man, who seemed to be a cop advised me to try some sweets and a drink of water when the train stopped at Orai, but it was no good. He asked me who I was, and when he learnt I was a magistrate he took me to a first class compartment, with a big block of ice to keep it cool [there was no air-conditioning then], and introduced me to a handsome man dressed in a silk shirt smoking the most expensive brand of cigarettes, It turned out he was an excise inspector a low-ranking post, but notorious for soap. The man who took me to him was not a cop but an excise-peon. I told the man sitting there. I had only a third-class ticket. He said not to bother, he seemed to have complete command over the railway staff for the ticket checking inspector [T.T.I] peeped in at one stop and didn't say a word. It was my first acquaintance with the importance of money, however it is earned, but for the moment I was glad to have a respite from my ordeal. We chatted on and I learnt he too was posted at Jhansi. We became friends and I met him often.

It was time to say goodbye to my colleagues and acquaintances, for I was transferred to Barabanki. My father wanted me in Lucknow for he had become so much used to his friends there–he had just three who went together every evening for a stroll – that he was uncomfortable anywhere else. He knew the officer who dealt with our postings, so he gave me this one, he couldn't manage to get me Lucknow, he told him but Barabanki was next best. It was only seventeen miles from Lucknow, just forty or forty-five minutes by car. I had to get a waggon to carry whatever few duds I had and also my old car which couldn't go that distance by road. When I went to book one the station master told me to freeze out. 'No waggons', he said. 'there's is a shortage of them'. 'But then how can I take my traps' I protested 'and my car, it's not roadworthy and I have to take it by train to Barabanki where I've been transferred'. He asked me who I was, and when I told him, he was all attention. I got a chair to sit, a nice hot cup of tea, and the hard-to-get waggon. That was my second lesson in the Indian Carnegian school and ever afterwards when I had any tough job in hand I would first tell the man who I was, instead of just my name, for in this country what you are matters, not who you are, and the ordinary citizen is a tin man one, no great shakes.

10

DISENCHANTING THE RURAL MASSES

Princes and lords may flourish or may fade
A breath can make them, as a breath has made:
But a bold peasantry, their country's pride
When once destroy'd can never be supplied.

OLIVER GOLDSMITH

At that time, 1948, Barabanki, while being a district could easily be mixed up with a progressive village. There were just a few houses, curiously each one having a qeer name to go by, for example the one I was ultimately allotted was known as the 'Station-wali kothi' and the one adjacent the 'Phoos-wali'. There was no electricity in the town and to begin with I was given a small dark room to live in, pending the vacation of the house, which was later divided into two portions to accommodate two officers and their families. I was alone during most of the period of my stay, as Lucknow being so close, my wife and children lived with my father. For some time an officer of the education department and his wife (they had no children) occupied a portion adjoining mine for they were houseless and had asked me to accommodate them till they could get a house. The very first night, I was woken by a woman's cries, 'O don't ! you are killing me ! O stop, O I'll die!', and so forth. I was alarmed and thought I'd go and find out, but fearing getting involved in trouble and partly because I was sleepy, and it was bitter cold outside, I just went to sleep again. Next morning the man was strolling about as usual in the compound. 'What happened?' I asked him, are you both all right? I heard screams in the night'. The man smiled and made no answer, and it came suddenly to me that I had guessed all wrong. They had been making love, but I never heard a woman scream like that when coming.

It is ironical that we should have started off when free, by whittling down those areas which we ought to have benefitted. The whittling down of the freedom of expression which reached its highest point in the period of Indira Gandhi's prime-ministership, began when we got our freedom. The Press (Special Powers Act) 1941 was ostensibly to 'better control dissemination of undesirables matter', giving obviously a wide scope to determine what was desirable and what was not. The Press (Objectionable Matter) Act 1951 barred 'the printing and publication of incitements, crime and other objectionable matter'. Again the political leaders at the top could call anything said against them as 'incitement' or 'objectionable matter'. An independent press is a pipe dream, and quite a few of the papers in India remain bound to party loyalties, stemming of course from the proprietors who own them.

As a sub-divisional officer I had to work for two government schemes for the United Provinces (renamed Uttar Pradesh), the zamindari abolition scheme (ZAF meaning zamindari abolition fund) and the compulsory procurement of wheat from farmers. They sought to assist farmers but they did it *over the left*. The aim of zamindari abolition was to get rid of the zamindars, who were believed to be cruel to their tenants, and to create a class of farmers who would have real rights in their land, the ones authorized to transfer their rights being called 'bhumindars [from *bhumi* = 'land'] and others, 'sirdars'. For getting these rights they were respective by to pay twenty and ten times their annual rent. We, the revenue officers, starting from the chairman of the board of revenue at the government headquarters right down to the tahsildar were involved in it, and the most vital links in the chain, the real doers, were the sub-divisional officers and the tahsildars. We were told to collect the ten times rental (the twenty came later) but on a voluntary basis – no big stick, no putting the screws on . We would go to the villages, the whole lot of us, SDO, tahsildars and naib-tahsildars (some posts of these being specially created for it), along with a posse of the police force, quite about two dozen persons in all, and in the height of summer when the scorching *looh* (hot breeze) fiercely rages. Summer is when the wheat ripens and is harvested and whatever little the farmer earned (the majority being poor as *Job's turkey*) went into his pocket, or more likely, was tucked away in the thatch which was the only savings bank he knew. We would go to the village where the *patwari* (village official) had gathered the men, and they would sit and listen to our pep talk about the advantages of paying up; listen and then just go away to their work on the field. Thus it went on, our talks and their listening, and the whole thing ended at that there was no response, as perhaps the government expected, and it was all playing possum. But the chaps at the top weren't convinced, and they kept sending stinkers to the district magistrate who in turn hounded us. What the people sitting at their desks out there in the revenue board, mostly the last lot of the fading away Indian ICS who were peeved as children when they couldn't get something they wanted, done; didn't know, was that in this country nothing is ever done voluntarily. As Chanakya would say, 'No *danda* (punishment) no state'. Anyway it was they who were to order and we to deliver, so who were we to argue? We learnt that the top brass wanted the collections anyhow, so we put on the squeeze. The carbine toting VIP security brigade for politicians and such others is mere ornamentation, a status symbol; but in the village a gun is sheer necessity, for the mudbuilt houses are easy targets for burglars and dacoits. The suspension or cancellation of a gun license is something looked on with horror. Then there is the pit before each house in the village in which the sullage and rainwater accumulates. The local rules say that a villager can be *challaned* (fined) for keeping this pit (*nabdan*) dirty, though how he can do it is anybody's guess. So we went about *challaning* those whose *nabdans* were dirty and that meant anyone who didn't cooperate in having the ZAF collected. Threats to cancel gun licenses were even more effective. Where even this did not work, we used a little twisting of the arm, Sometimes this created awkward situations, as for example when in one village the cops of the PAC (provincial armed constabulary) compelled some respectable persons to carry their baggage on their heads. The whole village was up in arms, and to quieten them I had to reprimand the erring cops and ask them to carry their own dunnage. It satisfied the villagers, but incensed the cops and I had to pacify them too. The money came pouring then, but we also incurred the villagers' ill will , and whenever they got news of our coming word went round that the ZAF people (*das sala wallahs*) were on the way, and they put the padlock on their doors, the women folk inside, and hid themselves in some nearby grove. The government were happy, but we had a problem, for no arrangement was made for the safe storage of the thousands which poured in. The banknotes had to be stuffed into cloth bags, and I remember I had to empty out the attache case containing my shaving-kit to put them in! Once an amin (village official) who was soused, dropped a bundle of notes, but luckily it was soon recovered.

The bureaucrats of today can hardly imagine what moving in the villages was like then. We had to walk daylong in the blistering hot June days, the sun above and the scorching *looh* mercilessly lashing us. We would move thus from village to village, some five miles apart, others even more, do our work in the evening or early morning, sleeping in the night under some tree on rough charpoys after a meal of thick *puries* and whatever the obliging zamindars supplied, whose zamindari we were engaged in taking away! We bathed by the nearby well and went to the open fields to empty our bowels. It was hard and tough going, and the drive was the first measure after independence which left the villagers chafed and distressed. Besides it was a fruitless endeavour for it replaced one class of zamindars with another under a different name.

The next scheme undertaken by the U.P.. government which had to be executed by us, was still worse for it was immensely more oppressive on the cultivators, particularly the smaller ones who ought to have been helped the more because of their poverty. This was the compulsory procurement scheme. Procurement of wheat at the support price is not against the farmers' interests and is a normal feature after freedom. Not all cultivators, however, are able to sell their wheat and almost three-fourths of them have holdings so small that they eat up all the grain they produce. In this maiden post-freedom scheme cultivators had to part with a certain proportion of their grain whether they wished to or not. This was obviously very hard on the poorer lot and a queer beginning to the 'remove poverty' (*garibi hatao*) campaign of the government. Anyway we were merely the executors of the policy that elected representatives of our democratic system made, so who were we to question its wisdom? The procedure was the same as for the ZAF scheme, and we were again going round at the height of summer with the *looh* blasting away. But this time we were armed with the full powers of the government to seize the wheat, the amount each cultivator had to make over being noted on the *parchis* (the slips denoting it). The farmers used the same tactics. Their men would go away and hide in groves and they would remove the wheat from their mudhuts and hide that too. Whenever an informer gave us the tip we searched places for hidden wheat sometimes making a hit and at other times drawing a blank. When we took the villagers by surprise and they could neither hide their grain, nor give us the slip, we entered the huts to get at it. And as I went from hut to hut I was distressed to see the wretchedness and squalor of the people who were truly representative of this sub-continent, for it seemed that heaven's sun did not shine there. On the bare cow-dung coated mud floor under the thatch scantily clothed ill-fed children looked at us, and especially at the cops, with round frightened eyes. The women hid huddled together terrified in a dark room scared stiff, peering with awe stricken eyes and in the dim light the tall earthen jars protectively sealed against decay containing the harvested wheat, they had gathered by the tough grind in wind and sun – all that they possessed, apart from a few odd utensils and earthen pots to hold their germ-infested water from the village well. I wondered what benefit freedom had brought these poor people and what good those who had been raised to power by their votes had done for them. My heart was not in my task and I felt much like a robber snatching away food from hungry mouths, but the people down there in their cosy chairs who imagined they had brought about an era of prosperous liberty had thus decreed. So we got the tall jars opened or emptied the wheat-filled gunny bags and had the stipulated amount written in the parchis weighed out, and departed leaving the poor farmers poorer and more wretched and miserable. Resistance? What could those helpless people do against the authority of those who governed them? At one place, however, opposition came from a mere teenager, a lovely rustic beauty who lay upon the sack and dared us to touch it. She was a very lovely girl. Though we have plenty of up to dick misses, products of beauty parlours, and the loveliness of Indian girls wins world fame, the paragon of loveliness is in our far-flung countryside. Anyway no one could have the brass to remove her from the wheat-bag and for once we were thwarted and that too by a lass!

All these ill-advised and fruitless schemes only succeeded in estranging the farmers more and more, They lost faith in us and since we represented the government, in the government too. And the most troublesome aspect of these measures was that we harassed them when they were most needed on their fields. After sometime they came to believe that whenever a government man visited them it was to take away something. There was plenty to give too, but the giving was most uncertain for most of it did not reach them at all, instead it went into the pockets of those who were supposed to give it to them. It's not that we haven't progressed but the advantages have not gone to the people who need them most. As London based non-resident Indian tycoon, Swaraj Paul says ' benefits had not reached the common man.... India has announced good policies but their implementation is poor' [23] That was later, but to begin with, in the early years of independence, it was the other way about. Implementation was all right, it was the schemes which were faulty. The various schemes also failed to achieve their objectives. The ZAF scheme substituted the bhumidar for the zemindar, compulsory procurement brought much misery to the farmers without having any impact on the prices of food-grains, and the consolidation scheme which aimed at bringing together small holdings and consolidating them into *chaks* (bigger areas) had only a temporary effect, for soon the law of succession split them up again. It was much labour lost.

There were no inspection houses then, at any rate not in the faraway villages in which most of the work of revenue officers was. All touring was in tents which were pitched in some grove near a village. *Rasad* (foodstuff) was obtained from that village and we had our own arrangement for cooking. When camp was over a bill was drawn up for the *rasad* and we paid up. No lavish dinners or lunches like the ones which have now become the fashion. At times the weather was hard on us, as for example once when we camped in a grove there was a sudden storm and it rained tadpoles till the whole place was a sheet of water. The lanterns had gone out and it was dark as the inside of a black cat. The straw spread in our tents was soaking wet and the water had entered inside, making us toss about all night uncomfortablly on our charpoys. Luckily the trees stood firm despite the branches swaying crazily, for had even a branch ripped off and fallen, it could have been fatal.

We had the lighter side as well as the tough moments. The tenor of the district is set by its head, the district magistrate and the executive officers under him, just as the fate of a nation lies with those who are at the top, the minister and the prime minister in the case of a democracy like ours. I will speak of the latter afterwards, here I speak only of our district. I was taken for a ride, but I must explain first. By some chance, it was *whoopee water* which reigned supreme, so much so that a senior officer from headquarters had to be sent to rap us over the knuckles. 'You may all get delirium tremens and die for all I care' he shouted at us holding a finger aloft 'but I won't have you making the district a tavern' But he didn't know half of the goings-on , and that was where I was spoofed. I had gone to meet the boss but found that he and a few of us of the gay life gang' were all set for Lucknow. I though that a good opportunity to pay a visit home as my family were there. So I asked if I could come too and on being told, yes, squeezed myself into the car. I hadn't the faintest idea of where exactly they were going but the roads in Lucknow we were passing were quite unfamiliar and whenever I wanted to ask 'where?' there was no answer. One of us in the car was the proprietor of a certain factory in Barabanki and I didn't have the foggiest idea of why he was there, and then, hey presto! we were on the first floor of a house in a fair sized room with a carpet for us to sit on and round cylindrical cushions for backrest (*gau-takias*), bottles of Scotch and glasses, the usual things for a rantan – and something more, a man with *tablas* (small tambourines), and a slim fair teenager, bangles on her wrists and lovely long waving tresses! That explained the presence of the factory chap. There wasn't any backing out and I thought it would some be over and I could drop on the way back, but no, it went on and on, and the Scotch was too good to resist. The girl danced and sang on, with the *tabla* - man beating his *tablas* merrily in tune, and to my embarrassment when they found me uneasy they started beckoning to the girl, who took the hint and squatted before me. Maybe that was a kind of encouragement, but it fussed me up all the more and I just sat there red in the face, even more so when the boss, soused by then began to dance about himself! It was four in the morning by the time the spree was off and there was no other course except to return from where we had come. Home would have to be next time.

There were the tough days too, as when a communal riot broke out in a village of my sub-division. I was resting content at home as I had go the okay report from almost all police stations telling me that Moharrum had passed peacefully, when I was told it hadn't for the rioting had taken place in an interior village of which I had never even heard, as I had taken charge of the sub-division only a few days back. The Muharram processionists carry *tazias*, [models of the tomb of Imam Hussein] which are buried by them under the earth. [124] They had concealed weapons inside these and all of a sudden they fell on the hapless Hindus round about, stabbing many of them, some fatally. The Hindus, caught by surprise became victims of this communal frenzy. The village, a couple of miles away from the road, was unapproachable and the PAC cops who went there on trucks had to lop off overhanging branches and hew out a path for the vehicles. I had thought my stay there would be for a few days, but I was mistaken. Quite possibly the officials at Lucknow had become panicky, for there would be some order or the other from them almost every day, passed down the line to us. A few of these made hardly any sense, as for example one day the district magistrate said that the government was not satisfied with the numbers of arrests made and we should make some more. That meant nabbing some more Moslems for it was they who were the aggressors. But nab whom? The riot was a slapdash affair and by then everything had settled down, with perhaps a little tension remaining. I called the police inspector in charge and told him the problem. 'It's easy sir,' he said, 'you'll have them in by tomorrow'. We went on the police pick-up. Whenever he saw a poor scraggy man of no consequence (he know all the respectable ones and avoided them) he asked him his name and if it was a Moslem one he'd roughly order him to sit behind. After we had thus rounded up about thirty absolutely innocent and unconcerned persons, I sent of a message that so many arrests had been made much to the relief of the district magistrate and the satisfaction of the authorities at the headquartaers, who passed on the information to the press and the AIR (radio) so that everyone, the people and their rulers knew action had been taken. That's how our democracy functions!

It was tough going for me with the PAC gong clanging out the hours all night outside my tent. Communication being difficult we had to depend on local supplies from the village we were camping in. They grew some vegetablels but only potatoes and *ghunia* and so we had to live on these alone during our long stay there of about a month and a half!

Why should the processionists attack unarmed people all of a sudden, killing some too? To answer that question we have to consider the attitude of the Moslems towards non-Moslems. According to them everyone born in the world is really a Moslem, only he is misguided into following other faiths. The Moslem is therefore duty bound to see that these misled people who do not realize that Islam is the only true religion, should be brought round to accept it and thus understand that they are really Moslems who have been bum steered into untruth.[125] A report from Washington (*Pioneer*, 10 March 1995 says that even the in worried over Pakistan's role in training Moslem rebels for *jihad*. The *Washinton Post* reports: 'On the third Thursday of every month a bus with about two dozen young men pulls away from a secret rendezvous point in this port city [Karachi] and travels 600 miles north to a base in Afghanistan, where the men spend the next 40 days in basic training for a worldwide holy war.... The group has "sworn to fight for the global supremacy of Islam...."' It wouldn't be proper to criticize scriptures, but it often happens that they are misinterpreted by zealots. A verse of the Holy Quran says 'Fight those who do not believe in God nor in the latter day, not do they prohibit what God and His Apostle have prohibited, nor follow the religion of truth, out of those who have been given the Book, until they pay you the tax in acknowledgment of superiority and they are in a state of subjection'. and at another place we are told 'So do not follow the unbelievers and strive against them a mighty striving' [referring to *jihad*].[126] Whatever these observations may be taken to mean, it is undeniable that in practice when the Moslems invaded India they gave the alternative 'Islam or the sword' to the Hindus, infidels as they called them. Later, perhaps they realized the impossibility of wiping them out altogether and settled for the *jizyah* (poll-tax) which was about six per cent of each individual's total monetary worth. We will not go into the details of the *zimmis* as all infidels were called or of the *jizyah*. The point is that slaying an infidel (unless he accepted Islam) was believed by Moslems to be a gateway to heaven and such a slayer became a Ghazi ('Victorious in a holy war'). Largely because of their aggressiveness, the Moslems remained a class to be reckoned with. The Congress was always under the illusion that it represented the Moslems as much as the Hindus. It never learnt that only a purely Moslem body like the League could really do so. The same misconception prevailed right though independence, and now an additional factor has given them more significance, namely the vote-bank scramble. After agreeing to truncate India in order to give the Moslems a homeland, when the birthpangs of Partition were over, India, which according to the logic of it, ought to have become the homeland of Hindus, ended up with more Moslems than in Pakistan! The expression 'Indian Moslem' then came into vogue though it was a rummy concept for there is really nothing to separate this kind of Moslem from any other. There can only be a Moslem Moslem. With the rejection of family planning by Moslems, their population as compared to HIndus accelerated at a greater rate with the result that the Moslem block in India is the deciding factor in any party being brought to power, so all political parties are prepared to *get down on their marrowbones* to curry favour with them. Thus, strangely enough, it has turned out that the Hindu is being passed up in that very country which was earmarked as his homeland! It sounds quite absurd, but then reason has never triumped over the lust for power or the lure of ambition.

11

DOWN TO THE DESK

I have in general no very exalted
opinion of the virtue of paper
government.

EDMUND BURKE

After a long spell of roaming the countryside I was at Lucknow, as my father had desired. Now I was tied down to an office with the opportunity of going round districts—no more village roving. Apparently, however, the boss of the evacuee property organization in which I joined, a judge, was fishing for some other person, his favourite, and he didn't take kindly to someone who had been thrust upon him. Though I was the same caste as him, he thought otherwise and with his resentment at not getting his man he gave vent to his chagrin by giving me a bad chit the first year. But thereafter he found out about the caste affair and gradually set things right for me. Caste has been one of the most remarkable and damaging features of Hindu society. This was the second time when I had to face the hideboundedness of our caste system. Beginning from a casteless society long ago in the Vedic period, centuries before the birth of Christ, the first social division was spoken of in the most sacred scripture of the Hindus,the *Bhagavadgita* as the four *varnas*. The division was on the basis of *svabhava,* (i.e., the nature of the person) and occupation (a priest, warrior, trader, or the service class). It wasn't caste but class. Gradually, however, this concept degenerated into caste and among these of the high and the low, which was never the intention of the teaching of the *Veda* or the *Gita.* Whenever a division takes place two things happen. The chasm becomes wider and wider, and secondly, unsoruplous or ambitious people take advantage of it to further their ends. That's what is happening to Hindus now. The British exploited castes by separating the so-called scheduled ones from others, with freedom, the Indian politicians stepped into their shoes and were even one up, for they created many other privileged castes like the backward the other-backward and so on. This is such a *boob stunt* that an SC candidate got a place in the merit list of a pre-engineering test with just *one* mark out of 900! [The *Pioneer* UNI. 16 June 1995] All these are of course a vote-catching devices but they have managed to completely fragment Hindu society and pitch one caste against another. The Hindus were never a strong or closely knit organization from the time of the Moslem invasion. They have been, and still are a weak and timid race ever fighting among themselves an easy prey to domination and gullible to pretenders who promise them the moon when all they are seeking is their own aggrandizement. The only Hindu state in the world remains the small one of Nepal, and Hinduism does not have a universal acceptance like that of Buddhism, nor does it have the tenacity of races like the Moslem. HIndu civilization has doubtless had a long spell but its intrinsic nature is such that it is bound to be extinct like the civilizations of the Greeks and the Romans, particularly when pretentious Hindu politicians are engaged in putting the kibosh on it.

In the department I found myself, the task was one of the offshoots of Partition. As has been said, the whole process of carving out a home for Moslems from the Indian sub-continent was an ill-planned, illogical and hasty affair. The division of assets brought out the littleness of Oriental minds. Colliris and Lapierre calls it 'The most complex divorce in history'. The Moslems wanted the Taj to be dismantled and shipped to Pakistan! while HIndu holy men wanted the Indus to be diverted to India because it saw the birth of the sacred *Vedas*![127] Liaqat Ali wanted one of the six presses transferred to Pakistan. In Lahore the superintendent of police Patrick Rich, divided his equipment between a Moslem and a Hindu deputy. Everything was distributed till just one instrument, a trombone, was left. Said Rich, 'Before my unbelieving eyes my two deputies, who had been comrades for years, got into a fight over which dominion would get that last trombone'![128] One of the consequences of Partition was the resettlement of Hindus, mainly Sindhis and Sikhs, uprooted from what comprised Pakistan. They had fled the Moslem wrath gathering whatever little they could carry and had to make a start from scratch. The refugees who poured into the truncated India, however were enormously more than the Moslem who fled India. While only 7,900,000 Mosleme migrated to West Pakistan, almost five million Hindus and Sikhs were driven from the Punjab side and another four million from East Bengal.[129] Moslems left behind property valued at 1,000 million rupees as against that of 5,050 million rupees of that of non-Moslems.[130] this was because the Hindus coming from Pakistan were much more prosperous than the Moslems as even Pakistan's paper the *Dawn* admitted, 'The people who migrated to India belonged on the whole to the capitalist class, and those who replaced them in Pakistan to the toiling classes'. There were many meetings and committees to solve the problem of rehabilitation, but nothing came out of them for the values of the property were disproportionate and in any exchange Pakistan would be a much bigger loser. As regards land left behind, Pakistan feared that India might divert the flow of the waters of the Ravi and Sutlej thus making the agricultural land in it unproductive, and so it kept linking this with the canal water dispute, However the demand of the refugees in India could not long be ignored and so an Act was passed for compensating them from the proceeds of evacuee property, Pakistan doing the same there. The task was a huge one and the evacuee property organization was constituted for this with an army of judicial and administrative officers in the districts appointed for it, designated as assistant and deputy custodians (the judicial ones to decide disputes arising). An office to oversee their working came up at the headquarters, and that was where I found a place as deputy custodian (headquarters) on the executive side. The job entailed considerable touring in the districts for inspections, but it was goodbye to the villages. Here I mention an incident which again confirms the inevitability of destiny. i had fixed up a tour in a certain district, but because of a last moment change, I decided to go the next day instead. That same evening my peon went to bathe in a rivulet, almost a nullah, called Kukrail. A stay dog had bitten him, and according to a popular superstition a dip in Kukrail would cure it. He wasn't cured, he got drowned and died. Had I not put off the visit, he would have been with me miles away from Kukrail. It was the Moving Finger again. There never is any escape from it.

My work gave me the opportunity to go to various districts, and one of these was Agra where stood the Taj Mahal, one of the seven wonders of the world, built of pure white *makrana* marble (the best available) and its inside walls inlaid with precious stones. The Taj did not impress me and as Aldous Huxley said in one of his essays, 'it was a disappointment'[132] But the reasons were different. While Huxley deprecated its monotonous architecture, and the lavishness of its decorated panels, I thought of the way it had been built and its purpose. With all its extravagant grandeur, it was just a mausoleum and it did no good to the memory of the woman whose tomb lay in it seeing the way in which it was built and the conduct of its builder which belied the deep love he professed for her. The Taj was raised by the blood and sweat of the poor. More than the candle light (with which the guides show its glittering embellishments) it is the agony and the tears that are reflected in the roses and poppies depicted on its panels and on the royal tombs, 'filigreed and patterned with an inlay of precious stones'; for as Bernier said 'it was the cudgel and the whip which compelled men to incessant labour'. Clearly therefore Shah Jahan's architectural monuments, among them the world famous Taj, were built by forced labour. Besides, after Mumtaz Mahall's death and her entombment in the Taj, the faithful lover seemed to have drowned her pious memory in a flood of debauchery, and as Manucci tells us he violated the wife of his brother-in-law and that too with the aid of his own daughter![133] He ordered a huge hall to be built adorned throughout with great mirrors, the gold of which alone cost a fabulous fifteen million rupees! 'The walls were of jasper and huge clusters of pearls hung at the corners of the mirrors. Here he ravished his women observing his lovemaking reflected in the mirrored walls and roof.[134] The Taj was not a monument to fidelity, it was merely the embodiment of the wasteful lavishness of an egotistic potentate. All this came back to me as I gazed at it, and I thought of how the pain of its builders turned out to be a curse on the king who spent his last days imprisoned by his own son in the Agra Fort's 'hall of mirrors', no girls to delight him, for this one was not for pleasure but for torture and the mirrors in it reflected the Taj so that to the end of his days he could remember the love he had betrayed.

Then there was the fort at Agra, desolate, with bare walls, where once jingle-bells jingled on the ankles of lovely women gyrating seductively, and wine flowed freely and the light of ornate chandeliers lit up the magnificence and lasciviousness of its halls. We went on to Fatehpur Sikri where once lovely women went to splendid bazaars, now a ruined city with its massive gate. Here, as everyone did, we ate *moghuli-parathas* and omlet the special delicacy of the place. Agra is one of the places the foreign tourist never misses, the other one being Benares (now Varanasi) the holy city of the Hindus. Benares is famous for its temples, its ghats and its holy men — as the saying is *rana sada sirhi sanyasi in se bache to seve kashi* ('One can see Kashi, i.e., Benares, only if he doesn't get taken with the widows, the bulls, the steps of the ghats and the ascetics'). Dying in Benares is believed by devout Hindus to confer *moksha* and many, the aged, and the widows shunned by HIndu society, go to seek *moksha* by spending their last days at Kashi (*karavat-kashi* as it is called). It is the city of virtue as well as of vice and many a *cat house* masquerades as a temple, disguised by an ornate facade with figures of gods and goddesses. Inside there are no idols, but girls and in a small open yard where drinks are available, a kind of secret bar. When one had them he is led inside and offered girl after girl till he chooses one. There are the genuine temples too, some of them grand like one within the Benares Hindu University campus and the illustrious Kashi Vishvanath, one of the most sacred temples alongside of which there is the inevitable mosque, which the Moslem rulers always built to demonstrate the triumph of Islam. The bulls jostle along with the walkers in the serpentine lanes of the city which wind on and on as if they would never end, for cows and bulls are considered sacred by Hindus. When I was working as administrator of the municipal corporation long after in 1977 I had to look after the upkeep of the Kashi Vishvanath temple as the trust in charge of it had been superceded. I thought of constructing small pillars at the entrance of the lane leading to it to keep out the stray bulls and cows as also the rash scooterists who would often go speeding in and out of it. But I found a lot of opposition to this despite the fact that it would be protection for the worshippers and pilgrims. One man to whom I spoke about it remarked 'Cows! ah, have you ever seen a cow which is not docile?' I thought it fruitless to argue for an orthodox Hindu (or a Moslem) is guided by emotion, not by reason. It was futile to tell him that I *had* seen a bull rather averse to the human species, who had unceremoniously given a woman in the lane a push which sent the score or so lighted earthen lamps (*dias*) she was carrying on a tray for offering worship, flying off and shattering to pieces. Luckily no one was burnt. Benares city goes on and on alongside the sacred Ganga. It does not spread out breadth-wise. As for all other Indian cities, there are two marked divisions, the posh civil lines (a remnanent of British seclusion which along with other traditions of the Raj, we have found advantageous to continue) and the city proper for non-VIPs. The city is one bewildering mass of tall ancient structures having the nineteenth century look, winding lanes, bits of which are skirted on both sides by houses whose roofs almost touch each other, where the sun never shines, and the roads one seething mass of pedestrians, rickshaws with ever-tinkling bells, vehicles squeezing in and cows and bulls rubbing shoulders with the moving mass of humanity. The last movie shows are over it midnight and it takes another good forty-five minutes for the waiting rickshaws to take the people coming out, home; and early at four in the morning the bathers appear chanting the holy name, playing on various musical instruments like the *kartal* (a kind of small cymbals). So the only time a light sleeper can sleep is between one in the night and four in the morning. Just three hours, only an hour short of Napoleon's doze on horseback!. There was one particular man who stood out from the conventional bathers. He would play on the *kartal* and dance as he went, swinging from side to side, chanting *Rame Rame satye hain* (approximating to *Rama nama satya hai*- 'Rama's name is the truth' (which HIndus utter when they take out a funeral procession). I wondered why he went like that every morning, exactly at four, and on inquiring from some bathers, learnt that his young son had died and his mind had become deranged by grief, so he went imagining that he was taking his son's body for cremation each morning. It was more sad than odd. Among the ghats of Benares which serve as funeral places there is one, the Manikarnika, which is exclusively for the rich and the powerful. Having space for a funeral pyre here is a costly affair unless the corpse is that of a man of importance, for the belief is that the souls of those who are burnt here go straight to heaven and are not again reborn. It seems a stupid belief for it's the deeds of the person which are significant, not the place where the body, shorn of the divine soul, is burnt, yet we find sages as renowned and godly as Shri Ramakrishna giving credence to it. He says:

> 'I saw [at the Manikarnika ghat]' a tall white person with tawny matted hair walking with solemn steps to each pyre in the burning ghat, raising carefully each *jiva* (soul) and imparting into his ear the *mantra* (holy words) of supreme *Brahman* (The Absolute). On the other side of the pyre, the all-powerful Mahakall was untying all the knots of bondage, gross subtle and causal of the *jiva* produced by past impressions and sending him to the indivisible sphere by opening with her own hands the door to liberation. Thus did Vishvanatha, the divine Lord of the universe, endow him in an instant with the infinite bliss of experiencing non-duality, which ordinarily resultls from the practice of yoga and austerity of many cycles. Thus did he fulfil the perfection of the *jiva's* life?[135]

Thus do religions auction salvation to the highest bidder. The Hindu gets it by paying through the nose for cremation in Benares's Manikarnika ghat when he dies. The Roman Catholic confesses and is absolved of his sins. For the Moslem it is simpler still. All he needs is a sword to hack off the non-believer's head , and lo! heaven is his. It was Benares which drew the observation from Huxley 'If I were an Indian millionaire, I would leave all my money for the endowment of an Atheist. Missioin'.[136] But it is not only the Indian millionaires who need to contribute, for religious fanaticism is not confined to India There are fanatics in all religions. It is Islam which is the most assertive one, and HInduism is perhaps the least, for it has in its fold devotees of all shades—those who believe in a formless God *Brahman* which is much the same as the Moslem concept of Allah, and those who believe in image worship like the Greeks and the Romans. Hinduism even accepted the Buddha, making him one of the incarnations of the Lord when really Brahminism and Buddhism were in direct opposition.

Other distinctive features of Benares are its tradition of music, for it is the home of distinguished musicians like Pandit Ravi Shankar, the renowned sitar player of world fame, Gudai Maharaj the famed *tabla* player and Sitara Devi the talented dancer, Benares was also the centre of Sanskrit studies and in ancient times no education was complete without a stay in this city. I found that the betel of Benares had a taste and flavour not known anywhere else. It is hard to chew it without the spittle spilling out and many a *kurta*-front is spattered with its bright red!

In 1956 my father died. The end was sudden and a coronary carried him away. It was the first time I was face to face with death, for all my life I had been kept away from such unpleasant things. Although death is an inevitable consequence of life, it is always a shock to see our beloved friends and relations die. Despite all the soothing things religion and philosophy say about it, nothing can remove its sting. Time can only dull its sorrow but not remove it, and homilies are no salve for the wounds. Despite all the researches on after-death and out-of-the-body experiences the fear of death remains because it is the snapping of years of association and a leap into the unknown. The ceremonies which follow are as exacting as they are illogical. Among Hindus as well as among Moslems curiously enough, death is mourned by a feast in which relations and friends are invited. In fact there is hardly any difference between celebrations and obsequies. The *bhatti* (improvised oven) is made of bricks and a *halwai* (cook) engaged. There is a string of relations who keep pouring in one by one so that arrangements have to be made for all. Besides, the whole affair is a considerable drain on the pocket for according to the Hindu custom the brahmin priest who conducts the ceremony has to be given gifts consisting of all the articles needed for domestic use. Almost all that the priest gets, he sells off in the market, for he already possesses them. And so the merry-go-round moves with the duds being bought and sold, the shops dealing with them happy with the profit they thereby make!

Our administrative system of evaluating the achievement of those working in the government by annual character-roll entries leaves much to personal prejudices, for with us taking an objective view of anything is well nigh impossible. In this, as in many other matters, such as transfers and postings, while adopting the British pattern, we have debased it, for in the Raj the only relation between the employer and employee was work. I had a taste of this while at the end of my tenure in the evacuee property department. The secretary got biased against me and due to certain personal reasons wished me to make an inspection of a western district in order to find fault with the officer there. That was a district which my boss had reserved for himself and so I had to take his permission for inspecting it. That irked him and he rang up the secretary saying 'What right have you to order my officer to inspect a particular district?' That set the secretary against me and I was preinformed by a wellwisher that I was on for being transferred to an obscure district on an indifferent post. The only way out was to take medical leave which I did and then managed through recommendation, the Indian panacea for all such ills, to get into the local board of revenue office as an assistant land reforms commissioner. Such things were unknown in the Raj for there was no *darbardari* euphemistically known as 'paying one's respect'. The social circles of the British rulers and the Indians over whom they ruled, were quite apart and subordinates went to their bosses only on official business. In the absence of any personal relations there were no partialities or prejudices.

The board of revenue of those days comprised senior ICS officers at the top, the last ones of the vanishing Indian officers of the covented services so called because they had been appointed, before the advent of freedom by the secretary of state. Of these there was one, Siddique Hasan, whose memory I particularly treasure and another, A.N. Sapru, who was remarkable for his fortitude. The greatest stumbling block for us humans are arrogance and vanity. S. Hasan was completely free of them. There were various incidents illustrating this. On one occasion he is said to have invited an old orderly of his to a dinner thrown out to his own brother ICS officers, and in which he paid special attention to his orderly to the wonderment of his colleague. This is but hearsay, but I had my own experience of his large-heartedness. On the day he took over he went round meeting all his subordinate officers. A few days after my father-in-law died and I applied for two day's leave. The application went to the secretary of the board, my immediate superior. He sanctioned it, but just to inform Siddique Hasan, who was a member of the board in charage of land reforms with which I dealt, he sent it on to him too. As soon as this reached him he called his steno and dictated a personal letter to me, getting it sent immediately to my home, expressing his sympathies and he wrote 'as regards leave you may take as much as you like'. This was a human gesture and the mark of godly persons, sages in worldly garb. A.N. Sapru's case was peculiar. He had been bitten at one time by a dog and had taken a course of anti-rabid injections, which in some rare case, one in a thousand, react and result in paralysis of the limbs. Unfortunately his was that rare case. He was paralyzed waist downwards and his hands were shaky so his notes (he wrote very long ones) were penned in a rather cramped writing. But despite his disability he was the member who toured the most! Two orderlies would lift him bodily and seat him in the car and he'd be off. It is very difficult to fight against our disabilities and the struggle is hard and uphill As a noted physician Dr Naomi Ramen says when illness strikes it's like hitting a wall at 90 miles per hour'.[137] Every permanent disability is taxing and nerve-racking. There are those who give in and spend their lives in profitless self-pity and depression And there are those whom the disability gives the spur to added effort so that they can prove that with it they can do even better than if they had been normal. As Dr Remen observes, 'There are people who are very healthy physically who are not living what I would call a healthy life. For them life has no value, direction or purpose. There are also people who are quite ill who lead a very rich life in terms of those parameters. I would call them healtheir than the people who simply have physical health and no reason to live'.[138] The religious philospher, Reinhold Neibi, whose advice was used by the USO to inspire troops during World War II had perhaps the last word on how to meet disabilities, 'Give us the grace to accept with serenity the things that cannot be changed, the courage to change things that should be changed, and the wisdom to know the difference'.[139] I particularly recollect the occasion when I went to wish A.N. Sapru a happy Holi. After offering me the customary sweets he said something which I feel has proved true and is proving truer as time passes. 'These days' he said 'one visits another person either because he can do him some favour or do him some harm'! That has become in reality the sole purpose of our social intercourse.

At this time the sage and social reformer, Acharya Vinoba Bhave was propagating his *bhoodan* and *gramdan* movements (*bhoo* = 'land' *gram* = 'village', *dan* = 'offering'). He was a very well-meaning person, a recluse and an authority on the *Gita*. Averse to medicines he died without taking recourse to any, a kind of spiritual hara-kiri. The main idea of *bhoodan* was to persuade those afflulent farmers who had surplus land to gift some of it so that it could be allotted to the landless and provide them a living- It was the same with *gramdan* which involved the gifting of whole villages. The Acharya's scheme was doubtless well-intentioned and for the public good, and it got the full support of the government who promulgated a Bhoodan Act and a Gramdan Act to give validity to the land donations Siddique Hasan had particular interest in it and he and I as his assistant got it going. But it was a flop because most of the land given with much outward show was barren land, quite useless for cultivation. The figures went up and up and the government and those associated with *bhoodan* were elated, but it was all a mere triumph of statistics and didn't mean a thing for there were no takers. The landless could hardly do anything with the unculturable land and it was all labour lost, just *flimflam* and *spoofery.* the entire effort only resulted in *sham workerism.* The authority of the board of revenue has been considerably eroded ever after the exit of the Raj. In the British days the English ICS officers aspired for postings in large towns, mostly the headquarters of the government because only these had clubs where they could have the kind of social life they were used to in their country, like balls and cocktail parties. One of the officers working in the Secretariat thought he represented the government and passed up the board. He was promptly transferred to a district and when he wanted to know what his fault was, he was told 'You have been transferred so that as a district magistrate, you may learn how to conduct yourself with the board of revenue'! But all that vanished after the Indian ICS and all the more so when their successors of the IAS took their place. It was partly because the governments of independent India became overbearing, but more because of the steady deterioration of the officers themselves. The British officers drank, but they never expected drinks at public parties. Their Indian counterparts had no such reservations. An Indian ICS member of the board would on his inspection visits, when invited to dinner by the senior officers of the district have several drinks after which he was just fit enough to sit in his car and be taken back to the inspection-house to seek his bed. Another, an IAS member, got so drunk that he started misbehaving with the women invited to dinner and had to be bundled off! Of course this deterioration was visible not in the board only but all over; but of that later.

English, which remains the language used in the offices of the central government and in the high courts and the supreme court, was still continuing in the provincial government, and all our notings on files and the letters were in that language. The ehangeover to HIndi came long after.

On leaving the board, I was once again in the district as additional district magistrate of the pilgrim town, Allahabad,

12

AT THE FEET OF MOTHER GANGA

Even evildoers attain emancipation
by just taking the sacred name of
the Ganga

MATSYA PURANA

The name Allahabad is of Moslem origin, but the ancient name of this sacred city which was the virtual capital of the provincial government in the early British times, was Prayag. Now the only remnant of the old name remains the small suburban station which is near the university. Allahabad is still the city where the High Courts are, housed in a grand architecturally majestic building, one of the many which have come down to us from the British times. Essentially, therefore, the city is primarily inhabited by judges, lawyers and the professors and lecturers of the university. More than anything else Prayag is one of the most sacred places of pilgrimage for Hindus, for it is at the confluence of the Ganga and the Yamuna rivers with the subterranean Sarasvati believed to pass under them. One can clearly see the line marking the junction, the whiteness of the Ganga on the one side and the bluishness of the Yamuna on the other. This confluence is known as the Sangam (from the Hindi word of that name meaning 'union') and a dip here is believed by Hindus, to wash off all sins and if taken on a certain day — the *mauni amavasya* — on the occasion of the annual holy fair held there, is said to confer emancipation. A press report of the Ardha Kumbha of 1995 (mid-Kumbha), says: 'over a crore will bathe on Monday in the sacred waters of the Sangam on the occasion of the *mauni amavasya* which coincides with *somvati mauni amavasya* falling after 40 years and is considered auspicious by the devotees. An unending stream of pilgrims drawn from all over the country and abroad were pouring in....'[140] I have had the opportunity of seeing the Kumbha, the Ardha Kumbha and the Magh (held every year) for Allahabad is the city of my birth, my university days and again my posting as additional district magistrate. The ashes of every Hindu high or low (except of course of the poor who can't afford it) are strewn at Sangam. According to legend the Ganga flowed from the toe of Vishnu, the Preserver in the Hindu trinity. It is said to have been brought down from heaven by the austerities and prayers of the sage, Bhagiratha to purify the ashes of the sixty thousand sons of king Sagara who had been burnt by the angry glance of the sage, Kapila. thus it is also known as Bhagirathi. In order to check the torrential force of its descent from heaven, Shiva contained it in his matted locks from where it flowed down from the Himalayas and thence to the plains. The Yamuna (wrongly spelt 'Jamuna') is believed to be the daughter of the sun, and is associated with Krishna and the cowherd maids of Braj. The Kumbha (along with its allied fairs) is the largest religious gathering in the world. It turns almost into a mini-city with numerous tents and shops, and sadhus from all over India gather here. The prominent sadhus bathe ceremonially, arriving on elephants and horses, and take the traditional royal bath *(shahi snan)*. It is more or less a parliament of holy men. Their different sects camp in their own *akharas* to which flock a number of sadhus with various sacerdotal marks adorning their foreheads. The Kumba is an expression of the solidity of the Hindus and a demonstration of Hinduism's firm surival despite centuries of cruel repression by Moslems who wanted to wipe it out and on the *q.t.* conversions of Christian missionaries.

It was an embarrassment to me to find myself at loggerheads with the students belonging to my own university where I too had joined in the 1942 agitation, and all the more so because it was now in an independent India. The occasion of the confrontation has already been narrated earlier. The students were annoyed with a cinema owner about restriction on their entry either because they were refused the concession in rates they demanded or because they wished to force themselves in free. The resultant disorder and police firing has already been narrated.

That was the beginning of the nightmare. I was asked to man the control-room all night and I had to lie awake on an improvised bed at the police station. We had planned to get the provincial armed constabulary into the university campus at two-o-clock in the night. By then the students who would be studying in the hostels would be asleep and it would be quiet all round. The *jawans* would wear canvas shoes so as not to make any noise. It was well-planned and perfectly executed, and when it was daybreak the entire PAC force was camped inside, everyone, the students, professors and visitors taken by surprise. The government had decided on an inquiry into the whole affair by a single judge of the High Court who was an ICS. officer [obviously a continuation of the British practice of having the civil servants both on the executive as well as on the judicial side], and to prepare for it we had to hold endless fudge up sessions discussing to the *n*th degree what each one of us would say in the court. Here evidence is generally fabricated, for nothing can happen in the *fine whack,* and citizens are chary of getting involved with the police and courts, so if there are no eye witnesses, fake evidence can always be made available; in fact there is a popular adage 'come on, out with the truth now, you aren't before any court'!

The Indo-Gangetic plains are the most fertile and productive areas of the Indian sub-continent. As the mighty rivers the Ganga the Yamuna and their tributaries flow, they deposit sand (which is one of the ingredients used in construction of buildings) and damp soil which is highly productive. But sometimes these rivers change their courses and what used to be a water course becomes a stretch of alluvial land on which farmers, and often land-grabbers, cast a covetous eye. The sandy soil of the erstwhile river-bed is ideal for growing melons and watermelons and a kind of pumpkin from which a sweet delicacy (*petha*) is made. The land further down is just the article for bumper crops or it if is firm enough a boon for the mafia for they can usurp it for colonization. Often bitter struggles, fights and bloodshed are the outcome, for it is very difficult to say in land of shifting cultivation, known as the *khader* area, who is the real owner. I did not realize the immediacy of solving this issue till my district magistrate made it sink in. The course of the Ganga river had slightly altered leaving a chunk of land for which the people of the neighbouring villages were raising a ruckus. we went by boat to the other side — a narrowing experience for it was an open boat without any covering overhead and the torrid. Indian summer sun mercilessly beating down on us. We listened to the various claims and gave an on the spot settlement, returning late in the evening, with pleasent boating. That wasn't of course the end of the problem but I was in the district just about a year and it didn't come up again in my time. The changes in the rivers' watercourses also cause innumerable other problems too, such as rehabilitation, floods and so forth.

Lal Bahadur Shastri, the small man with an iron-like determination, winner of the Indo-Pak war of 1965, was, unlike the Nehrus, Indian to the core. Essentially a man of the village, he was straightforward, simple in habits, anglicized in virtues like punctuality, but not in his life style, unassuming and unostentatious. At that time he was home minister in the government of India. My district magistrate was going on a week's leave and before he went he told me that Shastriji was arriving next morning by the night train which reached Allabahad at four in the morning and in accordance with the protocol I should, in the DM's absence, receive him at the station. It was a beastly hour, but there was no escape. However , just a little time after he rang me again saying that Shastriji would not like to be disturbed. so no one need receive him. He would keep on sleeping in his special railway car and drive home (he was a resident of Allahabad) when he woke. The DM said I needn't go, and it would be enough to send the tahsildar, I felt relieved and went to bed. I was a late riser, and the ring of the phone woke me up at about eight. 'DM sahib, how's Shartriji?' someone was inquiring. 'Well, he must have gone home by now' I said 'and must be there, probably at his breakfast'. Luckily the person speaking was a neighbour of mine at Lucknow and we were friends. He had become the private secretary to the chief minister of the province and it was he who had rung me. 'Look' he said, 'Shastriji has got a heart attack and the chief minister wants to know how he is. So you had better find out and ring me back immediately.' That set me into action. Nobody had told me about it, although the attending civil surgeon ought to have done so. Anyway I rushed to Shastri's house, learnt that he was out of danger and asleep and I conveyed the information to Lucknow. Thereafter I had to keep a regular tab on his condition, a kind of two-hourly news bulletin, for the phone calls kept coming from Delhi and Lucknow and other places all over, 'How's Shastriji? How's Shastriji? Please don't disturb him, but do tell him so and so rang to inquire his welfare.' Baloney! They didn't care a fig how he was; they just wanted to put their names in Abou Ben Adhem's Book. For the next few days all I did was to hand out progress reports on the minister's condition till the DM returned and took it over from me. Shastriji was, in fact quite all right by then and fit enough to resume work, but the local civil surgeon would not give him the okay for he'd never soon get an opportunity to attend on a VIP of that stature! Ever since then I was wary about the health of VIPs coming to my district, and one one of them, a lesser one, had a similar condition, but that was more comical than of consequence, and will be related later. Those were the days of sense among politicians, and the times have gone, never to come. Now even if a minister gets a cold by an officers' sneezing on his face maybe he's in for a transfer!

The American ambassador, who must doubtless have been taken round to view an election in our democracy on a conducted tour, as he happened to be a VIP, observed about it, '... there has seldom been a more orderly or peaceful vote of a great nation .... In Asia as in America I know of no grander vision than this government by the consent of the governed'. *Buddying up* is of course necessary in an ambassador's attitude, besides the dirty side of things is obviously kept away from him; but our electioneering does not deserve such encomium. Orderly and peaceful voting is a chimera so far as our elections go, and the 'voice of a great nation' is largely the voice of the illiterate, the communally-minded, the casteists, men doled out small favours and bribes, and even goons and yobbies. In every election in our days there is booth-capturing, shootouts, running away with ballot boxes, goondaism, impersonation and dozens of other malpractices. In fact quite a few elections are fought not by the ballot but by the bullet. It was my first brush with an election, but it wasn't for the assembly or parliament, only for the local municipal corporation. In one of the booths some miscreants knocked down a wall, rushed into the room where the ballot-box was and before one could know what was happening they took hold of it and ran away. A repoll had to be held and the district magistrate was rightly furious about it, but he wasn't fair on the magistrate in charge there. 'Why didn't you use your revolver?' he said. As the magistrate told him, however, a revolver was of no use against a crowd of people storming in. Besides firing inside a closed room could have diastrous consequences if the bullets ricoheted. Ever since then I have been through many elections in different capacities, as a presiding office and a returning officer. In one of these I put misplaced trust on one of the clerks of my office who was a polling officer in my station, and gave him the ballot papers, asking him to be sure he came at least forty-five minutes before voting started. Everything was ready and the boxes arranged and sealed. Half past seven, a quarter to eight, nearing eight – yet no ballot papers! I was in a mess for the polling had to start at eight sharp. Just a couple of minutes before the time the chap came and I felt relieved, determining never again to trust anyone so. Elections are an exacting business for those who have to manage them. After they are over, there are innumerable statements to compile, the long wait for the truck which will collect the boxes, for one truck goes round several polling stations, and presiding officers, some quick workers others slow, take varying periods of time finishing their work. Then there is the endless waiting for depositing the boxes and the statements. By the time it is over most probably the dawn would be about to break, often with no conveyance in sight, meaning that one has to walk home, but with light steps, for the whole drudgery is over. In one of the elecations I was the returning officer (the district magistrate is designated so for the period of the election). During election time the district magistrate and the superintendent of police, who are expected to supervise the election, move about together visiting as many polling stations as they can. I was at Muzaffarnagar then, a place having a large population of Jats who are sturdy longlived and industrious farmers fond of the hookah and connoisseurs of wrestling. They are mostly an agrarian people attached to their fields, so much so that [as I learnt] the foulest abuse with them is *hal jutva denge* ('I will forcibly have your sown field ploughed'). At one place we were informed that a fight had taken place and there had been some shots fired. We rushed up to the place fearing the worst. When we reached there, sure enough, there were four persons lying on cots each covered with a quilt. 'We've had it' I said to the SP, 'seems they are dead'. Just then some people came and being the other party involved, they started telling us how it started, accusing those lying on the cots to be the aggressors. Then unbelievably to our amazement, the men whom we thought dead, uncovered their heads one by one and shouted out to their accusers that it was they who were in the wrong, and one man, apparently grievously injured with a gaping wound on his head walked a few paces pointing his finger at them to emphasize what he said. Such was the stamina and endurance of Jats. About elections in general something will be said later. Here I only recount my experiences about them. Incidentally the Hindi spoken in western U.P. is in a somewhat different accent. The 't' for example is accentuated and *roti* ('bread') is *rotti.* Some words are also typical. *Taparghas*, I learnt means 'a man of antiquated notions'. A favourite word is *dhumadhar* which means anything on a grand scale – a *dhumadhar kushti* for example means a 'great and entertaining wrestling bout'.

The *mukhya nagar adhikari* (literally 'chief town officer' had gone on three month's leave and I was put in his place. The municipal corporations which exist in the principal towns of the province, the KAVAL towns [Kanpur, Allahabad, Varanasi, Agra and Lucknow] work under the *mukhya nagar adhikari* while they are elected bodies, and when they are superseded and taken over by the government the supervisory officer is the administrator. In the smaller towns there are the municipal boards which too work on a smaller scale on the same principle. Local bodies existed from the earliest times in India. Even as early as the Mohenjadaro and Harappan civilizations four thousand years before the birth of Christ. Excatations revealed the existence of planned towns, streets and an elaborate drainage system. The British rulers merely introduced new methods in their working. In 1683 a corporation and a mayor's court was established in Madras under a charter given by

James II. The corporation levied taxes for the building of a guide-hall, a jail, a school-house and so forth. The first statutory enforcement of municipal administration was introduced by the Charter Act of 1793 by which justices of the peace were appointed who in addition to judicial work, looked after scavenging and repairing of streets by levying taxes on houses and lands. Between 1840 and 1853 elective principles were introduced in the presidency towns on a limited scale. It was left to Ripon, however, to introduce regular municipal administration by the government of India resolution of 18 May 1882. The areas of jurisdiction were small like the *tahsil* or the *taluka.* Some boards were independent, others under the district board and a system of election for the members devised. There was autonomy to some extent and supersession could be only by the consent of the government.

Thus a start was made in local self government by the British. After independence, however, the municipal boards did not show any improvement even though there had always been an outcry against too much government control. As in almost all other matters, there were quite some committees – the Balwantray Mehta Committee, the Santhanam Committee, the Rural-urban Committee, the Local Finance Enquiry Committee, the Taxation Inquiry Comittee and the Rafiq Zakaria Committee. They met, deliberated, wrote long reports which nobody had the time to read, noticed the shortcomings and suggested remedies, but that was all. In so far as acting it was a washout and the municipalities and corporations were soon *out of whack.* In fact we are not merely marking time, it's getting worse and worse. The study made by the Rural-urban Committee, 1963, revealed some shocking facts – no drainage system in medium and small towns, no connection with sewers in more than 60 per cent of the houses in large towns, lack of water supply and in Calcutta one latrine serving for 30 to 60 persons![142] True the municipal boards in the towns and the *gaon sabhas* and *panchayats* in the villages are plagued with lack of funds, but at the same time they hardly make any effort to fully realize taxes and get income from the properties in their charge. The two main reasons for their flopping are political exploitation and rampant corruption. The mayors of elected corporations are most of the time involved in party politics and keep funding their respective parties from the money of the corporations which should really be used for the tasks with which they are entrusted. The political affiliations of village panchayats are even stronger and a decisive force in our elections. Most of the time is spent in internal bickerings just for kicks. The curse of corruption is even worse, though of course the municipalities share this with other departments which are corrupt in varying degress (we will speak of corruption later). Thus the towns and the villages remain nauseating and garbage-stuffed, with no planning, interspered with slums, littered with open manholes, and overflowing sewers the dimly-lit roads constantly dug up by various departments of the government, having potholes left by repeated welcome-arches whose *ballies* (wooden supports) are wrenched out after they have served their purpose, traffic signals which have long ceased working, speedbreakers at VIP places which keep sending vehicles continually to workshops for repairs and hundreds of other ills too numerous to mention. Another feature of local administration is that like every other, it is an armchair affair. The officers entrusted with it remain glued to there seats when really they should be moving round to see things for themselves.

While I was on my three month's assignment with the municipal corporation (*nagar mahapalika)* of Allahabad I had a taste of these evils. The mayor who became a big shot afterwards, was, as all people who make their mark in our politics, a Moslem fan, though he was a Hindu, and had fished out something to show that Shivaji was a descendant of a Moslem! He was also constantly at loggerheads with the deputy mayor, as is often the cose in elected corporations, but as I was there only for three months, it hardly bothered me. The municipal boards are constantly plagued by demonstrations, strikes, *gheraos* etc., by the staff, and politicians can often be very nasty for most of the time they are engaged in wanting wrong things to be done and the administrators are the most vulnerable of officers. While working as administrator of the municipal corporation at Varanasi long back there was one guy, related to a minister belonging to that place, who on coming to me on the very first day of my tenure said 'You don't know me, I eat up men!' (I qote what he said in his exact words – *ap jante nahin hain, ham admi ko kha jate hain*). 'In that case', I told him why pick upon a bony chap like me, you'll get more to eat if you get hold of a person with plenty of fat on him!' That settled him. Then there was the minister in charge who came on an inspection and addressed the officials. In order to appear popular he left his chair and squatted on the table! But it didn't pay off, for later when he was scrutinizing some papers with us in a room, there were loud shouts and noisy slogans outside in the corridor., I hastily shut and bolted the doors, but the officials who were armed with sticks smashed the glass-panes, It was a trying moment and it was only when the cops came that the trouble petered off. Then one day I found myself *gheraoed.* The staff, who were on strike, squatted in the doorway to prevent my going out. Some mediamen were sitting inside at that time for they were fishing for something to print in their papers and for the 'advertisement' which would give their paper some money. I was in a fix, so I went to my steno's room which adjoined the toilet of my office room, telling the pressmen that I was going for a pee. Instead I went to the steno and asked him if there way any backdoor by which I could dodge the *gherao-wallahs.* There was. And guided by him I went out, and got into the waiting staff-car, and back home! Local self-government has pegged out in India, the village *panchayat* eroded by prejudices, intrigues, casteism, politics, dispensing a kind of wild justice, and the urban local bodies sunk in corruption and squandering the funds got by taxing citizens to get political mileage.

13

MAMMOTH MEETINGS AND CROWDING FILES

At thirty man suspects himself a fool;
Knows it at forty, and reforms his plan;
At fifty chides his infamous delay,
Pushes his prudent purpose to resolve;
In all the magnanimity of thought
Rosolves; and re-resolves; then dies the same.

EDWARD YOUNG

Back to the table. There wasn't any air-conditioning in the Secretariat then, and every room had a cooler fitted in summer, all making an awful din like hell breaking loose. The peons and orderlies sat outside in the corridors in the sweltering heat (electric fans were provided later). Like other things, we adopted the British system of administration with just changed names, the superintendent for example came to be known as the 'section officer' and the clerk as an 'assistant'. Time was the first casualty. Gone were the days when the work started punctually at ten and the offices closed at four-thirty. At opening time most of the chairs were empty and if someone who had some work asked where the assistant was the curt reply was *seat par nahin hain* ('he's not in his seat'). You had to be content with that. There wasn't any fixed closing time either. The day was spent in gossip with numerous cups of tea and coffee and soft drinks in summer, all at the taxpayer's expense of course, while visitors waited in anterooms or in the rooms of the personal assistants (PA's) and whenever someone asked when the sahib would be available he was told 'sahib is at the meeting'! There were the genuine meetings too, huge affairs in commodious halls. Many were roped in just because the conveners felt that to be on the safe side it was better to call them. They came, had the coffee and snacks and sat through without speaking a word. The meetings were more or less platforms for orataions each officer making a kind of speech. Of course it was all recorded, cyclostyled and circulated, but nothing really came out of it. The notes on the files, mostly written by the clerks have become longer, and even after that they end up with a 'please speak' by the officer to whom they are addressed. The reason is that everyone wants to put the responsibility of taking a decision on someone else. The Gian Prakash report on the recent sugar scandal observed 'The various departments had adopted an approach of passing the buck and were not concerned as long as the responsibility could be passed on to someone else'.[143] The present administrator works in an atmosphere of fear and tension for he does not have the kind of support from our governments that the British ICS officers had from theirs, so he keeps dithering. *X-teen* rules make it impossible for any administrator to remember them and so a decision could go against some rule or the other technically, even though made in good faith. This also makes the man at the lowest rung of the ladder, the 'dealing assistant' the only one who really knows anything about the matter concerned, for at his level these umpteen rules thin down to those only which concern him. That gives him the knowledge about the subject which others above lack, and with this the capacity to put things the way he chooses, for with so many rules and regulations, in quite a few matters there are two conflicting ones on the same subject. This is the inevitable result of the haphazard way these rules are made. As we have seen the British officers always wanted to have the letter under consideration along with the previous reference. With us this practice has fallen into disuse and it has become practically impossible to connect the letter with previous decisions. Therefore quite often conflicting ones are made and this provides a handle for corruption. Another factor responsible is that our ministers, most of whom have no idea about administration and merely wish to have what is to their personal advantage speedily done, get regulations made without devoting their minds to them. Rules are made not to govern but to satisfy the whims of those in power. No wonder the constitution has been amended 78 times in 47 years and when rules are made amendments are not far behind. It's not that no work goes on. In fact most of those involved in running the government work out of hours and are overstrained. But what is the outcome? Prices keep rising and these hit the poor and the middle class the most, particularly when they involve articles of food. The rich grow richer and the poor, poorer. The comparative wholesale price index for 1994 and 1993 for the month of December was as follows:[144]

WPI		WHOLESALE PRICE INDEX	
DECEMBER		Annual % change Base 1981-82= 100	
1993	1994		
250.33	276.66	All Commodities	10.5
289.18	316.00	Food Articles	9.3
254.30	299.20	Non-food Articles	17.7
135.60	143.74	Minerals	6.0
265.80	281.16	Fuel, Power, Light and Lubricants	5.8
247.10	267.88	Food Products	8.4
308.00	347.20	Bevereges, Tobacco and Tabacco Products	12.7
220.63	257.62	Textiles	16.8
403.60	429.38	Wood and Wood Products	6.4
327.23	328.18	Paper and Paper Products	0.3
249.60	258.70	Leather and Leather Products	3.7
190.10	199.62	Rubber and Plastic Products	5.0
209.25	237.34	Chemicals and Chemical Products	13.4
260.93	275.56	Non-metallie Munerals	5.6
279.70	310.54	Basic Metals, Alloys and Metal Products	11.0
235.98	264.92	Machinery and Machine Tools	12.3
225.70	241.30	Transport Equipment and Parts	6.9
142.30	166.90	Miscellaneous Manufacturing Industries	17.3

Thus it is evident that prices of all commodities have shown a rise during just one year, and what is particularly alarming is the fact that the increase has been quite substantial in articles of food. The wholesale price index for all commodities, base 1981-82 for December 1994 increased further to 276.66, up 10.51 per cent over December 1993 and inflation is edging up toward 12 per cent. Government has itself accepted that shortages in items like sugar and cotton have played a key role in inflation. Moreover while money supply was Rs 14,600 crore in early December 1993-94, the corresponding figure for 1994-95 is a meagre Rs 857 crore. Steep rise in the prices of essential commodities like sugar (largely due to the sugar scandal in which leading ministers of the central government were involved), kerosene oil, groundnut oil, coconut oil repeseed oil and mustard seed oil, wheat, rice and other foodgrains has been most taxing to the poor. Moreover it is they whom corruption and exploitation affect the most. Essential commodities are meant for them, but greed deprives them of any advantage. For example in a tahsil of Lucknow, the government headquarters, a press note says, 'these [essential] commodities, chiefly kerosene, have gone off the market.... a few workers of the supply department have been conniving with fair-price shop licencees.... who are selling off the quota of kerosene, sugar and food-grains in the black market at high rates.[145] As we have seen, villages are in a mess with uneconomic holdings, poor crops and ever increasing population and poverty. By the year 2050 we will have 1.5 billion people to feed, and with the much flaunted green revolution at a standstill it is quite impossible to find food for them. Even now when the government claims to have a stock of over 30 million tonnes of grain, 300 million people are hungry and go begging for food. According to a UNICEF study more than 5,000 children die of malnutrition each year, and many more will die when the population touches 1.5 billion. A study made by the Washington based Worldwatch Institute says that by the turn of the century the country will have to start importing foodgrains and continue doing so for the next 50 years thereafter. Whatever chances there are for getting through this tight squeeze, are rendered futile because of ever increasing soil erosion due to felling of forests. The Himalayan belt is denuded of greenery About 175 million hectares of land is affected by one or the other form of erosion. The subsequent loss of top soil – the top layer of the soil that sustains most crops – is no less than 5,333 million tonnes per year. Instead of irrigating the land, for which the canal system was planned and built by the British, it is causing waterlogging and already nearly one-third of the cultivated land is thereby rendered useless. About 16 million hectares of irrigated land has gone out of production by 1944 end, and no effort is being made to check this.[146]

The Standard and Poor (S & P) survey has the following depressing observation:

> 'India has a heavy external and public sector debt burden and its fiscal position is weak. The country's fiscal deficit which reached 7.3 per cent of the GDP and is expected to fall to 6 per cent during the fiscal year 1994-95 has contributed to a worrying inflation rate. India's currently comfortable balance of payments position is vulnerable to import growth and sustained high fiscal deficits, and its net external burden estimated as 200 per cent of exports in 1994 remains high for similarly rated sovereigns'.[147]

According to a PTI report the trade deficit in the first nine months of the financial year 1994-95 rose to $ 2.011 billion as against $ 731.65 million during the same period a year ago. Yet another reason for the *yes-noismness* of bureaucrats is their exploitation by politicians who make them fall guys for their own misdemeanours. Elected representatives have power without responsibility and paid servants of the government have responsibility without power. This curious equation keeps pulling the reins of the horses of the coach of administration in opposite directions so that it keeps stay put. For example after years, it was decided to take action against retired officers, an action which according to press comments was motivated by purely political considerations. This naturally puts decision makers on their guard, for they may be roped in whenever some slick politician wants to make political mileage or wriggle out of an awkward situation. Commenting on the charge-sheets against former bureucrats for their alleged role in the assassination of Rajiv Gandhi a columnist writes: 'They [the bureaucrats] are unhappy as they feel that Mr Narasimha Rao's government has of late begun trying to fight the ruling party's political battles with the help of bureaucrats.... Consequently, the confidence with, which most officials moved files for speedy action has been shattered. There is a perceptible reluctance on the part of many bureaucrats to move new proposals howsoever important they might be'[148] The politicians hardly bother about rules or the right and wrong of any matter. They just want the thing done. These factors, therefore combine to make governments ineffective and at times even oppressive. All the hard work that goes on is unproductive and does no good to the citizens for serving whose interests governments exist.

A factor which is responsible for the failure to benefit citizens is the standoffishness of administrators, what may be called the 'closed-door armchair' attitude. I worked in the departments of revenue, finance, irrigation, harijan and social welfare and the 20 points programme. It was slightly better then inasmuch as officers were more accessible than they are now, when the entry is only through the room in which stenos and PAs sit and entails waiting till Doomsday. Curiously enough the ministers who beg for votes from door to door when the election comes, are no better, their rooms resembling Moghul durbars in minature. In the finance department, for example, one hardly finds any officer going to see for himself how treasuries function, in irrigation, how the canals are working or in social welfare how the homes and institutions are being run. Statistics, statements and reports are considered to be enough information. Many committees and commissions are of no account and mere wastage of time and money. the only benefit goes to the members who get paid and go on jaunts for so-called comparitive study. It is evident that any taxation reform to increase revenues in impossible if the two-thirds people who live in villages are not brought into the tax-net. Yet a committee under the chairmanship of a renowned economist was constituted for this, knowing fully well that no politician in India can afford to tax farmers [beyond the nominal land revenue] and spoil his chances in the elections. This hiatus between ruler and ruled results in a lot of dilatoriness, customer-and-farmer unfriendliness, and frustration in the minds of those who have to deal with government departments, most of which believe more in harassment than in help. Corruption of course makes it worse, and in India a feeling goes round that *nothing at all* can be done without a get to . It is plain that all the work that goes on in our Secretariats is *donnish* and and ineffectual. This being so, there must be something wrong in the way the work is done, for the phenomenal labour put in by administrators and others in whose hands the country's fate is, ought to have taken the country miles ahead rather than stagnating. So where have we gone wrong? It's a million dollar question for to quote a cliche our Pandora box of ills has opened and one can only pray that Hope (as some believe) is still not out! Here only the system of administration is being considered, the ills in general will be spoken of later. We took over the British system, but adopted a method of dealing with files that was quite different. As we have said, it was the office then which put up the letters and the drafts, and the officers who wrote the notes setting forth their views. We reversed the order. It was now the dealing assistants and the superintendents (the 'section officers') who wrote the notes which became longer as time passed. Perhaps it was the involvement of the officers with meetings, briefing the ministers and the mushrooming of departments which was responsible; or maybe it just became a habit. The consequence was that gradually for the most part officers just signed, and the expression of views was left to the office. The natural corollary of this is that the vital part of decision making is now the prerogative of those who are at the lowest rungs of the ladder. With the expansion of departments we have reached a stage when it is impossible to revert to the old practice, although one of the ICS chief secretaries once had such a scheme in mind. It would mean large scale retrenchment of clerks and a very substantial increase in the number of officers. So the degenerated system continues, and everyone who has some work to be done knows that the way is to approach the lower staff, not the officers. Another factor which contributes to dependence on office notes is the ignorance which assails most officers about what they are dealing with. Frequent transfers is one reason for this ignorance. By the time an officer gets familiar with his work he is sent somewhere else for political or other reasons. Then there is the peculiar practice of manning technical departments like power (electricity) irrigation P.W.D (dealing with construction of building roads and bridge, medical and so forth, by administrators who obviously can't know anything about what they are dealing with. Engineers have to go through four or five years of study in the particular branch they take up and so also doctors and other technical people, before they qualify for their degrees. How can an administrative officer understand all that just by virtue of being conversant with administration alone? Perhaps the only work of technical departments which administrative officers are capable of is that dealing with transfers, postings and promotions, for in that they can act without prejudices, but barring that other things are best left to technical officers.

Then there are the innumerable meetings that plague good administration. Every business tycoon on top of the heap, knows that if a decision can be conveyed on just a piece of paper, it is pointless wasting time and energy in meetings. But in our administrative offices we have protracted meetings which often postpone decisions than arrive at them. The same, in passing, may be said to be the case with inquiries, more often just political gimmicks to underplay some embarrassing issue and put the spotlight off from it. Every department of the government and its offices spends a great deal of time on compiling statements which have really no utility and are just seen and filed. Not that statements don't have importance. They do. But only if they are given attention and convey some useful information. Private up-and-coming firms get statements of the achievement of their workers which give the exact picture of the work done, but that can't be said for statements which keep on being made in government offices.

A government service was considered to be the most aspired for occupation in the days of the Raj. Poet Akbar who lived in the latter years of the nineteenth century and the early ones of the twentieth – the heyday of British rule – having a dig, at this avidity wrote:

Shauke-lailaa-civil service ne mujh majnun ko/

itnaa daurayaa, langoti kar diyaa patlun ko//

['Desire for civil service made this man run so much that his pantaloons got so worm-out that they became a loin cloth!']

This eagerness for a government job has persisted in the post-independent period, despite the much less pay and other facilities which those working in reputed private firms get. The reason for this is the security and the importance which government servants have. The notion of feudalism still persists despite forty-seven years of independence and people flaunt their status as a tiepin. So anyone who's in the government, particularly connected with administration or those departments with which the citizens have to deal with, thinks himself to be a higher-up. The security umbrella is so wide and strong that it is extremely difficult to get rid of anybody in government service irrespective of whether he works or not, or even if his integrity is questionable. There are inquiries and punishments, but with the rules as they exist, ultimately the man is back. The result is that honesty and hard work are at a premium, and the worker and non-worker being treated alike, there is hardly any incentive for work. This can be remedied only by linking salaries and promotions with achievement not as is the case now with other factors like flunkeyism and *shifarish* (out of the way recommendation) and now, caste. This will take away the main attraction from government service, but then with the *in the bag* nature of it, administration is bound to remain off the rails. One reason why everything governments steps into, deteriorates–like insurance, electricity, banking and so forth – is that while private firms pay (and quite heavily too) for achievement only, government agencies do not relate work to that, with the result that a good few government undertakings keep on running at huge losses while the government provides them with crutches to limp along. Allied with this is the problem of overstaffing. We have a top-heavy administration and the imbalance keeps growing more and more with no consequent betterment in efficiency. More than two-thirds of the government revenues go in the payment of salaries and very little towards development, and of that too it is anybody's guess how much reaches those for whom it is meant. Once expansion takes place, there isn't a dog's chance for retrenchment. If any such move is made there are strikes, demonstrations and so forth and the attempt has to be abandoned.

To get on with the narrative, the 20 points programme, which followed the Emergency imposed during the regime of Indira Gandhi, was a double-edged measure. On the one hand it showed that we could work as a disciplined nation and work hard, on the other it also brought out our capacity to misuse power. The state of emergency proclaimed by the president of India on 25 June 1975 under article 352(1) of the constitution was said to be 'happenings in Gujarat early in 1974 leading to the dissolution of the state assembly and the symbolic protest and indefinite fast by Morarji Desai to hold elections in Gujarat when the state was passing through a period of drought, the concept of' total revolution of Jayaprakash Narayan and the extensive coverage by the press to the accusations made by them [the leaders of the opposition parties] against government and persons in office' Thus the main grievance was the activity of the opposition like fasts, protests, countryside tours and so forth, which have been the usual way of opposing measures by parties in the opposition after independence and by political leaders of the stature of Mahatma Gandhi in the Raj, against the British government, and as regards the press its very function is to publicize what's happening. The Emergency was, therefore a purely political measure. The Amnesty International in its report of 1977 observed. The MISA [Maintenance of Internal Security Act] and the Defence of India Rules in particular, had been used extensively to detain peaceful opponents of the government after the declaration of National State of Emergency on 26 June 1975.... precisely how many political prisoners have been detained without trial during the Emergency is not yet known. However official statistics published by the new government showed that 34,630 people had been detained. Of these 6,244 were held under the ordinary provisions of the Act, but the vast majority, i.e., 28,386 were held under the Emergency provisions of the MISA. Article 16-A, which permitted political detinues to be held without even being informed of the grounds for arrest.[150] 'The Shah Commission has by now a comprehensive view of the excesses committed in Delhi... the callousness with which arrests were ordered on false allegations to serve personal or party objectives and with a view to smother protest, the manner in which the Statutory provisions governing detention, confirmation of detention and review of the detention orders were honoured in their breach... the ease with which established procedures and conventions were subverted for the benefit of individuals who had contacts at the "right places" '.[151] The Supreme Court of India defined the character of preventive detention as follows: 'Preventive detention means no offence is proved nor any charge formulated and the *justification is suspicion* or reasonable probability and not criminal conviction which can be warranted by legal evidence'.[152]

The 20 point's economic programme aimed at price control and a better deal for the middle class, the landless and the economically weaker sections. The effects claimed did come, like the zero rate of inflation, fall in prices, better industrial production and so on. Trains arrived on the dot, and people began driving on the proper side of the road, paying due attention to traffic lights. Telephones suddenly came to life Office-goers were in their chairs at ten. Hoarders disgorged their grain and black marketeers no longer made their piles. But it was not civic sense which was oiling the wheels. It was fear. The lesson was that we could do the right thing only under compulsion, and the wonderful part of it was that we could work. Only hard pressure, Chanakya believed, could do the trick, and in a way he was right at least in so far as India was concerned, for the India that he knew had not developed civic sense, and it is doubtful if the India we know has by now developed it, for when that comes, the function of governments becomes not to tyrannize but to act according to the goodwill of its citizens. In fact the end of such an attitude is that government exists only symbolically, for when men do no wrong the question of punishment does not arise As Thoreau wrote:

> 'I heartily accept the motto: "That government is best which governs least", and I should like to see it acted up to more rapidly and systematically, Carried out, it finally amounts to this, which also I believe. "That government is best which governs not at all", and when men are prepared for it, that will be the kind of government which they will have. Government is at best but an expedient, but most governments are sometimes inexpedient....
>
> 'After all, the practical reason why, when the power is once in the hands of the people, a majority are permitted, and for a long

> period continue to rule, is not because they are most likely to be in the right, nor because this seems fairest to the minority, but because they are physically the strongest. But a government in which the majority rule in all cases cannot be based on justice, even as far as men understand it. Can there not be a government in which majorities do not virtually decide right and wrong, but conscience?– in which majorities decide only those questions to which the rule of expediency is applicable? Must the citizen ever for a moment, or in the last degree, resign his conscience to the legislator? Why has every man a conscience, then? I think we should be men first and subjects afterwards. It is not desirable to cultivate a respect for the law as much as for the right. The only obligation which I have a right to assume is to do at any time what I think right.[153]

We have not only overgovernment but governments which have become oppressive by framing law and rules taking away one by one the freedoms which the framers of the constitution had envisaged so that the Indian citizen who was meant to be free is now bound in chains. These draconian laws are really unnecessary as when we adopted the provisions of the Criminal Procedure Code there were already such provisions existing as for example sections 107, 109, 110 and 144 which provided the executive authority including the police to arrest any person they wanted to. The British government had inserted these sections for subjugating Indians over whom they ruled. It is curious that the same compulsions which necessitated an alien government to have rules to suppress their subjects should weigh with the government of the democratic republic we gave ourselves on 26th January 1950. The seven freedoms gifted to the citizen of independent India by Article 19 of the constitution were : of speech and expression, of peaceful assembly without arms, of forming associations or unions, to reside and settle in any part of the territory of India, to move freely throughout such territory, to acquire, hold and dispose of property, and to practise any profession or to carry on any occupation, trade or business. But apparently those who enforced the constitution trusted the citizens as little as the British rulers did for these were taken away one by one making the promised rights, directives and equality mere eyewash. The constitution secures justice, social, economic and political, liberty of thought, expression, belief, faith and worship, fraternity and dignity of the individual, minimizing inequalities in income and providing equalities in status, facilities and opportunities and prevention of concentration of wealth and means of production 'to the common detriment'. What happened and is happening is just the contrary. Justice is not only expensive but also dilatory, so much indeed that it may not be obtained even in one generation. Long back Ghulam Hussain observed in *Seir Mutaqherin* about Clive's Bengal (1757-65) '... to obtain justice is become a very difficult business, a very operose article'... 'A whole life is needful to attend their [the court's] long very long proceedings: and till a dicision is given, there is no comprehending what is going on and what is likely to follow, nor what is the probable end of the business'. It is doubtful if that has picked up much since then. Liberty of thought and expression exists only on paper, and there have been eases in which newspapers which have not gone along with governments have been suppressed and even burnt. The official *doordarshan* (TV) is decidedly an organ of the government, and as we have said elsewhere, freedom began with a curb on the press by the enactment of the The Press (Special Powers Act 1947 'to better control dissemination of undesirable matter', and when just a year after the constitution secured liberty of expression for us a bar was placed against 'the printing and publication of incitements crime and other objectionable matter' by The Press (Objectionable Matter Act 1951, giving free scope to put the kibosh on anything a government or a political VIP didn't favour. As for equality of status wealth and opportunity, the constitution makers couldn't have realized how deep these would be buried. Nothing counts so much as status today. The rich have become richer, the poor poorer, and as for equal opportunity it's nothing but a *four-flush*. Writing under the head 'As it Happens', Sean French says, 'When impoverished peasants or factory workers became dissatisfied with their lot and demanded what rich people had, the results endangered public order. They had to be taught that they would be compensated in heaven'. That is the position with us still. There is opportunity of course, but not for all. It is allied to various individual factors like how much one can pay for getting a job or something normally due to everyone, whom he knows, and now to what particular caste he belongs. Thus the liberty and equality so firmly embedded in the constitution remain a pipe dream. As a writer say's "The Indian constitution is peculiar. It gives enough of opportunities to the executive and legislature to bring in enactments which negate the very rights which it is supposed to confer on the people. It has been made possible to deprive these rights and make them devoid of any substance by a mere stroke of the pen'.[154] Today we have reached a stage when silence is really gold, for an indiscreet word may send the man years earlier to the other world than when he is due! It's as Confucius says, 'When law and order prevail in the land, a man may be bold in speech and bold in action, but when the land lacks law and order, though he may take bold action, he should lay restraint on his speech'.[155] What Confucuis observed long back almost six hundred years before Christ is strangely enough applicable to us today. The insecurity which prevails is such that freedom of speech is silenced and there is mobocracy on the slightest pretext. Politics is no longer a subject of passive disagreement, and violent disorder and disorderly conduct dominate it and political vandetta has found expression in frequent shoot outs. Long back in 1942 Mahatma Gandhi urged the British to leave India to 'God or what in modern parlance is anarchy' Apparently God seems to have stepped in now after fifty-three years!

The 20 point's programme was purely a political gimmick, though ostensibly it was aimed at the welfare of the weaker section. It was overseen by the ministers of the government and boiled down to statistics. Of the items the emphasis was on repressive ordinances like the MISA and COFEPOSA, family planning abolition of bounded labour and distribution of land to the landless. Though Indira Gandhi's intention in launching on the scheme was doubtless laudable, towards the end it led to the use of force instead of pensuasion and a great deal of witch-hunting and roughing up. The method employed in family planning (already spoken of before) led to a lot of resentment and the MISA and other such oppressive measures were used to smother public rights of redress and to crush political opponents. One senior officer who had the temerity to go to the court against his suspension from service was put into jail and left to languish till the end of the Congress regime. Some proprietors of wine-shops who dared to file a writ against a government order affecting them financially were treated likewise though they managed to get out of prison sooner because of their resources. Thus in its implementation the programme was outrageously oppressive and with 'the best of intentions Indira Gandhi managed to do the worst'.

As I have said earlier, the premier of U.P. was Pandit Govind Ballabh Pant a man of integrity and fairness in politics and administration. Indira Gandhi had a great regard for him. The magnetism of her personality was unquestioned, and she was one of those rare prime ministers who went through some of the hundreds of letters and complaints addressed to her. Once at a conference on her favourite 20 point's she pulled up one of the chief ministers attending it when he addressed her as 'Honourable prime minister'. '*Not honourable*' she said frowning on him, and he quickly corrected himself by saying 'Madam prime minister'. Another thing at which she would flare up was when the mikes set up for her speech had the name of the company advertised on them, and someone would quickly rush and remove the offending nameplate. Once she was on a whirlwind election tour and on the way had to address a gathering at a roadside village. I was the district magistrate then at Bulandshahr where that place was. A makeshift path was made leading to the podium and since it was a dirttrack I took care to water it thoroughly to prevent dust being raised when her car arrived. But I had not anticipated its speed and the suddenness of the driver's applying the brakes to stop it, and when it came with a rush and suddenly stopped, a little dust was raised despite all the watering. I thought I was in for a dressing-down and looked quite miserable in the freakish buttoned-up coat which our government for some unaccountable reason has prescribed as the formal official dress (sweat-drenched in India's hot summer). Perhaps seeing me all hot and bothered, she just smiled and walked up the steps leading to the dais with her usual alacrity.

The early politicians might have erred in their policies but they were mostly honest and well-meaning. The rot set in later, and some of the ministers whom I encountered were also rum. One was an oldish man who must have been round about eighty and rather absent-minded. When I called on him he asked me 'DM sahib, what's going on in your district?' I told him about the various schemes which were the government's hot favourites - family planning, small savings, procurement of wheat and so forth. But he seemed not to hear and asked me the same thing thrice. That put me out for a moment and I said. 'Well sir, if you wish to know what really happens, it's eating, meeting and cheating'. I regretted it at once, for it was a most inappropriate thing to say, but instead of ticking me off the old man laughed jovially and repeated 'Eating meeting, cheating eh! eating, meeting cheating! ha! ha!' Then there was another minister who was to inaugurate the opening of a newly built eye-hospital. He motored from Delhi, but his car didn't have the usual pennant or red bonnet-light and the cops posted at various turns of the road naturally couldn't make it out. So driver asked someone the way to the hospital and the minister arrived at the district hospital – the wrong place. Anyway after making many inquiries, he finally arrived at the eye-hospital. There were some people there, mostly politicians, awaiting him, but they had been told that the minister would first go to the inspection house, where we were all expecting him. When his car arrived at the place of inauguration [as we learnt afterwards] there was a *bhisti* with his leather-bag watering the approach road. The minister peeped out of the car window and asked him if the inauguration was to be there. The *bhiste* just glanced at him and kept on spurting water and raising dust in the minister's face, and not caring a *scat* for him, said, *are jao, jao, jab D.M. sahib aur S.P. sahib ayenge tab hoga,* 'Fade out, when the district magistratic and the supreitendent of police come, then it will start'. Some people who were inside came out to see what is was all about, for the enraged minister was raising cain. Since no one had seen the minister before, opinion was divided, some saying it could be him, others that he was just kidding. Just then someone who knew him arrived and removed the doubt. The peeved minister was taken to the place where the audience were waiting, and give a speech, and meanwhile we were informed on phone that he had arrived. We hastened to the eye-hospital. The minister had already cut the tape and was halfway through his speech, and giving us a surly look went on with it. At the end we explained how we were waiting for him at the inspection house but missed him because of his car not having the usual distinguishing bonnet-light. Ministers were then more tolerant, but if had happened now we would sure to have been transferred, as occurred a short time back in the case of one who wasn't even a member of parliament, but still politically an important person, who despite not being entitled to it, was given a police escort, but the inspector somehow took a wrong turn and took her by a ciruitous route. The inaugural ceremony was followed by a dinner. The minister, apparently hungry, gorged on half-a-dozen *puries* which restored his good humour.

It was past ten in the night when my phone rang. It was the private secretary of a minister who had come for an overnight stay. It was election time and he was campaigning. The voice was frantic 'D.M. sahib' said the PS, 'the minister has suddenly taken ill. Please hurry'. I rang the civil surgeon, a Sardar, 'Doc, the minister's in a bad way, quite possibly a heart attack. Please reach the inspection house immediately [I recollected how it was with Shastri when I was posted at Allahabad]. When I reached he could hardly speak and kept muttering in a hoarse voice 'DM sahib, I don't know what's happened to me. Please call a doctor'. 'He's on the way' I assured him, and just then Sardarji arrived with his medical equipment in an attache case. He took out his stethoscope and gave the VIP a look-over, asking him open his mouth wide and flashing his torch inside. 'That's it,' he said, 'you've been giving speeches?' The PS said '*Mantriji* has had a dozen meetings and has been giving speeches the whole day.' 'Grand gatherings,' he said proudly. 'Nothing to worry about' the civil surgeon said, 'just an over-strained larynx'. He placed some capsules on the table 'One just now and another early morning. He'll be all right'. Just then a blind man walked in led by a lad. 'It's *vaidyaji*' the PS said. The minister gave him a welcome nod 'Ah *vaidyaji,* come on I was waiting for you', he said in a hoarse voice. Sardarji wasn't going to compete with quacks, so he snapped his attache case shut and abruptly departed. The *vaidya* took hold of the minister's pulse and held it for two minutes. 'Did you have rice for your dinner?' he asked. The minister nodded. 'Did you have *urd-ki-dal* (a kind of pulse)?' The minister nodded again. *The vaidya* took out a packet of powder from his pouch 'You may have it with water or with *rabri* (a tasty milk product)'. At the word *rabri* the minister's face lit up. 'Yes, yes *rabri'* he said. It was eleven by now, and it was rather difficult to get any *rabri* in that small town at that late hour. Nonetheless the VIP's wish was beyond being ignored. The PS asked for my jeep to fetoh it . He got a shop opened and it was by midnight that the minister was gobbling up the sweet delicacy after taking the powder, and I could get my jeep and go home to face a rather miffed wife. But I thanked God the minister hadn't a heart attack. Next morning first thing I rang up to inquire how he was, but was told by the PS who was preparing to leave 'Minister sahib has already left, he has to give an election speech early at ten in the morning'. It wasn't the *vaidya's* powder, it was the *rabri* which had restored him. These were just *priceless* episodes. But there were the jarring ones too, and I shall have to speak more exhaustively about politicians and ministers later, for I believe this country will go to sticks and staves or be in clover, depending largely on the conduct of those whom our democratic republic puts in power.

The British ICS officers were mostly concerned with realization of revenue and maintenance of law and order and order and of their rule in India. Still they were the initiators of many other things like the railways, post and telegraphs, canals and road construction. True, most of these were to assist them in maintaining the Raj, but they were the foundation on which we developed them for public utility. As I have said before, however, we have committed the unforgivable folly of maintaining the laws governing these as we got them from the British so that they remain overbearing and anti-people. The reason for this is that our governments of the independence era, while making a pretence of being citizen-friendly, are in truth hostile to the citizens and believe in *baffaloing* them. Many of the British ICS officers wrote valuable and original works about the fauna and flora, castes, tribes and cultures, philosophy and history of India. Doubtless they had the time for the number of departments of the government then existing were fewer, but at the same time the staff was also very much less, and the entire strength of the United Provinces Civil Secretariat of those times was just about that of one of the innumerable sections of today'. Apparently the government of independent India, while closing their eyes to administrators spending long hours at local clubs playing bridge or rummy, false fronts for gambling, took umbrage at their writing books. One day I got a letter from my commissioner asking for my explanation for writing a translation of the *Bhagavadgita* in English verse! The letter said that reports had reached the government that the district magistrate was writing such a book 'which might be creditable in itself but left him no time for administration'. Luckily I had written the book about twenty years before, and my explanation was simple – that I couldn't be writing it again. But what amazed me was the attitude of our governments who would rather have their officers *cut the deck* than be at books!

We have carried on the British tradition of concentrating power in individuals. The drawback of such a system is that the quality of administration then depends on the ability and integrity of these individuals. In the long run, therefore all demoncracies in which power is so centred in individuals, tend towards dictatorship. The American essayist, poet and unitarian minister, Emerson, even says 'Democracy becomes a government of bullies tempered by editors'.[156] So long as we cannot have any alternative system, the administration must remain so concentrated in a few hands. Incidentally while being in the district I had some interesting experiences. There was the case of a young couple who came, the husband wanting a licence for a pistol his application bearing the recommendation of a member of the legislative assembly. Since it was rather difficult to sanction a pistol license, I tried to talk him out of it. 'Look ', I said 'a pistol is a tricky thing. Quite often it might not work if a bullet fails to go off . It gets stuck. Why not take a gun. That's safer and surer.' Much to my relief the man agreed. Some time after he came again, saying the clerk concerned was holding up his licence even though I had sanctioned it. His wife also urged that it should be given to him quickly. I called the clerk and asked him to give the man the licence immediately. He and his wife went away satisfied. Next morning it was in the papers that he had bought an English double-barrelled gun and shot his wife with it and then himself. That's why he had agreed to take the gun license instead of one for a pistol. My argument that a gun was surer had worked, for all the time he was planning to get rid of his wife, who was pleading his case for the speedy issue of the licence! There's certainly no art to find the mind's thoughts by looking at one's face, as the bard said. After about 9-10 years in the districts [Pilbhit, Bulandshahr and Muzaffarnagar] I had a brief spell as administrator of the municipal corporation of Benares [Varanasi] before my last but one assignment, inspector general of prisons. I go on to this.

14

WARDERS AND HIGHL WALLS

To whom the goodly earth and air
Are bann'd and barr'd - forbidden fare.

LORD BYRON

The British reserved th top posts for Britishers. They didn't trust Indians for them, though there was no reason for doing so. Attlee, whom we have already quoted, had said 'The ICS Indians worked extremely loyally but it was idle to suppose that they weren't just as patriotic as everybody else and just as enthusiastic for Indian nationalism'. This was, evidently self-contradictory, for how could they be extremely loyal and at the same time 'enthusiastic for Indian nationalism'? For the lower posts from a deputy collector downwards, there was no competitive examination for selection as we now have. The Indian subordinate officers were nominated to the posts, and this was purely discretionary and governed by caprice. My grandfather, for example, was a head-clerk in an office. He was very good at English, and a letter drafted by him happened to be seen by a senior British ICS officer 'Who is the man who wrote this?' he asked. 'It's in excellent English. He is fit to be a deputy collector'. And he got my grandfather fixed up as one. Howevser, there was one thing the British were very particular about in appointing Indians – family background. After independence this still mattered but it was for other purposes like marriages, which with us are mostly arranged ones.

I wanted to stay on in Lucknow to be able to look after my family. Besides I had only a few years left before I retired from service. But a *hard-shell* who suffered from the low family background syndrome, wouldn't have it so, and I had to go out as administrator of a municipal corporation. Our municipal government I found is a complete wash out. Financially they are a *bust* for they are not able to collect taxes or raise their own resources and are more or less parasites, ever sucking up government funds. But by far the most cogent reason for their failure is corruption in every branch of their working. The sanitary inspector, whose monthly income perhaps exceeds that of the highest salaried officer gets a fixed sum from all the sweepers just for filling up their attendance so that they may be left free to work in private homes. It is his job to detect adulteration in foodstuffs and other commodities, and the shopkeepers in his circle pay him hush-money to carry on his nefarious activities. In this country there is no limit to adulteration and businessmen are callous about it, caring a damn what happens to the people so long as they can make money. There are spurious drugs which do not work and instead of saving life, destroy it. Non-permitted colours are used in edibles without any compunction. So much is the grabbiness of unethical manufacturers, that it was discovered disposable syringes used for injections or taking blood samples, which are a dime-a-dozen, were being repacked and sold, not caring a *scat* for the victims who mkght be put on the spot by contacting serious infections like AIDS, hepatitis and so forth. So these inspectors keep on exacting their cuts and woe betide anyone who doesn't pay up. The usual method of giving him a lesson is this. The inspector fixes the date of his visit and his favourites know from before about it but not these who haven't paid up; and so they are caught unawares. The branch for removing garbage has trucks for picking it, and the truck-drivers show fake journeys selling the gas thus saved in the black market. The department for road construction and buildings, houses and plots makes fortunes on contracts and property matters, and the octroi department (now abolished) charges a small sum from every vehicle entering the limits of the corporation, which is then shared by all concerned. Corruption therefore rules supreme in our local bodies. Besides there are *gheraos* strikes and all kinds of diorderly conduct both on the part of the staff as well as of the people who come with complaints thus making the job on an administrator most trying. The corporation development auuthorities are generally more corrupt.

After a year I was back to Lucknow as inspector general of prisons, a job entailing supervision of the jails of Uttar Pradesh. The prisons present a rather dismal picture, for their buildings are very old and there is little provision for their upkeep. Besides they are jam-packed with all kinds of prisoners hunddled together, whether accused of heinous crimes or simple offences like larceny. Quite often juvenile offenders are mixed up with murderers and dacoits. and this has a very adverse effect on them. This chumming together leads to a great deal of homosexuality in the men's barracks and lesbianism in those of the women, so much so that in some jails condoms were distributed to prisoners to prevent AIDS – an acknowledgment of its prevalence. In the women's wards girls usually pair together into active and passive partners and are always seen together. As in the men's barracks, there is no real segregation and prostitutes are mixed up with young girls who become targets of their libidinous advances. Sometimes lesbianism is practised by objects resembling a dildo. There was a newspaper report that in one of the jails a being 'half-human and half a beast'would wander in the women's barracks in the darkness of the night and forcibly ravish young girl often causing them pain and injury. On investigating into the affair it was found that a middle aged woman, putting on a mask and posing to be a hybrid monster, would tie an improvised dildo round her waist, violating the girls in prison, a few of them happening to be virgins. The erring convict was punished and put in isolation for some time.

One of the astonishing features of jail-inmates, particularly those convicted for atrocious crimes, like murder and dacoity is that they are most innocuous in appearance, and the most impressive recitation of the *Ramayana* of Tulsidasa was heard by me in prison by these convicts. Crime is often unpremidated and on a sudden impulse or caused by provocation and what the criminal does in haste he repents at leisure, though of course there were others for whom revenge was wild justice. For example while going round the cells of convicts with death sentences hanging over their heads, I found that they invariably had books of scriptures before them, the Hindus the *Gita* and the Moslems the *Holy Quran,* and doubtless for those who could read them a kind of deathbed repentance. An experiment was made to bring peace to the minds of inmates through Transcendental Meditation, a kind of Patanjali-type yoga practice sponsored by Mahesh Yogi which was believed to have a beneficial influence on convicts. Howeaver it seemed to me that it did not make any great impact, for the practice is a rather stern bridling of the thought process and in no way an *easy as a pie* affair. Even the renowned sage, Patanjali, puts it in the last few steps of yoga, so it couldn't be gulped down as a sort of reformative-pill by persons who have not undergone the preliminary steps. Another thing I noticed was that these dacoits and murderers looked deceptively innocent.

Women criminals were, I found, much rarer than the men. In December 1973 a study conducted found only 42 women prisoners in the Nari Bandi Miketan [the jail for women in Lucknow][157] and in January 1979 there were only 142 women prisoners in all the jails of Uttar Pradesh! of which the majority. 57, were convicted of murder.[158] In proportion to men, women convicts are less than one per cent. In Uttar Pradesh there are, according to one study, only 302 women prisoners as against 34,370 men, which works out to 0.87, while in America the percentage of women prisoners in 7.3 [2,02,098 women against 675,66,000 men]. In other countries however the percentage is less.[159]

The main reasons for murders committed by women according to the aforesaid study were for sex, gain of land or money, enmity, to avoid social disgrace and on sudden or repeated provocation, the mode of killing by stangulation, weapons, pushing into a well, burning, poisoning and illegal abortion. Of four women questioned, three said that their children were killed by their sister-in-law or brother-in-law due to enmity. A widow said that her *jeth* (elder brother-in-law) tried to seduce her as he wanted to many her for getting her property and when she resisted, threw her child from the rooftop. The brother-in-law of a widow repeatedly urged her to poison her children and then marry him. He brought her the poison for this, but the astute woman mixed it in his food and got rid of him! Another woman was repeatedly seduced by her *jeth* when her husband was away to in a far off place. She plied him with liquor and kept on urging him to drink till he was drunk and fell asleep. Then she hacked off his head.[160] Thus the lust of brother-in-laws for their sister-in-laws is quite often the reason for murders by women. Most of them come from the rural areas and are illiterate or have very little education. Very often men leave their village homes to take up service or some small business in cities, and they leave their wives, mostly young girls, behind. These girls are in some cases involved with men of the village, and hence the urge to murder the husband, who is in the way of the affair. But more frequently it is the husband who seeks extra-marital sex. The brother-in-law sister-in-law tangle is also very largely the cause for murder. Occasionally the cause is ill-assorted couples, the girl being very young and the husband very old. In one case a father-in-law tried to have sex with his daughter-in-law and she killed him, and in another the bride was too young to know about sex, and on the second night when her husband, who was very much older, tried to make love, she mistook his motive and killed him! However most of these murders committed by women in India are the consequence of ill-adjusted relations in joint families, leading to illicit relations between various categories of relations, sister-in-law and brother-in-laws, uncles and nieces, aunts and nephews, cousins and so forth. It is not possible in this brief acount to go into the details of all the various cases of convicts of which I had made a study. It was not always that convicts admitted of being actually guilty of the crime for which they had been punished. These cases often come to light in the prison when the convicts have no reason to *taradiddle* as it couldn't possibly then be of any help to them. There was the case of a Moslem woman of forty-eight who was undergoing life imprisonment for murder. Her ailing mother died when she was yet a child. She was abducted by a *maulvi* who said he would take her to her 'uncle', and kept her in a huge box with a slit for breathing. While carting the box to the railway station he was caught by a vigilant constable who heard moaning sounds coming from the box. She was placed in the custody of a *maulvi* who lived near a mosque, who got her married when she was grown-up, to a Moslem boy. The lad, however, was keeping another woman. Despite this she continued to look after her new home and gradually she had a family of a son and two daughters. She fixed up her daughter's marriage with a young man, but she [her daughter] was enamoured of another lad. One day when the convict went out with the younger daughter, the elder one who was then alone in the house, fearing she would be married to the boy chosen for her and thus be deprived of her lover, put the noose of a rope round her neck and committed suicide by hanging. When her mother came she was shocked, and taking down her daughter's corpse began to weep. The dead girl's lover informed the police and told them that there had been a tiff between mother and daughter. The police arrested her and the crime was hung on her. Another case was that of a poor unmarried girl of eighteen who was searching for a job. She happened to go to a house for this purpose. When she opened the door there was no one in the room, but soon a woman came from inside and said 'You are a thief and have stolen the things here!' [Maybe someone else had done it]. However, the sons of that woman called the police and she was handed over to them and convicted of theft. Here again, it was the wrong person who was hauled up. Then there was the case of a married woman of forty who was her husband's second wife. The first wife of this man had eloped with a certain lad whose young sister aged fifteen used to visit her husband's brother-in-law living in the adjacent house. The two (the husband and his brother-in-law) were on inimical terms. The brother of the girl took advantage of this and got the woman implicated and convicted of the crime. Yet another case of this kind involved Rahim (not his real name), a eunuch dancer who had homosexual relations with a man and both of them would take part in dramatic performances. The man was murdered by some persons, and at that time the eunuch, who was a Moslem, was on his way to offer homage at the shrine of a renowned Sufi saint and was at Delhi. But it so transpired that at the time of his death the murdered man uttered the name of his eunuch lover, *Hai Rahim* ('Ah! Rahim') and it was thought it was really the eunuch who had killed him! These were, of course, the convicts' own versions, and one could believe them or not.

There was the case of a woman belonging to a good family, who had studied up to class 9. Her marriage was an arranged one as most marriages among Indians are, and her husband was a well educated man having landed property. But she discovered that he already had two wives, the second one of whom was highly educated and in government service. This began to worry her greatly, particularly she feared the two previous wives may choose to come back and she would then have them as *sauts* (cowives). Her husband's uncle was a next-door neighbour whom she considered to be helpful, and she would often go there to talk over her problems. But in fact there was a property dispute between her husband and his uncle and the uncle was planning to kill him to grab the land. The woman (convict) was rather perturbed because of her marital relations, for often her husband would be cruel to her. Once when she was in a fit of depression, the uncle spoke to her about his plan to get rid of her husband and being very angry at some harshness he had shown her, she reluctantly consented. The uncle invited her husband to his house for breakfast and got him murdered by one of his sons. He got the dead body removed to the house of the deceased. The whole household foisted the murder on her and she was given the death penalty which was later reduced to life imprisonment. So in this case though the woman didn't commit the murder, she was an abettor in the crime.

There was the case of a young girl of 24 convicted of murder. She was married when sixteen to a car driver much older, who himself had an 18 year old daughter by a previous wife. The girl had an affair with a boy who belonged to her village, while her stepdaughter too had a paramour. The two carried on their liaisons unhindered as the driver was away from home most of the time. One day the driver's daughter *peached* on her stepmother and when he became angry and gave her a thrashing, she in turn blabbed out about his own daughter's affair. However, they made up soon and began to carry on with their respective lovers. In order to do away with the risk of disclosure, they planned together to do away with the driver by strangling him. It was a curious and a diabolic crime which the victim's own wife and daughter together carried out.

In another case of a girl of twenty, the motive was rather uncommon. She was married when she was thirteen, though the consummation (as is usual in villages – the *gauna* ceremony) was later, when she was 18. According to her version she was given some powder (*taweez*) in milk before going to her husband's home [maybe to make her inclined for sex] which had an adverse effect on her mind. Whatever might have been the reason, she slept separately, and on tahe sixth day when her husband approached her, she attacked him with a *gandasa* (a sharp-edged weapon). He got hurt but survived. Apparently she hated men either because she was neurotic or a lesbian or just cold. The neurotic angle is quite possible as a study of women murderers showed that the neurotic trend appeared to be greatly associated with their personality[161]

Very often a woman was found guilty of murdering her own baby because it was illegitimately conceived, or someone else's baby to take revenge on its mother. In one such case a woman of the village was married when she was in her teens. Her husband took her to Delhi where he managed to get some work. She was *tickled pink* by the gay urban social life she saw for the first time, and soon had a lover there who belonged to her own village and had also come to Delhi for a job. Her husband did not approve of the sudden change in her and left her at the village while he continued with his work in the city. Her paramour would often go to her and as she was by herself they made love freely. Soon a baby was born to her which obviously could not have been by her absent husband. To escape the ignominy she killed her own child. There were other cases too involving women in smuggling and other such offences, but, as we have said; those of murders predominated.

With men dacoity, murder, rape etc., were found to be quite frequent, long back many dreaded dacoits like Man Singh and his son Tahsildar Singh operating in the Chambal ravines, surrendered at the call of Jayaprakash Narayan and the government promised to rehabilitate them by providing them employment and land. A UNI report mentioned one of them as follows: 'From dacoity to divinity. That is the story of dreaded dacoit leader Pancham Singh, who once struck terror in every nook and corner of the Chambal ravines and is now running a yoga centre at his village Lahar, in Madhya Pradesh. Pancham Singh, who surrendered before Jayaprakash Narayan along with his associates Madho Singh and Mohar Singh, was taught raja yoga by the Brahmakumaris in Moongavali jail a few years ago. "It changed my entire life" he told newsmen at a press get-together, adding that his 19 year old daughter, Rama Devi, had also become a Brahmakumari. Asked which had influenced him more – *raja yoga* or JP's dynamic personality, Pancham Singh said "I surrendered my weapons and body to Jayaprakashji, but I gave my soul to *baap dada*" (Lord Shiva as he is affectionately called by the Brahmakumaris)'. The Chambal ravines stretch on for quite a few miles. I saw them while motoring from Bulandshahr to Bhopal. Devoid of even a blade of grass the bare impenetrable never-ending barriers of earth zigzag on either side of the road, vanishing into the distance. Not a sound is heard there, not a face seen, and it is one enormous labyrinth in which anyone who is not familiar with the terrain would be irretrievably lost. On seeing the ravines one can understand the hopelessness of pursuing the dreaded dacoits whose shelter they were. It was impossible to flush them out from this secure hide-out and it was only the charisama of Jayaprakash which could charm them away. But not all of them were happy. As often happens with promises made by the government, they are not kept, and successive governments pride in undoing even the good work of their predecessors. I recollect, the legendary dacoit, Tahsildar Singh, who came to me complaining, with a great deal of truth, that nothing substantial had been done for his rehabilitation or that of his fellow dacoits. I had expected him to be a stern-faced harsh kind of man, but he was rather gaunt and carried a stick and he spoke gently but firmly. It was only when his bright eyes flashed that one could see in them the gleam of ferocity that reminded one of his former days.

Gangsters are not necessarily men. In fact a good few gang leaders are women for example the erstwhile dreaded Phoolan Devi and others. The motivation in the case of leaders of gangs is said to be the desire for power and such persons are 'creative psychopaths' according to the director of a Psychiatric Centre.[162] Quite often a woman gang leader has a lover to assist her, and almost always she is a victim of circumstances. The women gang leaders are as deceptive in appearance as the dacoits they lead. One, who became head of a gang of hired marderers, looked like a mod girl with short-cut hair. Her story, rather intriguing was as follows: Belonging to a middling scheduled caste family she was married when she was a child of seven, and three years after the boy died, leaving has a *balvidhiwa* (child-widow). Her father found her burdensome and she heard him say to a neighbour 'Oh! this girl will be a plague on me all my life!' These words broke her heart and she determined to make herself useful to her family. Putting on men's clothes – shirt, trousers and a pugree-she went out on the fields working hard so that her land had a bumper crop. The Thakurs of the village became envious and hostile to her father and they planned to have her kidnapped with the assistance of the leader of a gang of hired murderers. The man who took her away put her against a tree in the forest and was about to shoot her, when the leader stopped him saying 'You were hired to attack her father, not to kill this child'. However, the other man again threatened to shoot her, on which she yelled 'You keep throwing a scare into me all the time. Why don't you kill me and be done with it'. She lived with the gangsters a week in the jungle. The gang leader plaited her hair and taught her how to dress as a man and wear a turban, and taking her to a reliable friend in the neighbouring village got his wife to stitch her pants and shirts of the colour of the uniform of the military along with a belt for cartridges. He taught her shooting and other techniques essential for gangsters. She began to love her wandering life as an outlaw. Once on her entreaties she was taken to see her parents, but they refused to accept her and so she became a faithful member of the gang, promising allegiance to them. She learnt how to lie in ambush, be on the alert ot save herself from the vigilant authorities, and accuracy in shooting. Once the police chased them, but two of the gang covered the stump of a tree with a bedsheet, and fled. The police thought they were by the tree-stump and kept firing at it and then belaboured it with sticks! and thus got fooled. She became the gang leader's mistress and they would make love at night in the forest. One day the leader was treacheously shot dead by a friend in whose house he had taken shelter. The convict took revenge by hiding near the man's house and shooting him when he came out.

From then she took the dead leader's place, and all of them accepted her leadership. Led by her the gang committed many murders for money and also used to get a fixed ransom from moneyed people by terrifying them. There was an old poor couple living in a hut on the bank of the Ganga river whom she would help by giving them money. Once while she was resting there after her meals, the police who had got wise to her gave chase. The gangsters fled into the adjoining forest. She also ran desperately to get away, but there was no place to hide and the police were fast closing in, so she threw down her gun and held up her hand in surrender. The cops wanted her to be shot but the superintendent of polie said no, and finally she was sent to jail and on conviction got a five year sentence.

The other case involved a minor offence, the convict being an Italian girl, fair and beautiful, but a drug addict who had to be given a morphine injection each day in the jail. She too was a victim of circumstances. She loved freedom and wanted to live a peaceful domestic life, but her people would not let her do so. She was well educated, a dress designer and an artist.

She was adopted by a German family, and later returned to her parents in Italy. She was not treated well and the famiy broke up soon, her father marrying another girl and her mother taking a lover whom she ultimately married. Her mother's second husband hated her so much that he couldn't bear to have her in the house and her mother too wanted her out. So she went to Germany to stay with her grandmother and helped her in running her fashion saloon. She found a boy friend, a photographer, to whom she surrendered her virginity and became steady with him. At the college of applied arts where she studied she made friends with a girl who had a defect in her vagina and so was forced into lesbianism. One day this girl came to her grandmother's home and her grandma suspecting her granddaughter falsely of having an affair with her, complained, and insisted on sending her to a hostel of security (closed home). Rather than that, she left Germany and went back to Italy and earned her living by designing dresses. She met a boy working in a press and went steady with him, hoping to settle down and marry him. But he was having a secret affair with another girl, and deserting her, married that girl instead. Thus she was thwarted again in her endeavour to lead a family life. Later this boy came back to her and tried to force her to make love, saying he had made a mistake in marrying the other girl. But she repulsed him saying 'Look, you deceivied me, and now you want to deceive the other girl too. Nothing doing. Out you go!'

The shock of frustration made her a drug addict and when she lacked money for drugs she went bed-hopping to get them. Her drug supplier got her a suitable job in Milan with an artist. He and his wife used to go to transcendental meditation sessions and associated with sadhus from India. But she found no peace in TM. However the artist's wife who was going to India, persuaded her to come too. She got a good job there in an export company and for some time worked in a film festival at Delhi. But she ran short of money and her visa was also expiring. A gang who dealt in selling stolen traveller cheques approached her and lured her into working with them. They also got a forged passport for her. For some time all went well, but one day she was caught and landed up in jail, from where she was repatriated to her native country later.

The jail warders were given the work of seeing that no prisoner escaped and they made rounds of the prison handing a token from one to another so that they had their fixed beats. But as in other departments there was a great deal of corruption, some of it of the mean kind too, like cutting back on the prisoners' food. In fact anything could be procured in prisons provided one paid enough. Some prisoners escaped of themselves, but the majority of these escapes were with the connivance of the jail staff. There was one involving a very notorious prisoner who was an ace cheat and had been in and out of jail several times. At one time he lived a dissolute life with a *cat*, high and soused most of the time. In prison he was kept carefully guarded and in fetters, as he had escaped many times from different jails. After he had been a month or two in jail, he wrote to his brother to come to visit him, and from him he obtained money enough to distribute it to the warders and other jail staff and also to supply them various articles of daily use. An iron oven was got for him and all kinds of delicious dishes were provided to him. In this way he won over the jail staff and even the officers of the jail would wait on him and talk to him for hours together. He got the motorbike of the jailor's son-in-law repaired, gave him huge sums of money, sent him presents of dried fruits and had a taxi arranged for the jailor's son on the occasion of his betrothal ceremony. He also got a new motorbike for the jailor. The warders who had been obliged by gifts and money, loosened the fetters so that they could easily slip off his legs. A warder arranged for clothes which resembled the uniform worn by the staff–khaki jersey, khaki shirt, trousers and cap. On the day fixed for escape, the notorious cheat slipped out of his fetters, put on the dress made for him so that he could easily pass off as a warder, walked out of the main gate and rode away on a cycle which had been placed outside it by his brother. Thereafter they motored away on a car with a changed number plate. After some hindrances on the way they reached Kanpur and from there to Mathura. The sentry who had assisted the escape had been promised five thousand rupees as his reward. The money was placed in an iron box in the presence of the warder and the sentry who would take it away after the escape. But the cheat played his final trick by cleverly substituting a similar box containing a brick wrapped up in cloth, in its place. In this way he not only escaped with everyone looking on, but also cheated his helpers by handing them a useless box containing a brick!

The various crimes usually committed by women have been mentioned, but far more ignominious are those committed against them like rape, abduction, bride-burning, molestation (Hinglish 'eve teasing') and so forth. The impact of these which seems to have become much greater as the years of freedom flit pass will be spoken of later. Something needs to be said here of the miserable plight of mentally diseased and depressed prisoners lodged in our jails. Their condition is wretched and the indifference to it inexcusable and to be deplored. I had the occasion of to see some of these miserabel wretches and they looked like helpless animals in a cage often brooding in a corner, uncared for and unheeded. Normally such persons ought to be put in lunatic asylums or psychiatric centres after being examined by doctors. But the jail administration is hardly bothered about them. The examination keeps on being put off, with the red tape wrapping more and more around it, and these agonized prisoners who have done no wrong, keep getting worse and worse till they become mere vegetables. All the tall talk about rehabilitation of convicts becomes a farce so long as nothing is done to relieve the misery of these persons and it's a big blot upon our prison administration. I had brought the matter to the notice of the government, but apparently the politicians are more interested in getting their favourite murderers and dacoits released prematurely than in paying any heed to these poor suffering persons.

15

GOD'S LOVE IS MAN'S ANGUISH

He whom the gods love dies young

HYPSAEUS

On 17the March 1979 I lost my sixteen year old daughter. She died in just a week's illness, of viral hepatitis. My first reaction was a seething rage against God for taking away thc lifc of one so full of life, so spritely, and I flung the picture of the god Shankara I used to worship, out of my room. Then followed a feeling of guilt which would remain with me lifelong for in ignorance I had entrusted her to the treatment of a doctor (who I later learnt was a BMBS – not quite the adequate qualificatioin). I had thought of consulting my family doctor, and I had him on the phone when my wife somehow hearing me call him came running from inside and said 'No, don't call him, he gives very strong drugs'. Of course she could not have deliberately stopped me. The cutprit was God who had destined my daughter's death and would brook no interference in his plan. At that moment God seemed to me some diabolic monster as indeed Hindus depict him in his various repulsive and fearful forms and astride all kinds of freakish creatures. Hindus have a god for almost every facet of nature and existence much like the Greeks. There is a god for creation, for preservation and for destruction. Gods of love, learning, the earth, heavens, wind, sun and so forth and there is also a god of death, Yama: as if one God was not enough to control the world! Hindus seem to have a peculiar tendency to feature these gods (with exceptions) in uncouth shapes with tusks and horns, half man half lion, elephant-headed, monkey-faced and with many arms and faces holding terrible weapons that they call 'divine' or having a serpent dangling from the neck – hideous to look at. Yama is no exception. Dr Muir says, 'Yama is still to some extent an object of terror. He is represented as having two insatiable dogs with four eyes and wide nostrils which guard the road to his abode, and which the departed are advised to hurry past with all possible speed.'[163] Although thus the soul is made to *skedaddle,* death itself is usually a slow and painful process and the god of destruction is in no hurry, doing it breath by breath with gasps of Cheyne-stokes respiration, museular twitching, hemorrhage, shrieking and wailing and the final comatose, for in death we mortals, like beasts, are 'bound upon a wheel of fire and our tears scald like molten lead'.[164]

This was what my daughter's end was like and as she lay lifeless on the bed of the emergency ward I kissed her dead body while the shocked nurses looked on incredibly. But there were no tears for the deepest grief is expressionless with the heart halting in the breast like a frozen deer in the forest. For some inexplicable reason, which might have seemed foolish to others I wanted her home again and took the lifeless body back on my car. Beside her I laid a couple of Enid Blyton novels which were her favourite. It seems ridiculous now, but in moments of emotion reason is on furlough, and I fondly imagined she would have liked them to be there. That lovely child was wrapped up from head to foot in a shroud and I thought of those moments when her laughter filled the house, that voice that would every Sunday gleefully go round telling everyone to come and see the *citrahaar* (film-snippets) on the TV. The TV had just come to town, only black and white then, and she was all agog for it. I went to buy it for her and they said they had the one with a wooden cabinet, (the chic bakelite one would come ten days after), but I wanted to bring it quick for her and I took the one then available. She was over the moon to see it arrive. I remembered how she wished for a cycle, and even though knowing she would never ride it, I went the same evening and got one for her. And the red high-heeled shoes she saw in a shop and which taking her in the car. I instantly bought her, only a few months before she died. The kaleidoscope of remembrances keeps turning and reviving those moments of her exuberance and gaety, the rapture of the world just unfolding to her, that vivacity and zest for life, that lay buried in the white cloth tied round her. How could one associate that lovely lively child with that mace-and-noose bearing monstrosity clad in green and red sitting, of all creatures, on an ugly buffalo? How can one link a sweet smiling child with death? The Greeks would have it that those whom the gods love, die young[165] God alone knows what his measure of love is but for us mortals death is a terrible thing particularly when it comes to innocent children and heaven alone knows why he allows a bud to blossom but not the child whose heart is about to open out to the ecstasy of living, for 'God alone knoweth the praise of death'.[166]

I placed her body on the pile of faggots which would soon consume her and I gave her the goodbye kiss. The pundit looking on frowned and said 'enough, enough' for to him it was just another body for which he had to chant the religious *mantras*. I did not have the heart to light the pyre and my son did it for me. The flames soon engulfed her and I knew she had gone forever, the *Gita's* words that death is like a mere change of clothes sounded to me mere platitude, for it may be so and yet may not. So even then, despite all my wisdom I used to believe for some days that she would some time somehow convince God that she had to go back, and then I would look out for her in her school uniform with the bag slung behing, as she used to come in the days past. It was senseless to think so of course, but then as Antiphanes says, grief is madness', next door neighbour.[167] And when I used to go for my eveneing walks I would imagine I felt the tresses of her hair brushing my face. But the only way I could keep my mind off my sorrow was to plunge into writing, for I decided to dedicate the book to her and that kept me going on at a feverish pace. Visitors came, spoke their condolences and went, and I was again and again at my table. That was how I could cope with my grief, I learnt to keep it to myself, the hard way. I was pursuing a property suit and once when my counsel was chagrined at my not following it up, I told him about my daughter's death, and the old man just sat back and laughed and laughed. Shortly after my son who became a schizophrenic, soon after, and died next year, was in the KGMC hospital, when he had one of his fits. I rushed to a doctor lad under training and told him to attend on him. I mentioned by the way, that I was rather anxious as my young daughter had just died a few months back. 'What of that?' was his stunning retort. I wondered how he had got into the psychiatry department for it seemed to me instead of curing minds he would be spurring them on the insanity. I shall have to say more about Indian doctors, quite a few of them greedy, unscuplous inefficient frauds who are busy turning Hippoerates in his grave, but these experiences of callous insensibility put me on to Rahiman's snappy comeback; 'Says Rahiman, keep your grief to yourself. Everyone will laugh at it if you speak out and none will be able to share it'. I never talked about it again for I learnt the hard way what wise men already knew—that as Hobbes said in the *Leviathan* 'the life of man [is] solitary, poor, nasty, brutish and short'. Human nature is largely malicious. Gore Vidal says 'It is not enough to succeed, others must fail.... Every time a friend succeeds, something inside me dies. And wise man Confucius who was a close and accurate observer of mankind puts it thus,'There is nothing more pleasant than to see one's best friend fall off the roof of a house'. So one turns back to God, not because it is any more logical to expect him to do any better, but it is sheer folly to rely on what has assuredly been found wanting ; and there seems no option left, for there are only these two—God and man.

The same year, fresh from my grief, I had to carry out my elder daughter's marriage and I did it mechanically like one who turns from sleep to waking, for life has only one lesson and that is to go on. Soon after, just next year I had to face another shock, this time the sudden death of my son of twenty-three who shot himself with my pistol. He had been mentally ill and constantly under watch, but had been asking my wife for the key to my room, which I always kept locked and took care to take it with me to the office. But that day being a Sunday, I was at home and sitting in the veranda just adjacent to my room, hardly a few paces away from the door. My son came and said he wanted to see some back numbers of the *Reader's Digest* magazine which I had collected and got bound in several volumes. I felt happy that his mind was being diverted to good reading—a sign that he was getting better, and let him go to take the volume he wanted and went on with my work. A minute or two after I heard a bang and by the sound I knew it was a pistol shot. I rushed into the room It was horrible. There was a huge spot of blood on the floor where his head lay. The bullet had gone right through his temples and rebounded from the wall. There was still a weak pulse. We rushed him to the nearest hospital. Blood spurted on the wall of the veranda as he was carried along. The back seat of the car on which we laid him was soaked in blood. It was a wonder he lived on, in a coma of course, for eight hours before he died:

'Action is transitory,— a step, a blow,
The motion of a muscle, this way or that—
'Tis done, and in the after-vacancy
We wonder at ourselves like men betrayed:
Suffering is permanent, obscure and dark
And shares the nature of infinity,.[168]

People who came to condole would say 'Ah, you left the pistol unlocked'! And I felt too that a mental patient should not have been left by me to enter that room alone. It was the same feeling of guilt as I felt after my daughter's death a year before. As I said, I had a doctor attending her who was an ignoramus out and out. Ever since for the slightest reason I've been to a hospital, but I failed to take her then. In effect she had almost no treatment at all, till it was too late. It seems God never accepts the guilt of giving us our sorrows, he cleverly passes it on to us. The Moving Finger not only writes, before it moves on, it puts the poisoned chalice to our own lips. 'I do everything, yet I do nothing', that seems to be the divine conundrum. As Lord Krishna says in the *Gita* 'I am neither the source nor the agent of works nor am I responsible for their result, for the outcome of works depends on one's disposition [the consequence of works done in past lives]. I do not take on myself anyone's sin or virtue. Those who think I do, are ignorant'.[169] It is disputable, however, how much of the world's misery is the result fo past karmas. Maybe birth, death, loss and gain, honour and dishonour are the result of karma, even though the sage Tulsidasa assigns them to God. But surely what man has made of man—the social ills of poverty, unemployment, corruption, oppression and so forth—are not divinely ordained. In fact our tendency is to attribute to God many of the things for which our own society and polity are responsible.

Thus those three years in which I was in charge of the jails of Uttar Pradesh were years of torment and anguish, for according to our Vedic belief the greatest sorrow in the world is *dalidrata* (starvation) and the one next to it the death of one's young children. A tiff with the minister in charge of my department led to my transfer to the post of chairman of the administrative tribunals and the vigilance commission for the six month's service left to me. How this was foretold by the *jhariwale baba* has been already narrated. The short experience I had there [as chairman I had to decide cases of corruption of UP officers] convinced me that most of lthe officers guilty of corruption who got netted in were the small fry who failed to follow certain technical rules, while the shady two-timers of the highest echelons got away scot-free. The whole thing appeared to me to be eyewash.

More troubles followed after retirement. A speeding scooterist dashed into me when I was sixty, breaking all the four bones of my right hand and leg. That put me in a state of depression and I was taken, much against my will, to noted psychiatrist who prescribed a medicine which seemed to accentuate my other trouble of an enlarged prostrate. By chance I read the literature enclosed with the drug and it said that it was contraindicated in prostrate trouble. Next time when I went to the doc and told him about it, he gave me the astounding reply 'There isn't any drug for depression which does not contain this ingredient. You carry on with it and you can later get your prostrate operated!' That's how specialists work, I thought to mysl f. They're concerned with one organ of the body and pass up the others. I have narrated my experience with one psychiatrist before [the young apathetic one who reacted crassly to my daughter's death] and this one convinced me that it's best to stay away from these *nut doctors.* I still had my depression to deal with, and now I knew I had to do it myself. So I started looking up the back numbers of the *Readers Digest* in which I read many true accounts of severely handicapped people who despite their disabilities had accomplished feats that were tough even for normal persons—like the man who had lost both his legs and yet climbed the Alps, the girl whose one leg was amputated and who, wallowing in self-pity went crying herself out about it to a friend who listened to her patiently and then sitting up on lher bed and pulling out a pair of artificial legs strapped them on *both* her stumps! After going through these and many other such accounts I thought, well, if these people could remain active despite their impediments, so could I. And so I chased away my blues by my own effort — the only way, I believe, it can be done, for when the mind is vanquished it a man's victory and when he is licked by the mind it's his defeat. About ten years later I had the same problem. This time it was a greedy unskilled eye-surgeon, the than head of the department of opthalmology of the local medical college, with a string of foreign and Indian degrees, who operated on my eye and goofed it up, so that it got damaged with multiple defects. I had to go thrice then to a reputed eye hospital in Madras. They did their best of course, but the local doc had so gummed up the works that they couldn't do much and there was profound loss of vision. This was just three or four years back and now it has come to stay. This time it was another magazine, *Health,* which did much to put me back on the rails, though just somewhat. It has already been quoted and I would like to repeat some of that again, here:

> '...there are worriers, and then there are worriers. Broadly they can be classed into two categories. First, those characterized by the inability to discriminate between controllable and uncontrollable situations, feeling helpless, (i.e., they are not responsible for their fate) while simultaneously feeling guilty, (i.e., they are responsible for their fate).
>
> 'These kind of worriers generally end up by being depressed. They automatically assume that their efforts won't make any difference and so they won't act even when the situation is within their power to change. And so they come to feel helpless, victimized and depressed'.
>
> 'At the other extreme are the other kind of worriers: the people who believe that nothing is beyond their contol and take on every problem as their own. These people constantly worry about problems that they can never solve—a self-destructive type of

> behaviour characteristic of Type, as that can lead to frustration and burnout....
>
> "Most worries are anticipatory worries" says Barry Lubetkin Ph.D., a psychologist of the Institute of Behaviour Therapy in New York City. "We're afraid of what might happen. We're looking negatively and fearfully into the future."[170]

It boils down to this: One should not count his bridges before he gets to them. And suffering is inevitable because it is tied down to living. The only way to cope with that which can't be remedied, is to accept it. But then why is there suffering at all? Religions try to explain it in different ways. Hinduism and Buddhism believe that birth (or rebirth) itself involves suffering. But that is only a half-truth, for along with the sorrows there are joys too. Hinduism, which goes deeper into the origin of suffering than other religions, is rather mixed up about it. Somewhere it says that it is God who makes us do all works (*Gita* 18:61), but then it also says that it is works by which human beings are judged. The two views are self-contradictory. If works are controlled by God, why should man suffer for them? It seems to me that God is also bound by the law of karma just as our judges here are bound by mundane laws. But unlike our judges, he is the Supreme Judge, not enumbered by the Indian Penal Code! While human judges can only give the capital punishment by ordering death for the ace criminal, God punishes by giving him life, i.e., rebirth in various wombs of human beings and lower creatures to suffer punishment in proportion to his evil deeds.

Going to Madras (for the treatment of my eye) was a new experience for me, for I had not gone South before. It seemed to me I had walked into another country. The traffic was orderly, the roads clean and law and order which was *all U.P.* in the North, seemed to be yet surviving here. Besides, while in the North age does not command any respect and young men often make way for themselves on roads, pushing aside the old, this is not so down South. I was leaving the eye hospital there, my son holding my hand and taking me along, when a lad younger than him walked up from behind and tapped him on the back. 'Look', he said 'that's not how you take your father along. You should walk before him and let him place his hand on your shoulder. Then you guide him slowly along. That's how I conduct *my* father and that's how you should take *your* father along'. Having said this he went away. Then there was the Madrasi lady who saw me standing as all the seats were occupied. She got up and said to me 'You sit here', pointing to the place she had vacated. I declined saying 'That's your seat, don't worry, I can keep standing'. But she insisted 'No, you are a patient and I am merely an attendant,[each patient in the hospital had to have an attendant with him]. Another lady stopped and said while I was going up the stairs 'May I help you?' Then there was the Christian man serving in a company who came to see me. I learnt he had got himself purposely transferred to Madras to look after his aged father,'Yes, it's a debt you owe to him' I said. 'It isn't a debt' he said 'it's my duty'. No wonder a guide book says'The visitor who first makes acquaintance with the South will soon be struck by the warm hospitality, intelligence and the culture of the people. Madras is a city with a distinct individuality which has an instant appeal for the stranger'.[171] I found this to be the absolute truth. The people are devoutly religious. When I was on the operating table in the hospital one of the attending doctors asked his superior if he should take out the string round my neck bearing a small heart-shaped metal piece with the image of the Devi. 'No, let that be' the senior doc said. While we were motoring down a busy road a snake happened to be going across it to the clump of bushes along the roadside. Instantly all the traffic came to a dead halt [a privilege reserved in our parts to ministers and VVIPs only]. It was only when it slithered away to safety down to the greenery that traffic was resumed. The serpent is connected with the god, Shiva, who is represented as having one coiled round his neck, and that's why no vehicle would crush it. Hindi is, however, tabooed. Once while waiting for my turn in the corridor along the surgeon's room, an orderly came out with a sheaf of papers. I took care always to express myself in English, which surprisingly almost everyone can follow and speak, though the lower rung speak the pidgin variety, but at that moment I instinctively asked him *kya hamare bhi kagaz hain*? ['Are you taking my file too'.] *'I don't know Hindi'*, he exclaimed, almost shouting in my face, and I could read the hatred for that language in his angry eyes. With the tangle of tongues and the animosity to languages other than one's own, the only way of communication in this sub-continent is to speak English albeit with varying accents and intonations depending on the region to which one belongs. Thus English as 'Hinglish' in its various varieties has virtually become the lingua franca of India. It seemed to me, however, that the southerner's animosity to Hindi was in some way linked with the fact that a number of persons from the North had made Madras their mine of business opportunity. The Madrasi is by far more honest, conscientious and straightforward than the northerner. But it is the people from outside who are lousy rich. The reason is simple. Honesty and straighforwardness may be spiritual virtues, but in being successful in business they just don't do the trick. So the honest southerners who can't change their inherent nature and become unscruplous resent the commercial invasion of outsiders. The one trouble about the South is the food. What you can get and at what time is inexorably fixed. And like the schoolboy's uniform, it's the same everyday-with dollops of rice. It's doubtless very wholesome, but the despair of gourmets.

And so with impaired vision, one eye damaged by the *boggling* doc who made a hash of it, the other fast developing a cataract. I still struggle somehow with the books. And as for last words, if ever I have the opportunity of saying them, perhaps I would like to say something like what Gokhale said,'I have been seeing the fun on this side so long, now let me go and see it on the other side'.

16

THE GREAT INDIAN CIRCUS

Ill fares the land to hast'ning ills a prey
Where wealth accumulates and men decay

OLIVER GOLDSMITH

If a nation values anything more than freedom,
it will lose its freedom;and the irony of it is
that if it is comfort or money that it values
more it will lose that too.

W.SOMERSET MAUGHAM

We gave ourselves a constitution on 26 January 1950 which provided a sovereign democratic republic, and had an imposing preamble which sought to secure to all its citizens: justice, social, economic and political; liberty of thought, expression, belief, faith and worship; equality of status and opportunity; and to promote among them all fratenity, assuring the dignity of the individual and the unity of the nation. The directives of this constitution briefly are: adequate means of livelihood, equal distribution of wealth and other material resources, equal pay for equal work, prevention of the exploitation of child labour, equal justice and free legal aid to the poor, organization of village *panchayats*, securing the right to work and education, giving assistance in sickness, unemployment, old age, disablement etc., humane conditions of work and maternity relief, a minimum wage for workers, workers' participation in industry, free and compulsory education to children up to 14 years age, protection to the weaker section of the people, raising levels of nutrition and public health, organizing agriculture and animal husbandry, protection of forests and wild life, protection of monuments, separation of the executive from the judiciary, and promotion of internal peace and security.

Forty-five years have gone past since the constitution was framed and it is time to see how we have fared. Taking up the preamble first, it can't be denied that it is eloquently worded promising a kind of El Dorado to the people but getting down to the brass tacks all of the expectations from these avowals have been belied. The courts as constituted, do exist, but as we have said, litigation is strung out, complicated and costly. D.A. Desai, once Chairman of the law commission observed, 'The present judicial system suffers from the disease appelatitis—appeals upon appeals are filed where all sorts of funny arguments are brought up',[172] and Justice Shetty commented '*the major failure in the field of justice has been the inability to provide shelter to the masses....* The concept of the welfare state was to help the large number of underprivileged and those who are unable to look after themselves. The dispensation of justice has to move forward and break new grounds to make law an effective instrument of social change'.[173] 'What would the common man think', questioned the ex-chief justice of India Mr Y.V.Chandrachud, 'when a case is argued in the courts for months and months?'[174] According to one report [*The Pioneer* 31March 1995 PTI]. More than two crore legal cases were pending in the courts of the country...' Mr. M. Hidayatullah ex-vice-president rightly said that the laws in India, particularly the procedural laws, a legacy of the British, were lengthy and cumbersome.[175] According to Justice P.N. Bhagwati chief justice of India 'the judicial system is on the verge of collapse';[176] and further 'the Indian legal system as it is functioning today is incapable of delivering justice to the poor'[177] These are the observations of prominent judges themselves on the state of justice existing in the period following the framing of our constitution, one can imagine what the people affected think of it. Though one should not generalize there are counsels who pocket their fee and then forget all about the case, and a few who collude with the opposite party, and there is no let up in the fee so that the poor who constitute the major part of the people of the country can hardly afford the luxury of litigation. Equal justice and free aid to the poor remains a pipe dream for it exists only on paper. Maybe in some states there exists such a panel of lawyers who are said to offer free service, but in reality it is just window dressing. Perhaps what Anacharsis says applies closely to our laws: 'Written laws are like spider's webs,and will like them, only entangle and hold the poor and the weak while the rich and the powerful will easily break through them'[178] We have not only disregarded the promise made in the preamble and in the directives of the constitution, we have even lost track of the ancient wisdom of our scriptures which go back severeral centuries before the birth of Christ. The most important of the *Upanishads* says: 'In the society thus evolved [by Prajapati, the Creator] it was necessary to protect the weak against the strong and so Viraj created justice. Justice is the protector of everyone. It is truth. Because of this people say of one who speaks the truth "he speaks justly" and of one who speaks with justice,"he speaks the truth". For both truth and justice are the same.'

But we in India seem to have reversed this, and made justice the protector of the strong, and what some people say in courts after putting their hand on the holiest of Hindu scriptures, the *Gita,* is not truth but fabricated untruth.

As for social justice, whatever that means, instead of social justice we have achieved social inequality. In British India thanks to Bentinck, *sati* was abolished and declared a criminal offence. In the India under the Moghuls Akbar rushed or horseback thirty or forty miles to save a widow being burnt on her husband's funeral pyre. But in free India on 4 September 1987 Roop Kunwar wife; of Mal Singh a BSc student of Deorala (Rajasthan) was made to be burnt in the flames, with thousands looking on and cheering and the authorities unmindful. Almost every week a bride is being burned, hung or poisoned for not fetching adequate dowry. Investigations are made but there are very few prosecutions and convictions. Girls, and minors are raped, but no account is taken of them. Women belonging to the hill areas of Uttar Pradesh were raped in Muzaffarnagar district whose district magistrate came out with the astounding comment that if a girl is alone in lonely place the temptation to rape her is irresistible! On a court order an inquiry was institued by by the Central Bureau of Investigation (CBI) which concluded that the police raped some women Says Harish Chandola,'A Bitter Struggle', 'The tiny tortured body of Uttarakhand lies in trauma. In three months 30 of its people including women were killed in police firings and torture, thosusands imprisoned, women raped, people terrorised, hamlets placed under curfew and property brutally destroyed.[180] What is worse is that the Uttar Pradesh government is apparently trying to protect those guilty. A press report says:

> 'In a move to "protect" the officers responsible for firing on the Uttarakhand agitators in Muzaffarnagar, the state government has given an out-of-turn promotion to Mr Bua Singh, who was DIG Meerut range, at the time and had ordered the firing at Rampur Tiraha on 2 October killing at least 20 persons. Besides, seven women were raped and 24 cases of molestation were reported. The CBI has so far registered 27 cases of tampering with records. Apart from this the then IG Meerut Zone, Mr S.M.Naseem has been appointed IG Police Radio. It is noteworthy that most of the evidence gathered by the CBI is based on written messages and on the statement of radio operations Mr Naseem has been sent to the Police Radio allegedly to conceal facts and to hide the records if

> possible from the CBI sleuths. It may be recalled that in the two interim reports of the CBI submitted to the Allahabad High Court it had been established that criminal cases were fabricated against the Uttarakhand demonstrators and records were tampered with to hide the truth'.[181]

'One woman is raped in Punjab every hour and 29 minutes. Eight women fall prey to the dowry greed that covers both urban and rural Punjab now. Every twelve and a half minutes a severe wife beating takes place. Each day 31 women get molested in a State which has perhaps the largest number of religious places and preachers advocating non-violence. One case of a girl being mishehaved with occurs every nineteen minutes [*The Hindustan Times.* 9April 1995 'Saga of Untold Crime against Punjab Women']. What is disquieting is that the police who ought to prevent crime, not only abet it but quite often commit it themselves! A 25-years-old woman, a poor fruit-seller and divorcee is said to have been raped by a sub-insspector in the sacred pilgrimage town of Haridwar. The SI told her to accompany him to the police station, but instead took her to his friend's house and raped her there while his friend stood guard outside [*The Hindustan Times,* 10April 1995].

A body to listen to the victimization of women, the National Commission of Women (NCW) was recently set up. Amazingly even highly educated and wellplaced women were found to have been physically assaulted, tortured by their bosses and it became difficult for them to maintain their sangfroid. Among them were a sub-judge cum JMIC Karnal, Anup Yadav, Myra Dias: secretary to the regional manager western region, Vayadoot Ltd., who was demoted to the post of a stenographer for some 'pernonal reasons' which her boss wished to discuss with her alone at Juhu Centre! and Om Kumari Gupta, associate professor at Kariour Medical College who was abused and manhandled by the head of the department. Extracts from the press report about the enquiry are as follows:

> 'Packed auditorium. The audience is listening intently to the speakers on the platsform. Suddenly, a participant on th stage breaks up in tears. What is happening here? Some popular play being enacted by some famous troupe?
>
> 'The scene contained every element of drama. But the stories unfolded in the first public enquiry on crimes against women in

Delhi orgainzed by the NCW happened to be excerpts from real life. The participants comprised aggrieved women from all strata of society. Highly educated women with professions as varied as medicine or law, shared the platform with totally uneducated and harassed victims....'['the uneducated and less informed women simply narrated their horror stories of harassment for dowry, rape and so on. Mothers who have lost their daughters in dowry deaths, women who were molested, women who were divorced against their wishes, and the list went on. Most of them wept as they doscribed their torturous experiences. As the hearing proceeded, one victim from the audience waiting for her turn got up and began to shout in a frenzy of anger at the people who had wronged her...

'*Almost all the women who had come out with their grievances, did so only when several attempts to get justice in the existing system failed to bring them any solace....*

'*The cases cited here have proved the collapse of the police force, their inactive posture. It has exposed the inactivity complacency and corruption of the authorities*'.[182]

This is how social justice so grandiloquently promised by the preamble is being meted out to the citizens of India! And what is still more shameful is that the authorities who are the custodians of the constitution overlook it, connive with it and even in certain cases (as in the Uttarakhand affair), themselves perpetrate it. An editorial says:

'The sheer callousness of a Delhi police officer who wilfully neglected his duty when he asked a rickshaw-puller to dump a *two-year-old* victim of rape somewhere rather than bother him, is symptomatio of the law-enforcing agencies' increasing disregard for human life. For Mr Dharam Pal, the Delhi police officer who allowed the child to bleed to death rather than rush her to hospital last Friday, human life is worth Rs. 10. But it's not he alone who is guilty of such perversity. Most of our men in uniform who have been entrusted with the task of implementing the laws of the land have allowed themselves to be dehumanized to an extent that they are no longer seen as friends in need. What has made the situation worse is the near absence of any accountability– the police in many states has become indistinguishable from society's malcontents whom it is supposed to battle.

'Indeed the callousness of our police presents a sad, if not scary, picture. The brutality to which Ms Maya Tyagi was subjected years ago in Uttar Pradesh continues to be enacted with sickening regularity. Witness the rape of Uttarakhand protestors by policemen in Uttar Pradesh or the gruesome manner in which the body of a tribal was displayed in a public place by a DSP in Madhya Pradesh. In Marxist-ruled West Bengal there have been 183 custodial deaths between 1977 and 1994, while in Punjab policemen behave like outlaws, unmindful of the law of the land. These gross viiolationis of civil liberty could have been checked if civil authority had not chosen to abdicate its responsibility and turn a Nelson's eye. Tragically, if policemen are callous, so are administrators as well as politicians. The common man is of little relation to any of them!'[183]

It's not only the police who are making a mockery of the social justice which the Indian citizen was assured of in the preamble to the constitution, it's the politicians too, most of whom are a law to themselves. A resume of the year 1994 in India says:

'In Bihar a ruling Janata Dal MLA (member of the legislative assembly), Yogendra Narayan Sardar, had his private parts sliced off by a tribal girl after she was allegedly abducted and raped by him and four of his friends. Narayan Sardar who fled home following the incident reportedly got his penis restitched in a private clinic'.[184]

In Bihar, too, where the saying goes that anything can happen there, armed members of the 'Sunlight Sena' dressed in khaki battle fatigues charged into a Harijan village and killed nine Harijans and the police and administrative officials visited the site well after the killings. An IAS officer who had only come on some official work to Bihar and belonged to another part of the country was unawares caught in a demonstration and the supporters of a local politician literally lynehed him. The editorial in which these incidents are narrated, dismally concludes: 'With the administration virtually paralyzed, it is not surprising that more and more sections of society in Bihar are taking the laws into their own hands. There are large areas of the state where the police has lost all control and law and order is the preserve of local private armies whose only motto is that might is right.... To some extent this betrayal of the people by the political class as a whole has been the tragedy of the state right from its inception!'[185]

A columnist observes that for Bihar's chief minister 'social justice' [exactly what the preamble of our constitution promises to citizens] boils down to posting officer of the OBC (other backward castes) particularly Yadavs (26 district magistrates and 30 divisional commissioners in crucial field jobs. Booths have been changed to suit the Yadavs, and astoundingly one district magistrate Ms Rajbala Verma, has publicly declared Mr Yadav (the chief minister) of victory. Police officers of Danapur from where he is contesting are virtually campaigning for him. Kanchan Gupta, the writer, says:

> 'his [Mr Laloo Yadav's] dispensation of "social justice" has pushed the State further towards disaster. Bihar today boasts the lowest literacy rate, the lowest per capital income and has the largest number of people living below the poverty line. Bihari society has been irrevocably fragmented along caste lines and, to use a cliche', the State, for all practical purposes has withered away....
>
> 'Civil society has been all but crowded out and where it exists it does so in a permanent state of paralysis.... The list of crimes committed in this state is endless, the list of people punished for these crimes almost non-existent'.

The statistics of Bihar's home deparatment show, says the writer, that more people were killed every day there than in Punjab during the worst period of terrorism. 'Even today, life is cheap not only in rural Bihar but in cities like Patna, Dhanbad and Ranchi where gangsters rule the roost under the benign gaze of ruling party politicians. Bihar is perhaps the only state in the country where a parallel tax system [*rangdari*] exists to aggrandize the lumpen class'.[186]

The adjoining state of Uttar Pradesh does not appear to be any better. Says a report about the western districts: 'Gangsters are like cockroaches. Whenever the law enforcing agencies mount pressure on them at one place they turn up somewhere else. With the police either becoming indifferent to the increasing tribe of criminals the situation has assumed alarming proportions. To cap it, the shelter by the politicians has further worsened the situation'. The report goes on to say that a ransom of Rs 21 lakh was paid for the release of a youth. The police took the uncle of the suspect into custody to put pressure on the accused, but a lady,member of the Rajya Sabha who 'calls the shots in the state' directed the police officer to release him and escort him back to his home. 'In Ghaziabad, the fear looms large among the residents following a spate of dacoity, murder, loot and rape during the last one year [1994]. Roads in the city wear a deserted look after the dusk desends [*The Hindustan Times.* 9 April 1995 Crime Wave in West U.P.' Anil Maheshwari]. The report goes on to say that these criminals 'acquired respectibility in the Congress' way back in 1969. During the short BJP regime there was some respite, but the criminals fled to Delhi [then under the Congress and they were suppported by the Delhi police cops with whom the 'criminals did not mind sharing the booty' [*Hindustan Times* 10 April 1995]

Ms Medha Patkar, convener of the Narmada Bachao Andolan [in opposition to the Sardar Sarovar Project writes about 'the exploitation of one section of society by the other' in the name of development, and 'when the poor, who is deprived of his livelihood, raises his voice against exploitation, he is termed as anti-development'. 'When the poor villagers of Manibali, the first village to get submerged, refused to leave when the gushing waters of the Narmada river entered their houses, they were beaten up by the police. they were dragged out of their houses; one 15-year-old youth was killed and many women were raped: and still they were called anti-development'.

Recently in Uttar Pradesh it was reported that a person whose seat had been booked from before on a train was accosted by the nephew of an MLA who insisted on having it for himself. The nephew went and told the MLA about it, who picked up his gun and straight- away shot the GRP man who was 'interfering'. Leaders of the ruling party have been brazenly grabbing houses in the capital of the state. A report says:

> 'In a brazen display of muscle-power the sons of a senior Samajwadi Party leader forcibly occupied the house of a retired army colonel on Madan Malviya Marg on the night of 27-28 January 1995.
>
> 'The house-grabbing operation was carried out in the absenec of the sole occupant of the house, Mrs Pushpa Kapoor, the widow of an army colonel, at present in Bombay....
>
> 'It is learnt that on January 27, at around 11.30 p.m., a police inspector came and handed over an allotment order to the servant of the house and told him that the upper storey of (retired) Colonel PB Kapoor's house had been allotted in the name of Dinesh Verma via an order issued by the ADM (Civil Supplies) on January 24 1995.

'The servant refused access on the ground that the first floor had not been rented and the mistress of the house was in Bombay.

'The police inspector then left the place. At around 3 am on 28 January a busload of persons, fully armed, descended on the place and forced their entry into the vacant house by breaking down a wall. Before entering the house they roughed up the two security personnel manning the main gate of the colony.

'Having taken possession of the premises, these persons have begun terrorizing the residents by sending messages that they would soon occupy the other vacant houses in the locality.

'This is the latest incident in a long chain of such acts by those belonging to the ruling party.

'Their activities are manifest in several other areas of the state capital including [the localities of] Mahanagar, Badshahnagar. Gomtinagar and Butler Palace. *What is more shocking is that the police has invariably been in league with the house and land grabbers.* In this incident too, the role of the police cannot be said to have been above board'.[187]

This is only one example. During the 14-month rule of the Samajwadi-Bahujan Samaj Parties (SP-BSP) combine, 128 houses have been grabbed, the majority in the western part of the state which is the more prosperous one. Most of these were grabbed between September 1994 and January 1995, while police reports were recorded in only 22 cases. The report says 'The state president of the SP Mr Ram Saran Das refuses to believe that these houses have been grabbed by his party workers. But he argues "in a state comprising 65 districts if suppose they have grabbed 128 houses, what wrong have they committed?" ' [*Pioneer* 21 February 1995] The conclusion is that in order to have committed a wrong they should have grabbed many more!

In Uttar Pradesh also the police gunned down in a 'fake encounter' ten Sikhs. On the other hand 'highly aggressive men of the politically powerful Mahendra Singh Tikait could kill two policemen and "imprison" four others with apparent impunity. In fact, they refused to release either the captives or the corpses until the state government had capitulated to Tikait's peremptory dictates'.[188] Recently the Bahujan Samaj Party MLA Mr Uma Kant Yadav and a dozen of his armed associates are said have killed three people at Jaunpur. They were seeking to release another associate whom the police had locked up in an outpost. Their stratagem, which relied exclusively on a rather indiscriminate firing of automatic weapons while raiding the outpost paid off. On January 27, 1995 about two dozen armed intruders beat up, molested and abused at least six women in front of their family members. The police shut their eyes to this mass rape. Thus legislators who are supposed to set an example, themselves resort to criminal methods.[189] Then there was Biju Patnaik chief minister of Orissa who *threatened to secede from India* unless some demands of his were not fulfilled!

The behaviour of politicians and the state of our society indicates that the social and political justice announced with great fanfare in the constitution's preamble was just big talk. What economic justice means is anybody's guess. It is evident that the so called justice has only resulted in the poor becoming poorer and the rich richer. We have spoken earlier about the sad plight of famers, three-fourths of whom live below the poverty line, which with us means not even affording to have a square meal a day. The poor in India are really poor. A report says: 'In U.S every seventy person is poor. But that means a family subsisting on and annual income of less than 14,763 dollars as classified in 1993. In India an income amounting to this would be considered princely'. Delivering the 9th Fakhruddin Ali Ahmed memorial lecture at the Sakharita Bhawan on 7 December 1987 Mr Justice Rajendra Sachar, a former chief justice of the Delhi High court, stressed the need of the economic emancipation of the masses, particularly the millions who were still below the poverty line. With over 50 per cent of the people living thus, there were virtually two civilizations - one of the rich and the other of the poor – living in the country. The economic gap had to be bridged for it could not continue for long. On the one hand there was the 'five star' culture, multi-storeyed buildings and multi-storied projects, and on the other the basic needs of the people were not being met. Between 1953 and 1961 the share of the top tenth of the population in the national income rose from 28 per cent to 37 per cent, whereas that of the bottom two fifth declined from 20 per cent to 15 per cent.[191] According to a survey made by S.P. Gupta director Indian Council for Research on International Economic. Relations, the percentage of people below the poverty line went up from 35.5 per cent in 1990-91 to 40.6 per cent in 1992-93. People could buy less than 50 per cent of what was available at the shops of the public distribution system [but this could also be due to malpractices and the shopkeepers selling half of the supply in the black market and is no definite evidence of lack of the capacity to buy].

Grandeur and misery exist side by side. Bombay's Nariman Point, the Manhatten of the East houses a business of Rs 50,000 crore at the lowest estimate. Rs 66 lakh was paid by Forbes and Campbell, a Tata owned company for a flat with a carpet area of only 1,600 square feet. There are 21,000 air-conditioners (unit 1.5 tonnes) 120 elevators, 30,000 direct telephone lines and over 1,10,000 extensions in the complex of Nariman Point's 1,800 big and small offices.[192] that is the India of the stinking rich. On the other hand according to a UNI report between one fourth and half of the urban population in India's largest cities lives in make shift shelters, squatters and slums.[193] Squatter colnies exist against the backdrop of multi-storied buildings [194] About 37,017 villages did not have a single source of drinking water in 1980. In village Fatehgarh of Rajasthan 'there has been a famine for 16 of the last 20 years (1966-1986). Most people in the area live on a meagre meal of *bajra* (millet) and occasionally a wheat *roti* (unleavened bread) with salt and chillies. Pulses and green vegetables are a luxury which, like rice, only the rich can afford'.[195] As against this there are fabulous weddings. In one of them, says a fortnightly, invitations costing about Rs 30 each were issued to 20,000 guests. Orchids were flown from Singapore, pistachios and almonds from California and chocolates from Switzerland. A decorator specially flown from Calcutta, did up the place. A Meena Bazaar was recreated with rows of stalls stacked with bags, costume jewellery and other trinkets which the guests could take away with them. Foreign guests brought in on a chartered jet were gifted silk *churidarkurtas*.'[196] the picture has not changed, rather the gap has widened, and the middle class of our society are fast sinking into poverty with inflation rising to two digits and prices soaring almost every three months. Professor John Adams of the department of economics North-Eastern University, speaking on the theme 'India's economy in the 1990s: regress or progress' said 'the macro policy failure, which has been rolling forward since 1991 beginning with the problem of significant fiscal imbalance and balance of payments imbalance, and now it has become mostly a financial monetary problem, which is leading up to inflatioin rates of about 10 per cent for the decade'. If this was not checked, he thought it would have very adverse 'distributional effects'. He commented on the government's 'extremely disappointing progress in dealing with social programmes and social needs, education, literacy and health; disappointing not only to those who look at India from outside but to Indians themselves'.[197] The profligacy of 1993-94 made the fiscal deficit to skyrocket to 7.3 per cent of the gross domestic product at Rs 58,551 crore against the budgeted figure of a considerably more modest Rs 36,959 crore. Government has resorted to progressive increase in taxation but the increase in revenue thereby is likely to be offset by the expenditure increase over the projection levels. The biggest hurdle would be the food and fertilizer subsidies. The fertilizer bill is likely to touch Rs 6,000 crore. The food subsidy bill is likely to exceed the targetted Rs 4,000 crore by about Rs 1,700 crore because of an anticipated expenditure of about Rs 600-700 crore on sugar imports and increased carrying costs for buffer stocks of food-grains. While the common man is reeling under inflation and price rise and in addition exorbitant taxation, the politicians paint the town red with political sprees in which ice cream is flown from Italy and delicacies rivalling Moghul dinners served. When Lord Northbrooke was informed of a possible famine in 1873-74 he postponed the durbars to be held that autumn in Lucknow to demonstrate that government was not in favour of display at such a moment. Lord Mountbatten who gave lavish dinners when he was governor general of free India got Lord Listowel, a person of great importance, served just cabbage water in place of soup, and one piece of spam and potato, a biscuit and a small portion of cheese! when he stayed at the government house during the massacre following Partition, to show his government's solidarity with the people in their suffering. But while drought was having its greatest impact and the Indian farmer was anxiously scanning the sky for clouds, the Festival of USSR was launched on 21 November 1987 at New Delhi. The cost was Rs 25 crore [the inauguration alone costing Rs 4 crore] lit up by 1,000 lamps of one kilowatt each, 500 of five kw. and other imported light items and equipment weighing 300 tonnes – all this when the MACRO-model forecast warned of an industrial show-down in early 1988, worst drought since independence, food-grains output down by 10 million tonnes and overall GNP growth below 2 per cent.[198] From Madhya Pradesh comes the story of the chief minister's Relief Fund. Dhanno Bai 45, a poor woman suffering from cancer was sanctioned Rs 200 after a lot of effort of four months. Then the chief minister's office insisted that the bedridden woman should present herself in person. Three days later Dhanno Bai died 'clutching the bits of papers awarding her Rs 200' In contrast a Bhopal industrialist owning a printing press and a type foundry, was quickly sanctioned Rs 5000 for treatment for a heart ailment, a woman of status and wealth got Rs. 20,000 for cancer treatment without even a medial cortificate, which it was insisted Dhanno Bai must give, a former chief ministser got Rs 50,000, a man of property Rs 20,000 a doctor who had made a lot of money Rs 20,000 an MP Rs 3 lakh and an MLA Rs 5.5 lakh. In New Delhi three slum dewllers were shot dead by the police for daring to defecate in a park in the posh colony of Ashok Vihar. In Bangalore and Hyderabad there were organized rackets [we shall speak in detail of this later] where poor people were compelled to part for their kidneys for a pittance. In west Singhbhum [south Bihar] where steel companies have struck it rich, the poor tribals eat ants to fight starvatioin. This is how poor Indian's poor are, and that is how the preamble of the constitution promising justice social and economic, as also the directives of 'protection to the weaker sections of the people', equality and so forth, works. With a great deal of truth the veteran Congress leader, Kamlapati Tripathi, said 'Did we fight the freedom struggle so that our children should sleep half-belly and a number of people live in poverty? We elders had planned to create the statue of Lord Ganesha, but now we have turned it into the figure of a monkey'. Long back when the matter of giving freedom to India was being debated in the British parliament Churchill had opposed it on the ground that the people were not fit for themselves governing the country. He used rather strong language, as he always did to emphasize his point, calling Indians 'men of straw', but what he said about the country ultimately being lost in political squabbles, seems to be turning out true. What the constitution gifted the citizens as the liberty of political justice, has turned out to be license, not liberty. Politicians have stooped to calling each other names, like 'traitor', 'liar and even biff one another. There is no sense of propriety nor any honourable code of behaviour. Democratic norms are flouted, corruption, scams, scandals are no longer evils for them, the country's good is no longer their aim for they hardly care what happens to it, and their single objective is to retain power and benefit their own selves. In one of the most populous provinces, there exists the curious phenomenon of the governmetn itself carrying on agitations and one of the parties, the Congress, sitting on the government side in the state assembly, yet opposing it! In this way they bamboozle the citizens and make a laughingstock of democracy. Slogans like *halla bol* [*halla* = 'noise'; bol = 'speak' or 'make'] *inqalab zindabad* ['long live revolution,] and so forth which would be appropriate only when the freedom struggle was on, are still being uttered lustily by the henchmen of political parties. When the communal holocaust followed Partition. Nehru and even Patel India's iron man 'looking like a pair of chastened schoolboys' lost their nerves and piteously appealed to Mountbatten, free Indian's first governor general to take the reins of administration, Nehru confessed 'Our experience is in the art of agitation, not administration. We can barely manage to run a well-organized government in normal circumstances. We're just not up to facing an absolute collapse of law and order'.[199] After forty-seven years of freedom, things are no better. Agitation still is all that our politicians are capable of, indeed the art of administration seems to have gone on the blink so far as they are concerned, and where it is believed to repose, is with a spineless and committed bureaucracy fragmented castwise and chary of taking decisions because after casting on them the responsibility, their political masters foist their own misdeeds on them, even dragging officers who have long retired into diciplinary inquiries. Says an editorial:

> 'When the country was struggling to wrest independence from the British, the colonialists used to argue that Indians were not prepared for self-governance and independence would in fact be against their own interests since it would usher in an era of anarchy. The nationalists countered this by saying that freedom would also bring responsibility with it and the country would gradually mature into a full-blooded democracy. This firm belief promtpted the members fo the Constituent Assembly to decide in favour of a secular democratic polity with adult franchise. However, almost half a century later when one looks at the retarded development of our society and the behaviour of our leaders, the sad realization dawns that there was, after all, a grain of truth in what the British said about us.
>
> 'The superimposition of democracy on a society like ours with strong feudal and even pre-feudal tendencies has obviously had very limited success. And, barring a few honourable exceptions, the political class as a whole has developed an imperious attitude to treat the state as its private property. In no other country would an ailing and incapiciated politician be retained in an important portfolio like External Affair as Mr Dinesh Singh was. And even when he was axed, his Cabinet status remained unchanged so as to enable him to retain his bungalow and other perquisites. Mr Vasant Sathe too had refused to vacate his bunglow even after he had ceased to be MP and went up to the Supreme Court to retain it on health grounds. He too was accorded Cabinet status when the Government appointed him honorary president of the Indian Concil of Cultural Relations (ICCR) more than two years ago. Residences of the late Charan Singh and Jagjivan Ram are yet to be vacated by

their family members and, if the present trend persists, will never be. One also reads about the way our leaders behave – the latest being about an unapologetic former Union Minister relieving himself in full public view *outside* the toilet in an aircraft. This brings memories of Mr Ramarao Adik, the then Deputy Chief Minister of Maharashtra, misbehaving with an airhostess in an inebriated state. The way Mr Devi Lal and his clan treated Haryana as his fiefdom is fresh in public memory'.[200]

The minister of state for tourism, Mrs Narendra Kanwar, sent a guest to Khasa Kothi, a prestigious unit of the State Hotels Corporation, and rang the manager to see that he was looked after well. The 'guest' arrived with two kids and demanded VIP treatment for himself, his kids and his driver too! The report about this says 'So far Mrs Kunwar has not indicated her intention to pay the bill [of Rs one lakh], but it is apparent that she wants the guests should be treasted on State account' [*The Hindustan Times*. 8 April 1995, 'Minister's guest leaves hotel in quandary'].

Grabbing of houses by politicians is not confined to central ministers alone. In Uttar Pradesh, for example every ex-chief minister (with very few exceptions like Banarsi Dass and C.B.Gupta) retains a house in the poshest locality valued at several lakh rupees and they retain them in perpetuity from father to son, son to grandson so that their families can enjoy their benefit for ever. This is the 'equality of status and oppurtunity' which 'we, the people of India' sought 'to secure to all its citizens'! In fact as we have said before, exploitation of India has not undergone any change, only the exploiters have changed. The Turks plundered wealth and carried away gold and precious stones from temples. The British did it indirectly by ruining India economically. After freedom our political leaders are now doing it by corruptly amassing huge fortunes and squandering the country's wealth in order to retain power by giving bogus awards and huge grants to certain sections who would help them retain their chairs.

Coming to the second item of the Preamble, namely liberty of thought, expression, belief, faith and worship, this too has remained a paper promise. The government forcibly suppressed freedom of expression by persecuting writers and poets and kept putting the lid on creative literature. Any criticism of the rulers and their hencemen was brutally suppressed. In Uttar Pradesh, for example just a few months back, offices of a Hindi newspaper which dared to write against the state government were ransacked and bundles of the daily burnt. The Andhra Pradesh hounded and harassed such writers. In1969 the poet Subharao Panigrahi who was popular with the people and took up their cause was tortured and shot dead. The child artist who was only twelve years old was killed. Thus far from giving the right of freedom of thought and expression the governments of independent India are engaged in suppressing it with a ruthlessness which was unknown even in the colonial rule of th British when books written by prominent leaders like Nehru and Gandhi were doubtlessly proscribed but they weren't shot for writing them. In 1970 P.Krishna Rao was arrested and roughed up for writing his anthology of poems titled *March.* After a long trial he was fined Rs 500 by a magistrate. In August 1971 three writers, Jwalamukhi, Nikhleshwar and Charabanda Raju were detained under the MISA for writing verses which criticized the diabolic administration and the suppression of civic rights. It was only when protests of litterateurs caused a public interest litigation to be moved that the High Court get them released. Mrs Sandhya of the Jana Natya Mandali, was implicated along with others, on false charges, and she was so greatly tortured that she had an abortion. The list is endless Magazines and fortnightlies like the *Prabhanjanam, Jeevanadi* and literary works like *Jhamjha, Leh, Raktaganam* and *Ippudu Vistunna Gali* were banned and their writers persecuted. These are onlu some of the measures taken for gagging the press and literary writers and their works. [201]

The Indian radio and TV, controlled by the government are examples of how news is twisted so as to paint a rosy picture of a decadent and deteriorating administration. Curiously enough the English press, which under the Raj was a mouthpiece of the British government has, after a brief spell of unbiassed reporting, lately again become prejudiced, and editors find themselves unable to break away from the leanings of the political partisanship of the propietors who own the paper. Most English dailies and quite a few prestigious magazines too, have not been able to develop an impartial attitude despite the fact that a US based committee to protect journalists commented that the English press in India is free [though its Hindi counterpart was not because of the apparent desire by regional and local politicians to shape coverage in what is often the only print media accessible to their constituents. {*The Pioneer,* 21 March 1995]. This being so it is all the more surprising that the English press in India exults in underplaying Hinduism, branding it as 'Hindutva' and to *honeyfogle* minorities in the same way as politicians are doing, particularly by constant *jawing* the so-called

'Sangha-parivar'. This tongue-lashing leaves the English press free and yet fettered. Free because the politicians too rejoice at every such bashing, and solidly stand by it, and fettered by the narrow prejudices of its reporters and editors. For example an editorial says: 'The rise of extreme Hindu chauvinistic forces prepared ground for the rabidly communal element among the Moslems to multiply like a deadly virus, affecting their ability to think rationally'. Surely it's quite the contrary. It is the Moslems who are for Islam the world over, for as we have said 'According to the Holy Prophet every child is born in Islam, that Islam is the chosen religion destired to triumph over all others, and that the earth belongs to Allah and he causes it to be inherited by whom of by His servants He wills' [Harsh Narain. *Jizyah and the Spread of Islam.* New Delhi: Voice of India, 1990, p.,1] Yet our editor [*The Pioneer* 21 March 1995] insists that it is Hindus who are spreading the virus of chauvinism! The editorial is primarily about the film *Bombay* in which a Moslem girl is shown marrying a Hindu and has been for this reason banned in Hyderabad, a state with a large Moslem population. While condemning this rightly enough, the aforesaid editor remarks 'One is quite sure that their Hindu counterparts would have similarly objected had the film shown a Hindu girl marrying a Moslem boy', a conclusion which is purely a figment of the editor's mind. Hinduism has always been and is, a tolerant religion. Despite gibes and scoffings at it by 'secular' Hindus, there is no opposition or persecution. Hindus revile Hinduism and Hindu gods out-and-out, yet there are no *fatwas* like those against Nasreen or Rushdie. The warriors of *jihad,* says Kanchan Gupta, deputy editor of *The Pioneer* (22February 1995) 'stabbed an Italian who was translating *The Satanie Verses* shot the Norwegian publisher of the book.... at least 100 Moslem writers have been silenced forever since 1989', the journalist Rahman Hatefli had his veins sliced open and left to die and poet, Mehdi Shokri shot in both eyes.' Yet the Indian press and media keeps on drubbing the so-called Hindu chauvinists and the Indian politicians keep bending their knees to make themselves secure. An independent English press in India is a distand dream.

It is clear, therefore that the liberty of thought and expression spoken of in the Preamble is just not there. We have quoted Confucius 'When law and order prevail in the land, a man may be bold in speech and bold in action; but when the land lacks law and order, though he may take bold action, he should lay restraint on his speech'.[202] In India where there is violent disorder to speak out seems sheer folly.

Then there is the Preamble's guarantee of liberty of belief, faith and worship. For one thing this liberty has turned out to be rather taxing for the citizen who loves peace, for thanks to the loudspeaker through which it is expressed it is jarring to the ears. As Kabir says, God is not deaf and a silent prayer will reach him just as much as the cacophonies issuing from the loudspeakers of both Hindus and Moslems. As we will explain later, the politicians and their henchmen, fishing for Moslem votes are careful to see that full facilities are given to them in matters of faith, belief and worship. The same can't be said for the Hindus, the scared stiff majority, ironically in their own land! For example an English fortnightly cosiders it absurd that Rama was born in Ayodhya. Recently on the festival of Mahashivaratri celebrated after Shiva, one of the three gods of the Hindu trinity, *darshan* (having a glimpse) of the idol at Varanasi in the holiest of Hindu temples, Vishvanatha, was regulated by police force. In Ayodhya *darshan* of Rama must be had from a distance, so is the will of the authorities. The belief that Rama was born in Ayodhya is attempted to be disputed by certain people who wish even to take it to court. Justice William O. Douglas of the US Supreme Court observed in a judgment delivered by him in 1944 – US.V,Ballard 322 US 78 'Men may believe what they cannot prove. They may not be put to the proof of their religious doctrines on belief. Religious experiences which are as true to life to some may be incomprehensible to others'. Yet the Hindu must have the birth of Rama put to the proof! In fact the word 'communal' (which is fast becoming a cliche' here) is considered by the politicians and the English press in India to be synonymous with a Hindu, or at any rate with one who is unfortunate enough to belong to the so-called upper caste. But a Moslem is never communal, as concived by politicians who fawn on them, for it is the Moslems who have the capacity of bringing them into power and getting them a place in the parliament and the assemblies. The Hindu religion is perhaps the most accomodating and broadminded of all faiths quite the reverse of the Islamic condemnation of religions other than Islam. This is evident from the history of Moslem rule in India when thousands of temples were pulled down and the broken bits of demolished idols embedded in the steps leading to Moslem mosques so that they could be trodden on by those going for prayers. In consonance with the Hindu ethos, the destruction of the Babri mosque was most certainly condemnable but at the same time the massacre of Hindus on 2 November 1990 exceeded all norms of civilized conduct. The views of two veteran Congress(I) leaders Mrs Rajendra Kumari Bajpai and Mr N.D.Tiwari who visited the spot later was that it was worse than the Jallianwala massacre. People who had hid in houses to escape the violence were pulled out and shot and so too who tried to carry away the wounded: The demolition of the mosque where incidentally no prayers had been offered for long by some misguided Hindu extremists, which led to the fall of a government and a positive trend in elections, seems to have outbalanced all the horrors and indignities perpetrated by the Turks on their Hindu subjects under the Moslem rule. From the attitude of our present day governments it appears that they feel the Preamble's liberty of faith and worship was meant for the Moslems of India and not for the Hindus.

A later addition to the Constitution was that India should be a 'secular' democracy. 'Secular' means being irreligious. Surely those who introduced this word into the Constitution were either not aware of its meaning, or, if they were, perhaps what they meant was that there should be no public demonstration of religion – no loudspeakers atop the minarets of mosques or for recitations of the *akhanda Ramayana.* But aren't we doing just the opposite of that? In fact religion in India is no longer 'the opium of the masses', it's their *tootsie roll.*

The third item in the Preamble is 'Equality of status and opportunity, and to promote among all, fraternity, assuring the dignity of the individual and unity of the nation'. Very high-sounding, but it does not seem to have worked out that way at all: 'Sharda has taken a day off, she works as a domestic help. She knows the better half of the day will be spent in the queue at the ration shop. As she proffers her bag to the shopkeeper she winces at the dirt that is poured along with the grain and sugar. Her feeble attempts at a protest are answered by a rough *lena ho to lo nahin to jao* "take it as it is or else scram". SC Sharma is a property dealer in Noida. His telephone, crucial to his business, has been dead for ten days. He has forgotten the number of times he has booked a complaint and personally visited the Noida telephone exchange to plead with those smug officials. Roshan Lal has spent 35 years of his life in government service. He feels he'll spend the next 35 years in chasing his pension and gratuity. Geeta Batra teaches in a school in Daryaganj, New Delhi. For a good decade she has lived with the nightmare of travelling on DTC buses from Motinagar to her place of work and back.

'There is a familiar ring to these tales. In one way or another, we have all experienced something similar. But these, frustrating as they are, are only minor irritants. Power cuts, erratic water supply, trains running late [even by 20 hours or so!] The other day a person missed his train because the time of departure printed on his ticket was wrong. When he went to complain he was casually told that the computer information had not been updated. That impolite never-smiling man at the bank counter [and all other counters the citizen has to go to], shortages, inflation [price rise] and so on, there are any number of hurdles that ensure there is nothing in your life that ever goes smoothly'.[203]

'At any given time, 33 per cent of the phones in Delhi and 26 per cent of the phones in Bombay are out of order. In Calcutta seven out of ten phones are usually inoperative due to cable faults. Currently 842, 567 citizens who have paid deposits ranging from Rs 1,000 to Rs 8,000 to acquire a telephone may have to wait for over a decade for connections.... What the authorities are aware of but will never admit in public is that there is rampant indiscipline in the lower cadre of the staff, *Corruption at all levels*, poor supervision, slow execution of the work on hand and a general apathy towards work.... Not surprisingly, there are complaints galore – of frequent irregularities of billings, of blatant malpractices that unscruplours subscribers in collusion with linesmen and other technical staff indulge in, such as tampering with lines to ensure that their STD (subscriber trunk dialling system) calls are registered on another number'.[204]

India remains divided into a few people who are privileged and those multitude of citizens who are of no account. We have already spoken about the so-called equality of status guaranteed by the Preamble, quoting the case of the poor widow Dhanno. For the ordinary citizen equality of status and opportunity is a myth. For example a ten year old boy, Anshu, who had slipped out of home and was looking at the posters outside the Alankar theatre is reported to have been 'thrashed by the police in an attempt to force him to confess that he was a pickpocket. His father said that the police "used measures that were used on hard-core criminals. He was constantly hit on the elbow-joints, knee-joints and the soles of the feet to make him confess that he was a pickpocket and to admit to some crimes at the bus and taxi stands at Charbagh." He was beaten when he kept quiet till he became unconscious. Medical examination showed he had suspected fracture on the left leg with swellings on the knee ankles and elbows'.[205] One day when a *rehearsal* was being held for traffic contro when a VVIP was about to come (he had to come later) I was walking on the road when a cop said *Dadaji jara zor zor se kadam barhaiay* ('Old man, walk faster'). I stopped and told him that having long past 60, that was the fastest I could go. That is the kind of dignity a senior citizen has in free India, the Preamble of whose constitution assured its citizen, of the dignity of the individual. On another occasion, long before the VVIP was due to arrive I just wanted to cross the road so that I could get to the other side and walk home which was closeby. But no, I was told nothing doing. A report from the Indian capital says:

> ' "PAPA THEY WILL KILL YOU. The policeman is pointing a gun at you. Please stop". Scared and terrified, Poonnam Surendra Nath, a studen of Convent of Jesus and Mary school, got panicky when a police constable aimed his rifle at her father and ordered them to stop immediately.
>
> 'Mr Surendra Nath was not fleeing after committing a crime. He was on his way to reach his daughter to her school. Unfortunately he happened to take a route which was close to the one that the prime minister was to pass through.
>
> 'Driving through the calm and elite area of Moti Bagh, Mr Nath never imagined that driving at around 7.30 am could cost him his life. Short of shooting, the police personnel did "everything".
>
> 'Mr Nath had taken a by-lane which the PM was *not* going to use. Nevertheless stop he did because of the fear of the rifle muzzle. Before Mr Nath could utter a word, the police officials snatched the key of his car. Throughout the torturous incident the cop had his gun pointed at him.
>
> ' "Where is your driving license?" barked the rude police official. Not the one to take it lying down, Mr Nath reminded the police official that police officials had neither the authority nor the permission to inspect anybody's driving license. It was only when the official saw Mr Nath's visiting card, identifying him as a senior civil servant, was he allowed to go *on the same lane*!
>
> 'The incident would have been buried as yet another instance of the price that a common man pays for VIP security, but for the fact that Mr Nath, who happens to be the chief commissioner (labour), filed a writ in the High Court requesting to "punish the lientenant governor of Delhi, union home secretary and the police commissioner of Delhi, for commanding the police force at their control to commit offences like wrongful confinement wrongful restraint and criminal intimidation".
>
> 'Since then the phones have not stopped ringing at his office and residence'.[206]

This then is the much flaunted, loudly proclaimed, dignity the Indian constitution promised the Indian citizen – a dignity rust-cankered and corroded. And if one insists on preserving it the powers-that-be threaten him with 'dire consequences', and if he makes too much noise he is likely to be silenced for ever!

There are eighteen people in India with 'Black Cat' cover, i.e., guarded by black cat commandos. LK Advani is one of them, and perhaps one of those rare politicians with the human touch. While his motorcade was speeding down a busy Delhi road the commandos noticed a Sikh driving a jeep persistently trying to overtake them despite being signalled to move away. The commandos decided to shoot him down, but Advani asked them to stop the car, saying that he refused to be party to such drastic action. Menwhile an alert PCR Gypsy arrived and took away the jeep driver. On questioning it turned out the the Sikh gentleman only wanted to tell Advani's driver that a door of the car was not properly shut. One innocent life saved by a considerate politician ['Abou Ben Adhem may his tribe increase'!] 'Almost every citizen of Delhi has had his or her life overturned more than once by the security menace. Whether it is having your handbag rummaged while entering a cinema hall or having to bear with a Black Cat staring at you at every hole at the Delhi Golf Club because union minister, Jagdish Tyler, must indulge in his passion for golf, has only made life difficult'. Even as the police force was being alerted and constituted for the Bihar election in which violent disorder and affray were feared, a former Cabinet Minister rang up furious at the withdrawal of his security. It was restored, but now he demanded inclusion in the especially categorized Black Cat commandos for which he wasn't qualified. Despite 600 people being in the protected list in Delhi alone, demands for fresh cover keep pouring. The families of former prime ministers have also to be provided security. A municipal commissioner who ceased to be in office 15 years ago refuses to give up his security and if anyone's security is downgraded or struck off, he does not rest until he can by any means have it restored. Those under the security umbrella itch to parade it, attending every *mundan* (ceremonial shaving of the head) or marriage ceremony in order to show off their retinue of guards. Their personal security officers have free rides on the police escort cars and at the VIP's behest stay in the same expensive hotels and eat and drink with them and of course go with them on the planes. The government forks out the dough and has to arrange for prior reservations not only or the VIP but also for his entire security personnel, In 1994 the cost of this security was Rs 41 crore for Delhi alone excluding that spent on ex-prime ministers and the acting PM and the cost of air travel, hotel accommodation etc., for the thousands of personnel deployed with touring VIPs. An exasperated home ministry official asks 'Should we look after law and order, Kashmir and Assam or only look after VIP security [which in most cases is merely a swank]'. K F Rustamji former director general of the BSF (Border Security Force) says "VIP security in India is no longer need-based. It has become a status symbol. Excessive security has begun to offend the common man, and when that happens, it is a sure sign that it needs to be scaled down" ' 207

The above account will show that none of the promises so solemnly made to the Indian citizens by the Preamble has been fulfilled even during the course of forty-seven years of freedom, not to speak of the directive principles enshrined in it. We will now go on to that.

India has turned out to be a country of towering industrialists rich as Croesus, a good few of them afflicted with affluenza; the middle-class traders, the poor people moving about the pavements with wares on wheels or putting up a small [largely unauthorized] stalls and being chased about by various authorities like corporations, the police and so forth fishing for their monthly cuts and lastly a huge segment of those without any means of livelihood. The lousy rich housed in Nariman Point, Noida, Kanpur and other business centres are the ones whose huge companies are speculated on in our stock exchanges with crores of rupees as their assests. They form a minuscule of our teeming millions, and for them inflation and price rise are a boon not a curse and in any case does not bother them at all. They are in India but do not represent the real India. The middle classes who form a kind of halfway house are the ones who keep struggling against the price line and it is only a matter of time before they give up. But by far the greater lot are the lower rung who can barely eke out a living. These are the *oofless* and *down-and-out,* those who can manage just a meal a day and these constitute also the vast majority of the rural population who have uneconomic holdings. Ever since independence successive governments have been shouting themselves hoarse, the slogan being *garibi hatao*, some kind of magic word which could charm away poverty. But it is estimated that by the year 2000 about 468 million Indians will be below the poverty line. After more than three decades of planning and an investment of Rs 1,40,000 crore in development projects 6.6 million people are slipping below the poverty line. In the last rung are the landless labourers in the villages whose number is legion, and the educated unemployed whose number, according to figures of the employment exchanges was 26 million in 1985 [it would be much more now]. Of these 76 per cent were matriculates and 23 per cent graduates. Even those with technical degrees like engineering are to a great extent jobless. So much for the constitution's directive about means of livelihood. The other directives are largely about equal distribution of wealth regarding which we have seen how unequal it is, equal pay for equal work, prevention of exploitation of child labour, equal justice and free legal advice [which we have shown to be a myth], organization of village *panchayats*, education, assistance to the old in age, the disabled and sick, humane conditions of work, minimum wages, protecting the weaker sections, separation of the judiciary and the executive, promotion of internal peace and security. These have been mentioned earlier, but they are being recapitulated here. Let us see how these have worked out.

According to Pramod Kumar Rajpoot, the general secretary of the All-India General Mazdor Trade Union (affilated to the AITUC) 80 per cent of the electronic units in the capital do not pay minimum wages. An inspection of one of the electronic firms made in February 1995 showed that of its 61 workers, 26 earn a wage of Rs 1,382 per month, which is less than the rockbottom statutory minimum of Rs 1,420 for unskilled workers. In another company an inspection in December 1992 showed that 50 of its 99 workers earn between Rs1200 to 1500 after 10-20 year's service, a pitiable state of affairs for an electronic firm. The same holds true for many other prestigious electronic firms. Conditions of the workers are also deplorable. South Indian women stay in fours and fives in expensive cramped one room tenenents in Giri Nagar and Kalkaji areas. There is wide disparity in the earnings of various sections of the people of India. The reality is the output of work has hardly any relation to salaries and wages. A clerk who does most of the spade work in offices gets less than a third of the salary of decision makers many of whom are happier passing the buck than taking decisions! A labourer who toils the whole day in the exacting Indian summer get a pittance of Rs 1200 or so a month ($37.5), a mason Rs 2,400 ($75) while an officer of the central government sitting in an air-conditioned room gets anything from Rs 6.000 to Rs 8,000 ($ 187.5-250)

An executive of a well-established private firm might get anything from Rs 50,000 to 80,000 inclusive of perquisites, i.e.; $1562.5 to 2500 per month. Equal pay for equal work simply does not exist.

Coming to the directive in the constitution about preventing exploitation of child labour let us see what's happening. As far as legislation to stop exploitation of children is concerned there is no dearth of it – the Employment of Children Act 1938 banning employment of children in hazardous industries, The Plantation Labour Act 1951 prohibiting employment of children below 12, The Mines Act 1952 prohibiting employment of children under 15, Factories Act 1954 banning the employment of adolescents, the Bidi and Cigar Act 1966 prohibiting employment of children under 14 in these industries, and the Child Labour (Prohibition and Regulation) Act 1986. Law making is one thing and the enforcement of these laws quite another. The actual state of affairs shows that all this legislation was mere eyewash and window dressing. The prime minister Narasimha Rao announced in his Independence day speech, plans to *phase out* [not abolish] child labour from [only] hazardous industries. As usual with us, instead of implementation all decisions result in the formation of committee which after many extensions produce huge reports which no one has the time or patience to read; and so a 'national authority' was set up in 2 October 1994. This was to cover only 15 per cent of the child labour force which is 18 million according to official figures, but in reality above 100 million. As a report says: 'India probably has the largest child labour force *in the world* and it is growing every day despite increasing international conver and internal pressure for reforms. It is estimated that more than 100 million children are forced to work in organized and unorganized sectors. And that's not all. About 50 per cent of the children working in different industries in the country may come under child bonded labour. All in blatant violation of not only international laws, but also the laws of this country itself, showing how this corrupt and weak-kneed system does not care a bit about this horrendous exploitation'.[208] Coming back to the 'national authority'set up by the PM, firstly it relates only to hazardous industries, secondly it is only for 15 per cent, of these child workers, a mere handful, and thirdly the scheme provides that every child withdrawn from such employment will be given Rs 4,300 per year, i.e., Rs 358 ($11.19) a month. With this pittance the child would certainly much rather keep on the job than sit doing nothing on a monthly subsidy or unemployment allowance which will not bring him even a meal a day! The condition of child labourers in villages is worse, for the employer insists that every adult who comes to work, brings his child with him to work also. The wages are a mere pittance and many children flee the villages for towns, where conditions are bad enough. As the aforesaid report says: "Eleven-year-old Tipu wakes up at the crack of dawn. He gulps down a frugal breakfast and rushes off to a shantytown in north Calcutta where he, along with eight other young boys, breaks open batteries. It is tiring work. His back aches within half an hour, his head throbs with the hammering, but he cannot stop. At the rate of one paisa per battery, he makes around Rs 69 (28 cents) by sunset when he returns home, covered in carbon dust. There are millions of Tipus all over India – exploited, exposed to hazardous work conditions and paid a pittance. Forced to forego education, shouldering responsibilities far beyond their years, becoming wordly-wise when their peers have yet to leave the cocoons of parental protection, these children do not know what childhood is. All this makes a mockery of the noble promises enshrined in the Indian constitution'.[209] As if this was not enough, child rape has become a common feature in this country, and every now and then we come across reports of brutal sex assaults on minors, mostly girls, often with the connivance of relatives of politicians, with the police reluctant to take notice of them. A typical report reads thus:

> 'A five year old girl is said to have been ravished by the "mahout" of a BSP (Bahujan Samajwadi Party) minister in the khadra locality of the Hasanganj police circle on Sunday [12 March 1995] afternoon. *The Hasanganj police after first refusing to register a complaint, later bowed to the pressure when local residents threatened to gherao [surround] the police station.* An FIR (first information report) was finally lodged on Monday. According to the police, the victim, identified as Zeba, a resident of Khadra was first enticed by Guddu, alias Polle to his house which is in the neighbourhood of the victim's house. The police said that Guddu "criminally assaulted the girl and escaped when she raised an alarm".'[210]

In 1989, 2,317 cases of child rape were registered with the police countrywide. The figure rose to 2,481 in 1990 and jumped to a substantial 3,603 in 1991. In Delhi alone, in the first six months of 1994, nearly in two out of three rape cases, children were involved. These are the reported cases. How many go unreported is anybody's guess, and sodomy of young boys is almost never reported. Three years ago this problem was never even taken note of. It was only in a seminar organized by NCW (the National Commission for Women) in October 1992 that attention was focussed on this, but nothing tangible has been done till now. Surprisingly the NCW's recommendation are only for the rape of girls, who, *including those under 12 years old* are described as 'women'!

This *poppycockish* idea implies that if a girl of six or eight years is raped it can't be called such unless we term the child as a 'woman'! This is sheer nonsense and shows how demented such commissions can be. There was the case of a girl of two-and-a-half years being raped with profuse bleeding and ultimate death. What was more the local police officer to whom a rickshaw puller brought the baby for investigation, gave him Rs10 and asked him to go and dispose of the child. And on this day the capital of India, where this happened, was celebrating the International Women's Day! A certain doctor raped an 8-year-old child. 'He bolted the door from inside and stripped himself as well as the protesting and terrified child. He forced her to perform fellatio (oral sex) on him. Then he cuddled and pinned the child down, forced his penis into her and started kissing her on the lips. Even after ejaculation, he did not give up. He put on his clothes and laid the terrified child down on the sofa. He then lay down on her again and closed her mouth so that she could not scream. After whetting his sexual appetite, he opened the door and let the child out...' The father filed a case, but the trial court acquitted the doctor. An appeal to the High Court ended in a petty fine of Rs 3000! The Supreme Court, however, rendered justice by a sentence of 7 years' RI and a fine of Rs 25,000. But even after six months the police have not arrested the doctor as the victim's father says, his brother is AIG (Establishment) a high police officer of the Indian Police Service. Describing her traumatic state the girl [turned 19 by the time the Supreme Court judgment came], said: 'I cannot describe in words the sufferings a girl has to pass through after being a victim of rape. People have the false feeling of shame and it becomes difficult for the victim to live in such a society.... Often I've had dreadful dreams and even now I get up at night due to these nightmares... I hate all men. Whenever I see a man "his" face and the whole scene of my helplessness and his aggressiveness comes before me and I feel uncomfortable in the presence of men'. And the worst of this sordid episode is that justice was got with such great effort and so late and the police was even then reluctant to act. This is how we have carried out the directive to protect women. (Account from *Health & Nutrition,* January 1993). About 180 million women are illiterate in India. There were 999 registered cases of dowry deaths in 1985, 1912 in 1987 and 5,197 in 1991, From 1987 to 1991 there was a 37 per cent increase in cruelty by a husband and his relations a 26 per cent increase in rape and a 169 per cent increase in dowry deaths – all the crimes being committed most often by those closest to these women.[211] The various kinds of discrimination and deprivation to which women are subjected lead to malnutrition, illiteracy child labour and prostitution, particularly in the rural areas. In rural Rajasthan only 5.5 per cent women are literate. Bihar, Madhya Pradesh and Uttar Pradesh which account for 38 per cent of rural families, have a rural literary rate of below 10 per cent. Among girls aged less than 15 years in Hyderabad 65 per cent, in Delhi 69 per cent and in Calcutta 97 per cent had heamoglobin levels of less than 11 gm in their blood, leading to chronic anaemia. There are about 4,00,000 child prostitutes in India Most of them are girls under 16 years age. The way in which these innocent minor girls are pressurized into prostitution is appalling. A report says:

> 'Children are decieved or forced by violence into prostitution. Each one of these children is put through a process of seasoning. Most of them surrender within 7-10 days under psychological pressure, beatings, rape, starvation etc. Researcher Jyoti Sanghera says in a paper on the traffic of Nepali women into India that a 14-year-old girl put up a resistance for three weaks till whe was put in a pitch dark room with a cobra. She sat there numb for two days and ultimately yielded to their demands. Sometimes parents [obviously because of poverty] knowingly offer their children to sex traffickers'.[212]

Let us see how government, which prides itself on protecting the weaker sections of society, which is also one of the Constitution's directives, is faring. A report about it says: 393 Harijans were murdered in 1994 (against 286 in 1993 and 298 in 1992). Harijan women raped in U.P. in 1994 were a staggering 377 (more than in 1993's 250). Cases of arson against Harijan families were 342 (as against 243 and 225 in the previous two years). Cases under the SC/ST Act registered were 10,380 in 1994 (while in the previous years they stood at 8,995 and 8,462). Cases of atrocities against women rose sharply from 1,661 in 1993 and 1,444 in 1992 to 1,794 in 1994. Cases of rape (including those of Harijan women were 1,878 in 1994 (1,595 in 1993 and 1,569 in 1992). Molestation cases rose to 2,904 in 1994 (as against 2,442 in 1993 and 2,281 in 1992).[213]

Says Padma Seth there has been a collapse of the police force, their ineffective posture. The crimes against women have 'exposed the inactivity and corruption of the authorities'. [214]

Despite all this, the Shankaracharya of Puri says [reported in *The Statesman*] 'Sati is the only way for a woman to prove she's pure'! and a pamphlet issued in Deorala (Rajasthan) says *sati hona samaj ke liye gaurava* ('A sati does society proud'!) We have an unenviable record of what we are doing to our women. Every twelve hours a bride is burnt somewhere, and every two hours a woman is raped. Most of the bride-burning is among the middle and upper classes professionals, bureaucrats and politicians. Thus are we observing the protection of the weak and uplift of women directed by our constitution!

Clearly the 'social justice' so pompously proclaimed by the Preamble remains a nonachievement. Section 46 of the Constitution says: 'The State shall promote with special care the educational and economic interess of the weaker sections of the people, and in particular of the scheduled castes and tribes, and shall protect them from social injustice and all forms of exploitation'. We have shown how this pledge has turned out to be mere words, words, words. So also are the other tall promises made by it namely economic or political justice liberty of thought, expression, belief, faith and worship, equality of status and opportunity, dignity of th individual or any national sense in its citizens. The directives too have turned out just *ballyhoo,* with the ruthless victimization of women and children, the exploitation of child labour, lack of employment, increase in poverty poor nutrition and innumerable other evils. We go on to see how the directives about humane conditions of work, education, health, assistance in sickness, old age and disablement, separation of the executive from the judiciary maintaining peace and security and establishing village *panchayats,* have worked out. Let us see how much education has proceeded in the near half a century of our independence. Although Hindi is India's national language, it is spoken only in a few states in the Gangetic plains in north India and in anathema in the others, particularly in the South. How difficult the problem of this tangle of tongues is can be seen from the observation of a Goan MLA 'North Goa will blow up if the Bill [to make Konkon the official language] is passed, and the south if it defeated'! The issue of language somehow creates a lot of frenzy in India, and the Constitution solved the problem by including the large number of them all, and proclaiming English as the 'associate official language'. So English ramains the most popular and coveted language all over the country, as Macaulay and Bentirick wanted it to be, much to the amusement of foreigners. So an English education in Convents and Anglo-Indian or Public Schools remains the most prized one, and is termed as the best available. As Rajiv Gandhi said.'.. good education was available only to the elite, while the poor had to study in schools without proper buildings and blackboards. As for women, their education usually consists of home science and making pickles'.[215]

He was right as well as wrong — right about the boys, in fact an overestimation, for the condition of village schools is much worse, but wrong about the girls. Many girls now are much better educated, al least in the towns, quite a few graduates, post-graduates and even Ph Ds., for by and large girls are more serious and conscientious both in education and in work, than our boys. A class 10 student of the Emakulam Government School switched over to an English medium school, though he could hardly speak that language because, he said 'I will be able to communicate with big persons like the chief justice! Society willk respect me more'. 'Wanted a Convent educated girl' that's how a good few matrimonials in our papers begin. Wily politicians keep extolling vernacular medium schools but send their own children to those very Public Schools they keep deriding. In truth it is the politicians who are the worst culprits in ruining education by trying to exploit the youth to fulfil their narrow selfish ambitions for money and power. That's why they want to have unions in universities and degree colleges; and their machinations have turned the campuses into battlegrounds and strongholds of yobbists, who are equipped with *kattas* (countrymade pistols) daggers and even crude bombs. The academic atmosphere is lost in the haze of sex and violent disorder.

On paper, edcucation for all, and free education till the age of 14 looks very salutary, but the achievement has been quite the contrary. With 48 per cent of the people illiterate, the underclass remains as deprived of education as before independence. About 10 per cent of the figures shown enrolled in schools don't join up. A slightly higher percentage don't go to school beyond class 5, and those who reach class 10 are much less. Poverty and economic pressure make parents unable to continue their children's education after the preliminary stage; for higher education is a luxury for the majority of Indians struggling to make a livelihood. So boys are withdrawn from schools to be able to work and contribute to the family earning. Education, like every other thing that goes for carrying the country forward, is set off by the growth of population and the extreme poverty which too increases with each passing year. Despite our 200 universities and almost 8,000 colleges, the access rate of education is only six per cent, i.e., only six per cent get higher education . Says A.Jolly, a child psychologist and one of the early child education specialists: Uttar Pradesh has a drop out percentage of over 80 *which could be the highest in the world.* [*The Pioneer*, 13 March 1995]. There is of course no dearth of committees, commissions, commitments, plans and assurances, for politicians are fond of drawing old chestnuts and keeping the people pleased with platitudes, but in the doing one's stuff, its all a complete flop. The pledge of the constituion has not only drawn a blank on the provision of education but also on the quality imparted. The educated youth of today are an indisciplined lot, stealing cars to impress girls, unaware of the fact that it is not skill in crime which can catch their attention, but the cultured mind, looting shops, indulging in violence and hooliganism, overawing people to pay up 'ransom' in the garb of subscription. There are schools on which the government spends Rs. 10,000 a month in which teachers just sign the attendance register and go away, schools with teachers but no students, a high school with a staff of seven and a monthly expenditure of Rs. 13,000 the building of which houses a cattle-shed! [216] Students of primary schools are made to do the domestic work of teachers, who as compensation write the questions in the examinations on the blackboards and the answers just beneath them, so that all come out in flying colours without even having a look at their books! The English second paper distributed by the UP Board of High School and Intermediate had questions set different in different copies of the same paper, so no one could know which was the genuine paper! [217] In one of the universities over half-a-dozen students were awarded their PhDs without doing a spot of work. The students engaged a man who wrote their theses on getting an agreed sum. A section of teachers in the Hindi department and some members of the staff were believed to be in the racket.[218] Education is of primary importance in a democracy which has not yet turned into a dictatorship. With teachers not interested in teaching, students not interested in learning and politicians interested in keeping the masses of India unlettered so that they can do as they please and bring disasters on the nation and yet get the people's votes; education in India so grandiloquently announced as a diretive of the constitution remains a withering commedity. The sly politicians of India want it thus, for as a Scottish statesman and historian said, 'Education makes people easy to lead. but difficult to drive; easy to govern but impossible to enslave'. [219] This attitude on the part of our leaders, indifference in some and criminal neglect in other, is sad, for as Aristotle said 'All who have meditated on the art of governing mankind have been convinced that the fate of empires depends on the education of youth'.[220] But our leaders have neither meditated, nor have they been convinced.

We now go on to comment briefly on the other diretives. 'Assitance in sickness, old age, disablement etc., raising levels of nutrition and public health', thus says the constitution. But it is all *gobbledegook* when one considers what has actually been done. The allocation in 1995 for public health is about one per cent of the total (near two per cent if family welfare is included), when even the poorest Third World nations set aside 4 to 6 per cent for it, while the developed ones 8 to 14 per cent. Says Amit Sengupta of the Delhi Science Forum, 'India's is possibly the worst case scenario, barring a couple of banana republics'. From the First Five Year Plan there has been a decline in each subsequent year, showing that the constitutional promise to maintain the health of the nation has crapped out. Just as in everything else, in healthcare too there are two distinct categories of treatment available—the government and government supported hospitals, and the privately managed ones such as nursing homes, the clinics run by private agencies which often have government doctors too working part-time and also doing private practice on their own. The government has made half-hearted attempts to prohibit private practice for its doctors, but it has just not worked. They were given fixed allowances to compensate them. They pocketed the allowances and still continued working in their own clinics. The authorities are a dud in so far as this is concerned. One reason for their ineffectiveness is that the docs take jolly good care to attend on our VIPs. A cough or a bruise makes them rush to their aid, leaving the ordinary patients however serious their condition is [remember the Preamble, 'equality of status and opportunity' and 'dignity of the individual']. Once I had an appointment in connection with my wife's treatment with a doctor at the local prestigious Gandhi Memorial Hospital [KGMC] in the medical section at 9 am. Arriving on the dot I found to my surprise the main door to it closed with two orderlies standing by. 'You can't go in' they said roughly. 'And why not?' I asked, 'the doctor called me at nine'. Nothing doing, I was told. The reason?—the health minister was inside also to show himself to some doc, maybe he had a cold, and till the minister did not come out, nobody else was going in [even it he was on his last rattler]. When one Prime Minister was on a visit to Lucknow the entire operation theatre (OT) was reserved for him. No operations till he was in town. VIPs seldom condescend to get their treatment or surgeries done in Indian hospitals They go for it to some developed country like the US or Germany or UK. As non-public schools are not fit for their children, so too Indian hospitals are not fit for them. I had to stay four days in a private ward of the KGMC when I broke my right hand and right leg because of a scooter dashing into me while crossing the road. There was one bedpan for three wards with about 30-40 beds in each, i.e., one bedpan to say about 100-120 patients, all bedridden! Shouts and agonized screams would start for the sweeper who handled the bedpan 'Ah Ghasite, [his name] *ab to aa jao Ghasite* [come now at least, Ghasite]'. There was a child whose leg had been plastered. Every morning just about 3 am I could hear his agonized screams (something seemed to be pressing on his anklebone) *mar gaye hai rama mar gaye* ['I'm dying, O God, I'm dying']. Doctors came and went but never bothered about him, till one day a relation of his came from the village and did what the doc ought to have done. He brought a knife and cuting through the plaster set the leg free of it. The toilets of the wards were unapproachable yet essential. The entire toilet was full to the brim with excreta and the passage leading to it had lumps of it all over the place.There were of course departmental heads, an entire medical directorate, the secretaries in the health department and its minister, all of whom are blissfully unaware of this, for *they* have nothing to do with general wards which are only for the second-grade Indian citizen. Meanwhile hospitals, even the most prestigious one of this country, the All-India Institute of Medical Sciences (AIIMS) carry on with their callous indifference. A boy's eye has to be operated on. When he is taken out of the AIIMS's OT, his parents are horrified to see his good eye bandaged! The absentminded surgeon had operated the wrong eye!. Two girls go in for minor plastic surgery in the reputed AIIMS. One dies while under anaesthesia. Doesn't matter, get in the other. The same thing happens with her. In the KGMC the doctors held a camp for operating for cataract. They blinded 30 of them because, as it was discovered later, the surgery (OT) was infected! A child with gangrene in one lege was taken to a doctor who amputated the good one, and when the horrified father pointed it out, he said, 'Doesn't matter, bring him again tomorrow, I'll amputate the other one too'! A deputy inspector general of police having an eye problems asked the government doctor to send an eye ointment. He got a tube which he applied to his eyes and became wild with pain. It turned out it was for piles! He barely managed to save his eyes. On another occasion I was once more in a medical general ward for a check-up. They put me on a drip, but sometime in the night it started leaking and causing me pain. I asked my son to fetch a doctor (there was none in the ward). He came back and said he found three docs asleep in a room. When he woke one up, and told him the problem, he said it was none of his business and went to sleep again ! There wasn't even a compounder or nurse in the ward. One came late night and said 'I can't reset the needle, that's a doc's job but I'll put off the drip'. He took the needle out. Then there was the head of the opthalmic department of this hospital with a string of German Fellowships and other high-sounding degrees who operated me as a private case for a retinal detachment. When I was on the operating table he asked me *ap ka dil vil to thik hai*? ['Is your heart etc., okay'?]. I told him it was to the best of my knowledge. Then he got my *eyebrows* shaved (not the eyelashes) and the local anasthesia he gave failing, purformed a two-and-a-half hour operation with me fully conscious and writhing with pain, asking a man to catch my left hand and another my right and having a blanket put on my legs [it was the height of summer] so that I may not kick them up!. A right and proper Sushrut type op. which would be the kind performed several years before the birth of Christ! In September 1994 the plague broke out in Surat, said to be the dirtiest city of its size in the whole country, 80 per cent the slum dwellers defecate in open spaces, canal and river banks, railtracks etc. After the flood when the waters receded in Surat, carcasses were left to rot. The deputy municipal commissioner in charges health and hospitals and 250 doctors had warned the muncipal offical 'that epidemics of cholera and possibly even plague were imminent'. Jan Bremen told *Frontline* 'Public housing and public health were not municipal priorities at all'.[221] Clearly the health authorities were unmindful of their duties and responsiblities. The plague resulted in a loss of Rs 385 crore in foreign exchange because foreign tourists stayed away.

The Bhopal gas leak resulted in innumerable deaths and people going blind and sick. Here's how the government reacted. Says Zaitoon Bi, one of the sufferers : 'no one bothered to pay any compensation money for two years. We had to stand in endless queues and thumb-print endless claim forms, but to this day the only money I've received is Rs.1500. Although on paper the relatives of dead victims are supposed to get Rs10,000 as immediate relief, Rs. 700 per month as interim relief and then Rs one Lakh (or a house) so far I have seen no sign of any of these'.[222] The son of the then mayor of Bombay got a head injury in a car accident . Here's his experience at a government hospital, Nimhans (one of only half a dozen centres for neurological disorders in India): 'There I lay on the floor for five or six hours while the police went through all their formalities. Also they were waiting for some kind of deposit which it would have taken my friends an hour or two to organize. My friends were pleading with the medical officer "just treat him first, and we'll take care of everything". But it was of no avail. I lay on the ground for those six hours, waking up to occasional drifts of consciousness when I'd tell my friends "call my mom and dad , but don't tell them what's happened".[223] Being the son of an influential person, the boy could get a plane and be flown to Bombay and get the best possible treatment, but the constitution's directive was surely not meant for the privileged alone. The poor are only left to die, for elite treatment is beyond their means. They are not even left to die. To India's poorest of the poor death would indeed be a blessing. But death can come only at the allotted time. Meanwhile they live on like beasts unable to do anything about their physical suffering with unscruplous doctors, with their eyes on the pot, exploiting them, and our governments shedding tears for them much like the Walrus in Alice

' "I weep for you" the Walrus said
" I deeply sympathize." '[224]

A senior Shiva Sena leader, Pramod Navalkar; had exposed the kidney rakcket in 1994 on the floor of the Maharastra legislative assembly. On July 29, he had produced a list of all the illegal nursing homes and hospitals in Bombay that duped poor people into parting with their kidneys. Some very prestigious hospitals of that city were, according to him, involved in the racket. 'There was no follow-up action' he said, 'therefore I have decided to file a writ in the Bombay High Court for tackling the issue'. But the government wasn't worried [what did the poor matter, except at election time ?] These innocent victims were either coaxed to part with their kidneys for a pittance or had them surreptitiously removed in the garb of a medical check-up. They were then implanted by these doctors in recepients from the Middle East for $ 10,000 upwards [over three lakh rupees]. It turned out to be a wide racket involving touts who brought the 'donors' and got their cut and doctors who made the money. The recepients were foreigners from UAE, Turkey, Saudi Arabia, Germany, Yemen, Italy, Mauritius, Venezuela and other countries. Bombay's top doctors were involved in this 40 crore per year ramp, spreading all over the country from

Bangalore and Hydrerabad to Bombay, Calcutta and Delhi. Depite numberless exposes in the media, and even an article in the *Spectator* reporting that Britons were flocking to Bombay to buy kidneys and livers at throwaway prices, the government was asleep on the job. It woke up late, and then the Human Transplant Act was passed [mere eyewash providing a fine of Rs.10,000 to Rs.20,000 for middlmen, something laughable for the tout can earn much more on a single sale]. That too after years of lobbying by Bombay urologists and others who were all in the racket. Before this law is implemented it will have to be endorsed by a minimum number of states and there- after the rules framed. The police kept saying the racket wasn't there at all till faced by incontrovertible proof from a recepient in a foreign country. Despite the immorality and the large extent of the racket, a doctor of Wellingdon Hospital thought the ban was misconceived as it would force a patient whose kidney is not functioning to undergo dialysis till one becomes available and in the end the patient will have to foot a bigger bill and that the Act will drive the trade underground![225] In other words let the racket continue so that the surgeons can keep on making their ill-gotten fortunes and the touts bringing the poor needy victims and so the gyp could go on undisturbed. Why can't needy people in India itself get these kidneys instead of the select ones from abroad ? Obviously the ones who have the money can't compete with the recepients of the developed prosperous countries, and those who are poor can donate but not receive. In India no amount of appeal to the conscience will do any good because the consciences of most have long been dead. If we wait till there are no more poor in this country tempted to sell their kidneys, we may be waiting till Doomsday. The only way seems to be to deprive errant doctors of their right to practise the profession, so that they have nothing to sell. The kidney racket depicts one more ground of the failure to assist sickness and diablement and ensure public health', as provided in the Constituion's directive. Assistance in this regard is doubtless being given, but not to Indians, to those of the rich moneyed people abroad! It's as K.B.Grant, Trustee, Ruby Hall Clinic Pune, says. '...the Indian health system is deplorable; it is the *last* priority in our Government. [226]

It is not just one factor which creates misery for the people of this country. There are several [as we will point out later on]. In the case which follows it was a combination of carelessness and the poor condition of our power supply :

'An operation being performed on a patient had to be abandoned midway owing to power failure and non-availability of diesel for running the generator

This happend at the emergency operation at the emergency opration theatre of the LLR hospital, Kanpur'.[227]

The patient lay unconscious, bleeding profusely The ward boy ran to get the generator started, but the operator of it wasn't there He said his duty was over at 5 pm. and then when further questioned said the diesel had finished. Meanwhile the woman, Urmilla, bled on and the surgeons finding no other alternative sewed up her abdomen and sent her back to the ward in a critical condition Several bottles of blood had to be infused. The lights came on after 3 hours at 6 pm when Urmilla was brought back and the operation completed. This is how our hospitals function Meanwhile politicans are busy running after power and money, calling each other names, distributing awards to the already affluent from the government's funds, pitching caste against caste, grovelling to the minorities for their votes. They do not have any time to look after medicare Unscouplous traders taking advantage of government apathy, flood the market with spurious medicines and even repack and sell as new, disposable syringes. For them the Constitution remains a mere scrap of paper.

As for nutrition which is also on the constituional agenda, we hear of many programmes and schemes, but the truth is that instead of providing wholesome food for hungry months there is slow-poisoning. In Calcutta adulterated cooking oil caused swelling in the limbs. A test check made in Jamshedpur showed that pulse sold in the open market had germs which could cause paralysis. In certain regions of Bihar, wheat distributed in fair prices shops was moth-infected, rotten, and mixed with dust. Yet all this stuff was being ground into flour and eaten by unsuspecting people. *Kesari* is a kind of pulse, the consumption of which breaks down the central nervous system within two to six months paralysing the lower part of the body, and there is no cure for it. If the pulse is boiled before eating it is rendered safe, though it loses its colour and tasts. But the Madhya Pradesh government were reluctant to get rid of the poisons in *kesari* because 'after being boiled it loses its, colour, weight, vitamins, taste and consequently its *commercial value'* The argument amounted to this : it's better to paralyse the people [most of the users being the poor] rather than cause any setback in the earning of prosperous traders! It was found that the majority of vendors had been selling centaminated tea at railway stations in India. They made this tea from poster colour which contains chemicals the consumption of which may lead to diseases like asthama, heart ailments or even cancer. Ten litres of synthetic milk is made by mixing 15 mg of white poster colour in it. And by mixing on kg sugar and 50 gms of tea leaves in it, about 300 cups of tea are made. The tea made thus has an input of Rs.30 only and is sold for Rs.300 at a rate of two rupees a cup [Reported in *the Pioneer* 22 March 1995].

In Haryana's Karnal and Kurukshetra districts less than a fortnight after the rains began in 1988, thirty people in the village who entered wells to attend to the tubewell motors were choked to death. The reason was a steep fall in the water table. When the rains come, decaying bio-mass and organic material gives out gas, mainly carbon dioxide and carbon monoxide. Both gases are soluble in water, but in a drought the water is low. and the gases accumulate. The government showed its awareness only after people kept dying for a week. Then too warning was given the old defunct way 'by beat of drum'. Evidently loudspeakers are for politicians only ! The state education minister said 'This is the villagers' private matter as the wells are their private property. The people will soon forget about it as the monsoon will be very good this time'. The minister knew what he was talking about. Yes, the people do forget, and what is more forgive and vote those very callous politicians back to power. That is the grand wonder of our sovereign democratic republic. You may browbeat the people, keep them poor, starving illiterate, unemployed, impoverished and suppressed but they'll never put up a squawk. And when something goes wrong, the first reaction of our governments is to speedily deny it, the second to keep passing the buck and sweeping the dirt under the rug and finally if still there remains a murmur, to appoint a committee.

Coming to the other directives about the establishment of *panchayats*, separation of the executive from the judiciary, preservation of monuments, forests and wild life and internal security; though some have been achieved , the achievement is merely symbolic. In 1981 there were 2,28,593 village *panchayats*, 4,478 *panchayat samities* and 252 *zila parishads*. [228] There must be many more now. Some months back lovers, a girl and a boy who had got married against the conventional caste and orthodox marriage ceremony, were given the *panchayat* variety of 'justice' by having their heads chopped off in full view of the entire village. That's how our *panchayats* function in the settlement of disputes. In a village *panchayat* of Unao district in Uttar Pardesh, a woman having a three year old child and who was being ill-treated by her in-laws, was forced at the point of a knife to give in writing that she was willingly parting from her husband and whât was more that she agreed to leave her baby with him ! In this case too the people of the village connived with the husband. From Rajasthan comes the report about Bhanwari, a village-level woman worker of the Women's Development Programme who was gang-raped on 22 September 1992 by five Gujjar and Brahmin men in retalition for her role in preventing a child marriage. She lodged a report and the case went to the district court. But the local *panchayat* in collusion with an MLA of the Bharatiya Janata Party (BJP) are said to be making all attempts to make the woman compromise the case. Says the report 'The BJP MLA and the *sarpanches* openly asked her to cosmpromise and withdraw the case. One of them even offered her money if she did so'. Having failed in their attempts the *sarpanches* led by the BJP MLA decided on a social boycott of Bhanwari and other women workers of the Women Development Programme [The *Pioneer,* 24 March 1995 Raped woman being forced to withdraw case'] The *panchayats* suffer from insufficient finances, for corruption which has reached the top has naturally affected them too. They are also unable to put to good use the land vested in them like *singhara* (water cress) growing ponds and the like. Over the years they have turned out to be mere agencies of the various political parties in power to wangle votes for them. Lack of organization, poor leadership and political exploitation has made them a jestingstock. This is unfortunate, for they were intended to be the foundation and the grass roots of our demcoracy.

The separation of the executive from the judiciary too remains a half-hearted effort. The Union Territories (Separation of Judical and Executive Functions) Act of 31 May 1969 was enacted for it. However this mainly applied to the sections of the Indian Penal Code. As a district magistrate, the executive authority of the districts of India continue to be vested with provisions under the Criminal Procedure Code like sections 144,109 110 and so forth which are very often misused, their main objective being to get hold of persons whom the police don't like and to make up the 'quota' of such cases, for the police department insist on this and the response is to nab innocent person. Besides many Acts are framed by the state governments in subjects which are on the state list, and in most of them the court of decision is the district magnistrate. Let us take for example the Rent Control Act. For one thing it is very often misused. Recently it came to light that the members of the BSP-SP combine in Uttar Pradesh were, in league with Rent Control Officers, getting allotment orders issued without the house oweners' being aware of them After three such orders (none of them being served on the owners) the accommodation was forcibly occupied by sheer muscle power, the police colluding. Initially rent control cases are decided by the district megistrate or his representative the ADM. Quite often corruption rules such decisions. And even after going through the torturous, process of appeals, which is the prerogative of judicial courts, the case, if won by the owner is remanded to the district authority. Thus litigation keeps moving like a shuttle back land forth. In revenue matters the executive has sole competence, the ladder being, the sub-divisional officer, the district officer, (i.e., the district magistrate) the commissioner (again an executive officer) and the Board of Revenue which is also controlled by the officers of the IAS. While the separation was aimed at giving impartial justice, there remains the huge number of persons termed 'undetrials' languishing in jails whose guilt has yet to be established. The judicial process being tediously long an undertrial may, if found innocent, even before he is acquitted, have undergone a period of imprisonment which could exceed the maximum he could get it convicted! The aim of the Law Commission, established in 1995 and reconstituted in 1977-80 and 1981 (December) under the chairmanship of Justice K.K. Mathew a former judge of the Supreme Court, had as its objective elimination of delays, clearance of arrears, and making justice more just and less costly. We have already shown how none of these objects has been achieved. So much for people who reach the jails as undertrials or are put through the lackadaisical and balled-up process of law. But a good few do not and are shot dead in *hoked-up* police 'encounters' which a former judge of the Supreme Court described as 'deliberate and cold-blooded murder by an agency of the state'.

Preservation of forests and wildlife another constitutional directive, has been observed more in its breach than its performance. The Central Forest (Conservation) Act of 1980 makes it obligatory to get government's approval for felling reserved forests. But by the time guidelines were laid down for forest preservation about 45 hectares of land was deforested! The cutting down of trees continues, depite protests such as the Chipko movement. There are now no forests worth the name below 9,000 feet, and the tree-line ends at 12,000 feet. Thus the Himalayan region is denuded of forests. At least 10 million acres of forest land has been lost between 1951 and 1981. Apart from preventing soil erosion the forests provide fuelwood, essential oils, lac, resins, faltty oils and fats, gums, tanning material, dyes, animal products, bamboo and bramboo pulp for paper and so forth — all of which has been lost to us. In Lucknow, the capital of Uttar Pardesh the government uprooted a well-established nursery which used to supply rare plants to plant lovers, despite a lot of public outcry. And that to build a VIP rest-house which for years has remained built only in a very small part and the chances are it will never be completed. This is the government's own attitude to trees and plants!

The same is the case with preservation of wild life. Poaching goes on unchecked, even men in authority taking part in it. The forests are now almost devoid of the majestic Indian tiger of whom the poet admirengly wrote:

'Tiger! Tiger! burning bright
In the forests of the night,
What immortal hand or eye
Could frame thy fearful symmetry!'[229]

Lack of experience and expertness make the preservation of monuments a difficult task. The selection of those on which money is spent is also in quite a few cases more because of political expediency than their national importance. As for everything it becomes a political gimmick often to please the minorities and get their goodwill. The remnants of the Vijaynagar empire at Hampi, witness of the reigns of several rulers after its glorious days of the reign of Krishna Devarai are being ruined by unaruthorized constructions thus making a mockery of the preservation of these monuments, a treasure-house of Hindu culture. According to a spokesman of the Archaelogical Survey of India (ASI) 'the local revenue department is guilty of gross negligence'. Huge concrete buildings are disfiguring the monuments. 'The State Archaelogical department and the ASI have been complaining about those construction activities so close to the monuments *which were included in the UNESCO's "heritage of mankind" list in 1987.* Foreign experts who met recently at Hampi were of the view that these unauthorized constructions have disfigured the beauty of these monuments. The conference recommended demolition of all unauthorized constructions and a ban on carrying on construction activities in the vicinity of the monuments.

'In utter disregard to the experts' findings, a few days after the conference, a godown belonging to the *state cooperative department* was inaugurated in the area adjacent to the monuments!

'Way back in 1981 the State Archaeological department had recommended to the state government to declare an area of five kilometres around the "*mahanavami dibba*" as restricted'.

The report goes on to say that government has not issued orders on the aforesaid recommendation yet. Besides the monuments are by the river behind the Sun temple and tourists roam about naked causing embarrassment to the local residents and breaching the historical ambiénce.[230] The constituttion's directive about the preservation of monuments has thus been disregarded, except perhaps to some degrees for monuments which marked the rule of the Turks in India.

Lastly we come to the constitution's directive about preserving internal security, in other words having a condition of law and order which inspires confidence in the citizens and assures them of safety and security, as well as keeping out elements which may destablize the country such as militants and infiltrators, and the suppression of yobbism and disordely conduct.

The elections in India exhibit a sad and miserable picture of the behaviour of our political leaders a good few of trhem have criminal records and what is more *blow their bazoos* about it. In many parts of the country the state is that of yobbocracy hardly one of democracy. There are stickups and hold ups, with the police often mute spectators and sometimes the culprits themselvesd! Here's a report from one of the *tahsils* of the capital of Uttar Pradesh :

> 'Complaints of extortion of money by the police from passersby and specially tempo drivers, scooterists and jeep drivers have come from the Nigohan police station.
>
> 'Those who have been made victims of this practice complain that they are stopped on the roads and needlessely harassed until they hand over the amount asked for.
>
> 'A large number of people told this correspondent that some policemen have made it a practice to stop their vehicles and ask for the relevant papers.
>
> 'However, even when the said papers are produced they are not let off. They add that the main aim of the policemen is to extort money from them, that asking for the papers is just an excuse to stop vehicles. They also said that contrary to their expectations, those having the right papers were detained while those without the right papers were allowed to go immediately upon coughing up the

amount asked for. Those with papers have to wait for hours before being allowed to go[and that when according to a recent order the right to checking papers had been taken away from the police and givem to the transport authorities]

'They said that some of them were even forced to go to the police station and had to face the humiliation of being put in the lock-up on condition that they make some arrangements for the amount of money asked for before they would be allowed to go. They also said that their vehicles were held back in many cases while they themselves were allowed to go home and get the necessary amount.

'It is learnt that on hearing of the police high handedness, the block pramukh and prominent Samajwadi party leader, Mr. Ram Swarup Yadav, barged into the police station.

'He saw the detained persons himself and got them released only by resorting to threats that he would get in touch with higher placed police officials and complain to them of the open method of extortion that the police personnel of Nigohan police station were resorting to. Only then did the police let the inocent vehicle owners go.

'Most of the persons who went through the harrowing experience told this correspondent that the loss to them was not just in terms of time and money, but also in social status and self-respect. However, they said they were helpless and did not dare to retaliate as the policemen resorted to frightening threats'.

In this case it was a political leader who interceded for the victims. But politicians do not conduct themselves any better. According to a report supporters of a Bahujan Samaj Party (BSP) minister and of an MLC of the Samajwadi Party (SP) exchanged fire for over half-an-hour with 'about 50 shots fired by both sides', according to Hari, a guard who was present there throughout, in a property dispute. Government agencies like the police and magistrates are quite often so overawed by politicians that they underplay the gravity of a breach of law and order by them. In this case the circle officer of the police insisted that only five shots were fired, while the senior superintendent of police said 'Since I have reached the spot quite late, I am not in a position to relate the entire incident. In cases like this in which a minister and an MLC, *both of the ruling parties,* are involved the situation becomes "very tricky". We will however definitely take cognizance of the incident'.[232] The usual cliches for the official machinery to describe even the most serious breaches of law and order are 'the situation is *normal* and *under control*'. This ostrich-like attritude is neither here nor there, for long back the people have got on to it, and they would most certainly believe the non-official version rather than the official cooked up one. Crimes keep soaring with the police looking on. In the capital of Uttar Pradesh alone 95 vehicles valued at 50 lakh rupees were stolen in the first sixty-five days of 1995. In these two months there was a case of loot *every day*. There were 42 murders. 'What is lamentable' says the report 'is the lackadaisical approach taken by senior police officers towards the deteriorating crime situation which has failed to instil a sense of security in the public'.[233] A report from New Delhi gives many instances of crimes committed by teenagers. A 13-year-old walked up to the cashier of his school's bank took out a knife and asked him to hand over part of the money! On 29 March 1994 three teenagers raped a 22-year-old girl and took photographs of each other doing it! On the last new year eve five youths attempted to rape a married woman after forcibly taking her away, the poor husband vainly trying to rescue her. They said they were just 'looking for some fun'. Seven youths gangraped and then blackmailed a teenager for several months after taking photographs in various compromising positions. Two school dropouts stole over 11 cars so deftly as would amaze practised criminals — the motive, 'to impress girls and to give them joyrides'! Four boys of well-to-do families stole a number of stereos in west Delhi. 110 teenagers were arrested in 1993 — 24 for rape, 25 for murder, 25 for attempted murder, 20 for robberies and 14 for chain-snatching. According to Maxwell Pereira, additional commissioner of police, movies and satellite TV viewing are most to blame, it's quite true that the fascination for warnography and high porn has spoilt many young men and impelled them to daring crimes. Our films and video-cassettes show a lot of violence and sex. Since kissing is still out, we find the film heroes running after the girls, cuddling, hugging and adopting tantalizing and sexy poses — everything within an inch of the genuine kiss but not actually kissing, much like Keat's lover painted on the Grecian urn.

'Bold Lover, never, never canst thou kiss
Though winning near the goal — yet, do not grieve:
She cannot fade, though thou hast not thy bliss,
For ever wilt thou love, and she be fair!'[234]

This, of course makes the stuff sexier than if it had been just rounded off with a kiss. Besides the sexy scenes in Indian films and TV programmes, are often unconnected with the main story as in *superhit Muqabala, BPL Oye, Philip's Top 10* etc, and so too are the sex-provoking songs, like Karishma Kapoor's *sexy, sexy, sexy mujhe log boley* ['people called me a sexy girl'], Raveena Tandon's *main cheez badi hoon mast mast* ['I'm a wanton lustful chit of a girl']. Madhuri Dixit's *choli ke peechay kya hai* ['what's behind the bra?'], *rook, rook, rook, arre baba rook, oh my darling give me a look* ['stop, stop, stop, O darling, give me a look']. All this has an overpowering effect on our youth.

The mistaken notion that sex education is needed in schools, too, is misconceived and just a *wrinkle* of modernists who think it will enable teenagers to grapple with sex better. It has failed in its objective in UK and there is no reason to think it'll fare any better here. Analyzing th causes for its nonsuccess Ray Honeyford, a teacher who started teaching in 1961, says:

> 'I suspect there are two reasons why sex education has failed. First, sex is a much more powerful and complex matter than the sex educators realize. Sex is a wonderful servant, but a tyrannical master. Our ancestors knew this. They knew that without a panoply of restraining taboos, sex would get out of hand and produce social breakdown and personal misery.
>
> 'Thanks to the permissive liberal attitude of the' 60s which mocked morality, chastity and self-control, we abolished taboos on promiscuity, divorce, abortion and illegitimacy And instead of challenging sexual anarchy by creating a moral counter-culture in the schools, too many sex-educators went along with it. Instead of providing the youth with effective ways of saying no, they retailed the doctrine that all that mattered was that the girl should not get pregnant and disease should be avoided. The latest expression of this shrunken and offensive view of human sexuality is the condom culture [in modern parlance, "condomania" or the Ugandan goverment's "zero grazing" the realization at last of this excessive bu perverted zeal to sanctify promiscuity] and the myth of so-called safe sex.
>
> 'The moral collapse has been accompanied by the rise and influence of forces outside school, forces which far too few teachers have been willing to resist, and all of which in different ways subscribed to the discredited doctrine of sex education'[235]

It is significant that the teenagers involved in these crimes were from affluent families also apparently victims of affluenza. The lads who raped or molested girls were mostly kown to the girls' familier or even had previous acquaintance with the girls. Other factors responsible were the easy availability of porno literature, the need for easy pocket money to 'splash around', egoism, *dadagiri* (playing the muscle man) the curiosity to try out forbidden things, the glamour of attractive lifestyles outside home, insecurity, lack of parental attention and the leniency of law. The families affected are reluctant to lodge reports with the authorities for fear of social opprobrium. Poet Akbar who lied in the latter years of the nineteenth and the earlier years of the twentieth century, wrote:

taaleem ladkiyaan ki zaruree to hai magar
khatoone khaanaa hon vo sabhaa ki pari na hon
zeeilmaan muthaki hon jo hon unke muntazim
ustaad achebhachon magar ustaadj na hon.

[The education of girls is necessary, but they should be trained to be good housewives not Sharons. Their instructors should be learned and virtuous. They should be good masters, but they should not master the cutt of the risque].

With the women's lib and all that we have progressed much beyond this fogey concept. Women are excelling in almost all fields of work and in all departments, even as airforce pilots; nonetheless it seems we are treading the path which the condomaniacal west is now realizing to be the wrong one. With the craze for coeds in universities who no longer sit alongside the tables of dons, but romp about campuses with their galivanting boyfriends, barebreasted scantily dressed girls modelling for depiction on the covers of exiting images, books with lurid narrations of the sex act eagerly lapped up by publishers out to make a fortune sexy condomads and gender-benders and young casanovas hunting for forbidden delight, our youth has lost its moorings.

To come back to our subject regarding internal security, it is clear that this directive of the Indian constitution has also not been achieved. Faced with state terrorism from neighbouring countries and within too, the government has done little to protect the individual, and quite often even the national interest is underplayed. The well-informed editor of a prestigious daily writes:

> It is not altogether surprising that the defence establishment has become one of the major victims of the union finance minister's

budget for 1995-96. While on paper there is a rise of over 10 per cent, what has been effected is an actual decrease, if inflation and urgent operational needs are taken into account. Defence has never been one of the favourites of Dr Manmohan Singh, (the FM) , and it may just be a coincidence that the international financial institutions too have never ceased to grumble about what they perceive to be the inordinately high defence expenditure in India. That they appear to gloss over the abnormally high per capita defence expenditure in Pakistan and not make extra fuss about the gargantuan budget of the Chinese armed forces, is another matter. That India has to fight a covert war launched by a neighbouring country, and that it has to maintain a large army and equipment along a long border with an emerging superpower does not seem to occur either to the multilateral financial institutions nor the accountants in the South Block for whom threat perception cojures up visions of Mexco, rather than China or Pakistan.

'Still the budget has been exceedingly parlous to the two major arms - the army and the air force. Both have got less than constant budgets, but the air force in particular has received a shocking cut at a time when it was finalizing deals for acquiring hardware to fill yawning gaps and to replace its aging fleet. With its budget for the next year, the IAF will hav to put on hold its plans to acquire an advanced jet trainer (AJT) and to buy some frontline aircraft to set right the imbalanced fleet where most of the fleet have either passed or nearing the age of retirement....as for the army its plans to acquire a new main battle tank, guns for the artillery, remotely piloted vehicles (RPV), attack helicoptors, surveillance system,s all of which are needed to maintain parity with, if not an edge over foes, traditional and potential, will now have to be put away.

'The finance minister would have deserved kudos if his tight-fistedness towards the defence establishment had been juxtaposed by some real belt-tightening across the board, particularly in government expenditure. Indeed Dr Singh has dilated at length on how he intends to bring down fiscal deficit. Again this would have called for standing applause, but for the small detail of the Tenth Finance Commission report, presented to Parliament a day before Dr Singh tabbled his magnum opus-quoting the finance ministry-informing it that the centre's fiscal imbalance instead of coming down, is likely to worsen in the coming years'.

It is apparent that the mistakes we have been making ever since the disintegration of the Hindu empire centuries ago are been ever repeated.

The Hindus never bothered about arms, spending all their wealth on temples whose domes were of gold and the idols of precious stones. All of this was taken away in plunders and while ransacking temples like that of Somanath. They forgot that all was fair in war, a principle which the Mahabharata war had taught them. The Europeans came primarily for trade, but when they found how ill-equipped Indian armies were they turned to conquest. At St Thome (1976) a small French force had beaten back Nawab Anwar-ud-din's army of over 10,000. After the battle of Plassey (1957) Clive wrote to Charles Watson and the gentlemen of the committee of For William 'Mir Mardan and five hundred horse are killed and three elephants. Our loss is trifling not above twenty Europeans killed and wounded.' It was the superiority of arms that established British rule. Yet we seem to have forgotten the lesson of history, and are as mild, and careless about security, as ever, while our neighbour, Pakistan, our own creation, which had two wars with India, is quietly strengthening itself by building a new neuclear reactor which will enhance its striking power, and is lobbying with the US, its enthusiastic supporter, to modity the Pressler law and obtain sophisticated F-16 air craft, airborne early warning systems and other equipment, In contrast we seem so scared of loss of economic patronage by the US that we have suspended our Prithvi and Agni Programmes. Our scramblebrained leaders don't see what use wealth is when our defence is at stake!

The seventy-eight amendments of the constition in forty-seven years have taken away whatever rights and liberties the makers of it incorporated in it. Today the Indian citizen is left no dignity, liberty, equality or fraternity. Justice is long and dilatory and its cost prohibitive, character and discipline have pegged out, education no longer brings our youth refinement; the foundation of our half a century or so old democracy, even at its grassroot level today, is violence not votes, and our corrupt power-hungry self-centred *netas* are gleefully engaged in tearing its fabric apart. Economically we are be- becoming ensalved by powerful nation with GATT, Dunken and the proposed amentment of the Patents Act to bring it in line with the Trade Related Intellectual Property Right (TRIPS). Instead of the English East India Company we seem to be seeking the benign protection of another such Company. Liberty of thought and speech no more exist. Poverty, illiteracy, unemployment have increased during the years. The narrowness of politicians goes on dividing even more an already fragmented nation, on the basis of caste and religion - BCs, OBCS caste Hindus and so forth. The Republic seems to be breaking up with every state pulling its own way. Life is cheap and insecure. The people have become corrupt and indolent. We will speak of corruption in more detail later. In the words of Macduff :

'Bleed, blee, poor country;
Great tryanny, lay thou thy basis sure,
For goodness dare not check thee! wear thou thy wrongs,
Thy title is affeer'd.[237]

It seems that what one writer says is not far from the truth, 'None of these directives, [of the constitution] it must be noted, is yet within a shade of realization'[238], and another writer, that the directive principles of the constitution have not really been put into practice.[239]

17

THE SWANSONG OF INDIAN DEMOCRACY

No one can rule who cannot also
submit to authority

SENECA

The real difference between democracy and oligarchy
is poverty and wealth.
Whenever men rule by reason of their
wealth, whether they be few or many,
that is oligarchy, and where the poor
rule, that is democracy

ARISTOTLE

Fearlessness alone would, in my view,
meet the challanges thrown by dictatorial
forces. Unless fear is overcome by the people
through conscious effort, the fabric of
democracy could never be sustained, much
less strengthened.

MORARJI DESAI

Two police officers misbehaved with journalists. They were punished by the district head of the police, the senior superintendent, by being 'sent to the police lines.' The inspector in charge of the police station refused to relieve them, instead he sent in his resignation saying that either the senior superintendent of police who gave the order would have to go, or he. 'The choicest abuses were used by the policemen for the SSP. The cops also raised slogans against a senior officer who had ordered the inquiry against the cops'. The upshot? The SSP came over to the police station and had to announce that the order was withdrawn. It was said that the inspector in charge was 'reported to be enjoying the patronage of the ruling party.... The officers say that the number of officers enjoying political patronage was growing day by day'[240]

After the post-mortem examination (autopsy) bodies of persons whose relations are present (as also unclaimed bodies) are carted by people on hand-carts tongas etc., to be unceremoniously thrown into the Ganga river at Kanpur in Uttar Pradesh. Those who carry them earn between Rs 600-700 a month (about 19-22 dollars US). It's done with the connivance of the police of course. The superintendent of police was 'shocked' to know about this, a thing going on for yeara! He said that according to rules unclaimed bodies ought to be burnt in the crematorium and *government gave Rs250 for the performance of the last rites.*[241]

A man commits suicide by drowning in the Gomati river in Lucknow. His scooter with all the papers (license, registration etc.) stands by the pavement of the bridge across the river. The grieved parents get the mayor, whom they know, to ring up the senior police officer. The police go and instantly return with the *easy as pie* solution that the man must have left his scooter there and gone somewhere. The fire brigade, who are called, too, just come and see the scooter and go away. The harassed parents approach the boatmen and divers who live by the riverside who agree to search for the body on payment of Rs 2000 if they are able to find it and Rs1000 if they try but can't. They dive with a net stretched across. Thrice they draw a blank. On the fourth attempt they are able to get it, are given the money promised, and the parents are able to perform the last rites.[242]

The power keeps going off, in fact as soon as the breeze blows faster, presaging a storm, the power-houses themselves cut off the power, lest some overhead wires may break. These used to be copper wires, but were changed over to aluminium as there was a spate of wire-cutting thefts (off and on they continue, despite this). The telephones of all the subscribers on one road are out of order because once again, someone had cut the wire running through the poles on it. The replacement is a long process wrapped up in red tape—an ineradicable feature of our democracy. Sometime back a US firm, US Neal Adams Firefighters were engaged by the Oil and Natural Gas Corporation (ONGC) of India for capping operations at the Pasarlapadi-19 (PSP-19) gas well. They quit after a short time because of red tape. Said Neal Adams of the US company 'I had enough frustration dealing with the ONGC and its red tapism'. He charged that the ONGC could not bypass red tape and such procedures as calling for tenders for fire-fighting equipment even in a crisis situation. The system was considered worldwide the 'most cumbersome and archaic' in the industry.[243]

The Hindustan Times [11April 1995] reports that in Haryana the government appointed three members of the Haryana State Public Service Commission (HPSC) who had resigned at the chief minister's behest as they were involved in irregularities, in various posts of chairmen of vaious boards and commissions. Such appointments are prohibited under Article 319 of the Indian Constitution. Thus politicians invoke the constitutional provisions when it suits them [as for example in clamping president's rule in U.P after the demolition of the Babri Masjid, but not when the new governments's state of law and order is deplorable and women are mass-raped by the police]. And when it does not suit them, they keep flouting the constitution.

The problems that beset us do not appear to be solvable. The main reasons for this is that they seem linked up, a kind of round and round the mulberry bush, and each is a whopping one, a whale of a problem. Take population, the biggest of them all. The projected population figure for the year 2050 is 1,591,204,000 people,[244] while the census figures give India's area as 3,280,000 square kilometres. Thus by that time [which is not very far off] there will be about 485 people in every square kilometre of India's land!—a frightening prospect. The reasons for the failure of birth control, particularly in the villages, where it is most needed, have already been mentioned, and there does not seem any possibility of our governments' doing anything beyond paying it lip service. One of the primary causes for this apathy is the politicians' reluctance to have any truck with family planning because the Moslem population are against it and no politician today can dare annoy Moslems for fear of losing their votes. This, however, has a demographic consequence also. According to the 1971 census the percentage increase in population between 1961-71 was 23.69 for Hindus and 30.84 for Moslems. The rate of increase of the Moslem *over* the Hindu population during the decade therefore was 7.15. If the same rate is maintained, in about eighty years after 1971, i.e., by about the year 2051 the increase would have crossed over 50 per cent. The implication is obvious—that in the next half century or so, maybe a little later, the Moslem population of India would be more than 50 per cent of the Hindu population! Perhaps our *tall-headworker* politicians, being understandably eager to keep their seats and to remain rulers, have not exercised their minds about this demographical phenomenon. The unchecked rise of population has disastrous consequences, for despite all efforts, it blocks all progress. Long back in 1966 Geoffery Tyson wrote that with the population shooting sky-high "India is rather like a man running up a descending escalator—just about to make it'.[245] That was when some effort was being made to control population. Now that we have given up and have surrendered to the Malthusian way, the situation has much worsened, and the man's not 'running up' the escalator, he's only hip-hopping along.

As we said, all our ills are interlinked. Population is bound up with education, for only one who is educated can sublimate sexual energy into creative channels. Education is linked with politics, for our wily politicians are not so keen for getting the people educated as for turning colleges and universities into bastions of their power. Education really means the building up of character and discipline. By depriving people of the right kind of education, our political leaders are undoing all that our martyrs did to gain freedom, for a Epictetus says in his *Discourses* 'Only the educated are free'. With about half of India's millions illiterate and most of the other half not educated in the real meaning of the term, we cannot say we are really free. And what in reality does education mean? It is difficult to say it in just a sentence, but in the ultimate analysis it means acting as one's conscience dictates, for all that distinguishes human beings from animals is that the former act through their minds and consciences, sifting right from wrong and then accepting the right and rejecting the wrong, while animals behave as their instinct directs them (some even eat up their young ones!). Asked what qualities must one have to be called educated, Confucius said, 'He who is earnest in spirit, persuasive in speech, and withal of gracious bearing, may be called an educated man;— earnest in spirit and persuasive of speech with his friends, and of gracious bearing towards his brothers',[246] and John Ruskin considers education to be more than mere reading and writing: 'Education does not mean teaching people what they do not know. It means teaching them to behave as they do *not* behave. It is not teaching the youth the shapes of letters and the tricks of numbers, and leaving them to turn their arithmetic to roguery and their literature to lust. It means, on the contrary, training them into the perfect exercise and kingly continence of their bodies and souls. It is a painful, continued and difficult work to be done by kindness, by watching, by warning, *but above all by example*'.[247] Take for example, what happens in a Hindu marriage procession. The processionists, even the most educated ones, keep letting off noisy crackers even after midnight on the roads. This may go on intermittently even after 2 a.m. in the night. They care a damn whether they keep people who have no concern with their marriage ceremony, maybe some of them sick or in agony, from sleeping. These 'educated' peole are in truth uncultured and devoid of discipline and proper behaviour, for discipline means realizing that one is living in a society, not in isolation. India is full of such people who think they are educated, when really they are lowbrowed and half-cocked. Education in this country is in disarray. For most there is none at all, for some it is purely mechanical, learning by rote as a visit in any village school would show; for the greater part of the rest it is obtained by such dishonest means as copying and the spending of money as pelf, and the objective is merely to get into some coveted government job. Real education is the pursuit of only a few *egghead*s who can be counted on the fingers. Education is rendered ineffective by scheming politicians who exploit students and our universities have been turned into political arenas where hoodlums roam about and keep *kattas* (countrymade arms), instead of being temples of learning. With the absence of education, discipline and character, the pillars which support a nation are lacking. And this leads us to another major bane which makes a mockery of our democracy, namely corruption. Years ago Kautilya said, `Just as the fish moving about in water cannot be detected either drinking or not drinking water, so the government servants can't be detected while taking money for themselves'. It's not that the average Indian is basically corrupt. Long back there was a power failure in a city in a prosperous developed nation for just a few minutes during which shops were ransacked and looted in the darkness. In India power failures are frequent, yet no one loots shops. Customers patiently wait till the candles are lit (in the case of many a generator is a luxury) and shopping proceeds as though nothing had happened. There exists some form of corruption in almost all countries. But the deplorable thing about corruption in India is firstly that here corruption does not exclude the sort that causes loss to national property. The unscruplous government servants here are corrupt even in causing injury to the nation. Bridges develop cracks, roads don't last a year, dams burst, canals exist only on paper, the telephone departments cause loss to the national revenue by various underhand means, houses built by government agencies crumble and collapse, there are scams and scandals like Bofors, the sugar scandal, the Harshad Mehta affair and so forth, involving millions of rupees, and finally the whole matter is kept under wraps and public memory being short, forgotten. Another thing is that corruption has become all-embracing right from a *patwari*, cop, *peshkar*, peon, the lowest official and functionary to the very top officers and politicians in office. Today the country is engulfed in a haze of corruption and practically everybody in involved. A report says: `The higher echelons of the bureaucracy have been stunned by recent instances of two union secretaries (both of whom have been posted outside the country) being approached by touts promising them "immediate" allotment of bungalows for "fees" ranging between Rs 50,000 and Rs one lakh. This is not the first time that bribes have been sought from bureaucrats for allotment of residential premises. But never before have officials of the rank of secretary been so brazenly asked to cough up "speed money" from persons claiming to be close to the high-ups in the ministry of urban development. "Earlier it was influence-peddling and political pressure which determined how quickly an official was allotted a house but now only hard cash matters", remarked a senior bureaucrat'.[248] Edmund Burke says 'Among people generally corrupt liberty cannot last long', and the Populist party: Preamble, first party platform 1892 observed 'The conditions which surround us best justify our cooperation; we meet in the midst of a nation brought to the verge of moral, politial and material ruin. Corruption dominates the ballot box, the legislatures, the Congress [of America], and touches even the ermine of the bench'. Much of this could be applied to the India of today. But surprisingly in a survey made in March 1995, 58 per cent people in Delhi, i.e., among the educated classes, considered that it was right and proper to pay bribes and use influence to get work done! This showed of course that the people of this country have resigned themselves to corruption, but it is also a reflection on our system of education which make the educated feel that corruption is a good thing. Evidently it has not been able to equip the educated person with the mechanism of distinguishing betwen what is right and what is wrong. The corrupt give various justifications for their improbity. Government servants say its because of their low salaries and the desire to maintain a decent standard of living, politicians that they have to be corrupt because of the high cost of electoral politice [just as the Turks and Moghuls waded through blood to sit on their thrones!], and those who happen to have become heads of coveted schools and colleges feel that the doorway to the house of knowledge should be paved with gold, in contrast to the ancient *gurukuls, tols* and *ashramas* where the precious gift of learning was free, imparted with love and accepted with reverence. In truth these are just poor excuses and covert attempts to still agitated consciences. It is like what is often said about alcoholics — first the man takes a drink then the drink takes a drink and then the drink takes the man. That's how a bureaucrat justified himself, 'A bureaucrat moves from accepting invitations to dinner to gifts for his wife on Diwali and then on to taking hard cash. Once you cross the rubicon you fall in line'.[249] The right time to say no, is when one is first faced with temptation for if one then yields the fall is then rapid. There are umpteen people who have remained honest for the greater part of their lives and then are suddenly dazzled with the glint of ill-gotten wealth. A low standard of living or poverty, too, has nothing to do with corruption. Diogenes who lived in a tub snubbed Alexander's offer of domain by asking him to move away so that he could go on basking in the sun. Socrates preferred to drink the cup of poison than to escape prison or breach the law of the land. An honest rickshaw-puller returned a purse containing a lot of money to the person who had inadvertently left it behind. They say that every man has his price, but that is sheer nonsense — not every man, though most. The cause of corruption is lack of moral character which can be built up only by right thinking that stems from the proper kind of education. It is a mistaken concept that the poor are more prone to dishonesty than the rich. In reality it's just the other way round — `Arjun Singh's marble palace, Chandra Shekar's Bhondsi farm and Satish Sharma's marble tiles' (as says SC Dubey former director of the Indian Institute of Advanced Study).[250] The following are the views of three prominent persons, on corruption:

Maxwell Pereira, deputy commissioner of police (crime and railways) - One hundred and six of the elected MLAs of Uttar Pradesh have some sort of criminal record. But these people become legislators because people elect them. It is the same people, the same society that accepts and wants a corrupt way of life. In a country like Japan it is difficlt to get people to do something wrong. One look of disdain or disgust is enough. That is why two prime ministers stepped down when they faced charges of corruption [it may be added that here no one now steps down. Harshad Mehta alleged he paid prime minister PV Narasimha Rao 'rupees one crore to be let of the hook. The very fact that Mehta's allegation did not in any way damage Rao's political career showed the nation was simply beyond caring about corruption' - the *Roneer* write-up of 6 March 1995. And when a minister is removed on being found guilty, as food minister Kalpnath Ral was by the Glan Prakash report in connectioin with the sugar muddle, he goes with tears in his eyes. 'Mr Rai vowed *with tears in his eyes and a gruff voice* that he would dethrone Mr Rao's central government in the very near feature.... I vow, he said, that I will return to Mau (where he was speaking) after removing Mr Narasimha Rao from power'[251] —very much Bacon's 'Revenge is a kind of wild justice; which the more Man's Nature runs to, the more ought Law to weed it out'].[252]

K.J. Alphonse - Lands Commissioner, Delhi Development Authority - For a long time after independence the Indian bureaucrat was keeping his eyes shut while the politicians of the day were indulging in corruption around him. Gradually he began opening his eyes. By the eighties he was conniving with the politician, helping him making money and also taking a share in the booty. Now the bureaucrat is keeping all the booty for himself and not even telling the politician about the deals he is making. Even in a state like Kerala where bureaucrats are respected for their integrity , I know of a chief secretary who has *been making crores in a single deal.* And after him others have followed suit.

H. D Shourie, Director Common Cause and Chairman Coordination Council of India - We have come to a stage when everybody feels there is no alternative to corruption. Corruption has got built into the system. If you want to ply a truck or get a building plan sanctioned, or get a completion certificate for your house, it cannot be done without greasing someone's palm. And the payment for these things is no longer in hundreds but in tens or thousands of rupees! **The remedy?** Shourie feels the plethora of rules is responsible and wants them reduced and simplified. K.J. Alphonse thinks such offenders should be summarily executed, killed or shot, as in the Philippines, and the executions should be in public and shown on the TV. Alphonse is probably right, for now only drastic measures can end corruption, but then **who shall execute whom, when both the offender and the executor are corrupt!** Interestingly the MRAS-Burke survey concludes 'Often a bribe has to be paid *to expedite things that should be done in the normal course.* For instance 39 per cent of all the respondents said they had to pay a bribe to get a driving license — 30 present in the lower income category and 46 per cent in the higher income group. Similarly 35 per cent of all the respondents admitted to paying bribes or feeling the need to do so to sort out problems relating to day-to-day affairs like telephone services, power supply, water, etc. Another 29 per cent said it was to get a telephone or a gas-connection. As many as 23 per cent of the responents said they paid bribes to get the police to help them get things done unofficially. This view is held by 77 per cent of the respondents in the lower income group and 80 per cent of those in the higher category'.

Another major ill that plagues India [and perhaps along with it most of the developing countries] is the apathy to work and the phenomenon of millions of the poor toiling for the handful of the lousy rich. Work, as Ruskin says should be honest, useful and cheerful. 'No man minds or ought to mind, its [work] being hard, if only it comes to something; but when it is hard, and comes to nothing... that is the cruel thing for the worker'. And again he says that the things the dirty rich enjoy 'are paid for in deadly work somewhere, as many of us know too well. The jewel-cutter, whose sight fails over the diamonds; the weaver, whose arm fails over the web; the iron-forger, whose breath fails before the furnace— *they* know what work is - they, who have all the work, and none of the play, except a kind they have named for themselves down in the black north country, where "play" means being laid up by sickness.... You may have your fluting and piping; but there are sad children sitting in the market-place who indeed cannot say to you, "We have piped into you, and ye have not danced:" but eternally shall say to you, "We have mourned unto you, and ye have not lamented".' [253] So too is the case with us. A few people consisting of the poorest of the poor toil and sweat with ceaseless labour to cater to the needs of the big-rich. When they are sick there is only God to care for them for they can't afford any doctor. The corrupt government machinery consists of the class of workers who doubtlessly work hard, but as certainly achieve nothing. The lights keep on in the offices, but the towns become dirtier, the villagers poorer, the prices sky rocketing and things costlier, drinking water scarcer, the power more erratic, the poor poorer, and the jobless and illiterate multiplying. Thus the merry-go-round of India's democracy goes on — the population explosion diluting all development, abject poverty stalking the land like Banquo's ghost, with the politician exclaiming 'Avaunt!'; corruption spreading its deadly tentacles everywhere so that one can smell 'something rotten'; education for sale, but even when bought at a high price, failing to instil character or discipline; law and order extinct, administration paying court only to the privileged, governments which take birth morely to harass their citizens, liberty, equality, fraternity dignity and justice just catchwords: a country not one directive of whose grandiloquent constitution has been achieved, where planes crash and are delayed, trains collide and are derailed, dead men are unceremoniously cast in rivers, roads are blocked and loudspeakers blare at all odd hours — and all the time those in power have the sole aim of retaining it and quite a few of those who have the opportunity to get into the seats of power let the money flow like water, the blood spilt, the bullets speed, the booths captured and voters intimidated — anything so long as the democracy of India can make them rule again. And when the people [most of them the thumb-impression fixing ones or lured by caste or religion affinities or money] put them into their chairs, the government they give is quite often of this kind:

'A retail shop-owner dealing in garments in Patna asks for Rs 400 for an ordinary frock. When countered that he was charging almost double, he quavers forth in desperation "You are the first customer in the last four days. The government employees are not getting salary, university and college staff are starving, businessmen are reeling under the extortion and abduction menace, policemen are also taking their share from us.... what else could we do".

'His frustration is not unfounded. The whole of Bihar appears to share his concern. A noted doctor who did not want to be identified said the entire medical fraternity was affected by extortionists, most of whom enjoyed the ruling party's patronage.

'A teacher had a strange problem. She was posted to a school which existed only on paper. When she complained to the authorities, she was told that she could draw her salary without working provided she gave them 20 per cent of the amount every month. Dictated by her noble instincts, she decided to expose everyone.

'After a couple of months, paralyzed by the dead hand of a corrupt bureaucracy, she was found begging before the education department to forgive her and shift her to a school here she could work a little. Now the authorities were in a mood to punish her for her honest convictions. Thanks to an acquaintance, an IAS officer, she was forgiven by the hawks who were still demanding Rs 40,000 for a proper posting in Patna.

'If only she knew that the powerful Tatas were as much a victim of the system as she was. The industrial giant TISCO felt so helpless because of the hoodlums that it used to open its tenders in faraway places like Bombay and Bangalore instead of Jamshedpur and Calcutta to avoid a bloodbath and racketeering. It is said that the Tatas were so upset that they dished out a huge amount to get a dynamic superintendent of police posted in Jamshedpur.

'A top official in Laloo's [the Bihar chief minister] coterie has some interesting points to make... "When the entire teaching community of the state was agitating for salary and dearness allowance — not delivered for months together at that time — Laloo decided to buy a new helicopter (the BIhar government already had some planes and a helicopter). When the power stations threatened to cut off supply to Bihar, Laloo launched a gimmick of a scheme called Charwaha Vidyalaya (Laloo's children study in English medium public schools; one daughter pushed into a medical college), **and when Bihar was hiding its face in empty coffers, Laloo burnt money — some half a crore —**

to celebrate his birthday at Gandhi Maidan, Patna, which saw a massive congregation of Yadavs from all over".

'However, the chief minister rubbed the Bihari intelligentsia the wrong way most violently to **introducing chapters on his contribution to the state into the school syllabus.** To add fuel to the fire booklets singing his praises as a messiah of the poor were pumped into the market. This, when the naked truth of misrule was there to be seen everywhere in the state.

'The graphs of crime and cruelty, too, reached maddening heights. Cases of senior bureaucrats being beaten up by the Janata Dal goons were too common to take note of. The number of kidnappings rose to more than in Punjab, Kashmir or Assam. Why this culture flourished so fast could be understood by one incident. Laloo Yadav reportedly **scolded one depty director of fisheries so ruthlessly at a cabinet sub-committee meeting in Ranchi that he collapsed and died there itself....** many local Hindi newspapers.... in their editorials... used terms like "demon, dacoit, robber" for the so-called most popular chief minister of Bihar. 'Little wonder that Bihar hates to be called Laloo's Bihar any more'.[2534]

Such a state of affairs may not exist all over this sub-continent for in decadence, Bihar beats all other states pants off. The nearest competitor to it today could be its neighbouring state, Uttar Pradesh. True, a democracy is, as the worn out adage has it, a government of the people, and for the people; but who are the people in India who choose governments for themselves? By and large the voters are uneducated, bitten with the bug of caste, poor and therefore easily tempted with money and amenities, liable to be mobbed up into decisions, so they are easily gettable, and if all these fail, there still are the strongarm devices, so frequently used in our elections that it is needless to repeat them. Notwithstanding these hindrances the voters, even though bogged down by multifarious factors, retain a strong horse sense, and, as the latest trends of voting show, desire change. The trouble is that here, in the political field, change usually implies replacing one evil by another, for most political leaders, irrespective of the party to which they belong, are generally more interested in themselves than in the people, more in retaining power for selfish ends than for the good of the country; and those who are able to rise above self-seeking, find that they are faced with problems to solve which is catching the wind in a net. As has been said the main reason for this is the lack of discipline and character, and of moral values which are products of defective education. These turn politics into mudslinging, politicians calling each other names—traitor, *desh drohi* ('enemy of the country'or unpatriotic) and even 'animal'! Lack of character and discipline thwart administration, producing bureaucrats with a false sense of complacency, stuck-upness which puts a barrier between them and the common man, and turns out plans and schemes which remain paper promises, ill-conceived and badly executed, or not executed at all; and a police force more feared than endeared, more hated than admired and a dull thud in winning the confidence of the people. Indolence gums up the works for we are unable to 'fill the unforgiving minute with sixty seconds' of hard work.[255] But even if by shooting the works one can limit population, remove corruption, reform education, get rid of unemployment, illiteracy and poverty, improve the lot of women and the downtrodden, make the doctors aware of the hippocratic oath and make our villages like Auburrn; democracy will not be able to make it because of the multitude of political parties, still further fragmenting. Democracy needs stable governments and strong oppositions, while we are faced with the prospect of weak ones because the plethora of parties implies hung parliaments and assemblies, which in turn means coalition governments which can never come off because it is in our nature that we never can click. The British had a high sense of cooperation and discipline, which we unfortunately lack. In the Mutiny of 1857 Sir Colin Compbell was senior to Havelock when the English men and women were holed up in the Residency at Lucknow. Havelock had served under Sir Colin in Persia and was junior to him, yet he (Colin) instead of resenting Havelock being in charge of the rescue operations, encouraged him. As soon as Havelock was in the field, he sent him the following message from Benares: 'I shall join you with my reinforcements, but to you shall be the glory of relieving Lucknow, for which you have already so nobly struggled. I shall accompany you only in my civil capacity as commissioner, placing my military service at your disposal, should you please to make use of me *serving under you as a volunteer'*.[256] Our psyche is one of dissension and noncooperation, of airing our differences and insisting on rank and position even when faced by emergencies. Therefore weak coalition governments spell doom for our democracy.

Is there any way the rot could be halted? Any way in we can turn from agitation to successful administration? 'Impossible' is a word found in the dictionary of fools. So that couldn't be the answer. But certainly it's tough going and requires hard self-discipline, drastic measures, much austerity and a lot of self-sacrifice. Partition was a great blunder. It did not solve any problem and created many, and some day it's going to prove very costly. Now, with the number of Moslems far more than in the new Moslem homeland an ethnic fusion of the two communities—Hindu and Moslem—seems to be the only way out. Unfortunately the trends don't show that they are any closer, for fanatics and wily politicians can still fan the flames of communal disharmony. To take a recent example, there was a great furore when a movie, *Bombay,* depicted a Moslem girl marrying a Hindu boy, so much so that the film was banned in Hyderabad where there was a large proportion of Moslems. Clearly therefore there is no bridging the gulf between the two communities. Unless both of them think themselves as Indians first and Hindu and Moslem after and are governed by one common law, this problem cannot be solved. Religion is a private matter and while it is necessary, it is also a fact that, as a physician and writer of the seventeenth century says,'the religion of one seems madness unto another'[257] The difficulty with Islam amd Hinduism is that there couldn't be two faiths so unlike, making mutual accommodation a tough task. The other and more effective way (though how far it will be acceptable is anybody's guess) is to confine religion to temple mosque and church and not have any public demonstrations of it through loudspeakers, processions and the like. That, in fact, is the requirement of our constitution which conceives India to be a 'secular'democracy. Literally 'secular' means 'not religious' [Longman Dictionary of Contemporary English]. In 'Hinglish' it could be taken to imply showing religious tolerance, i.e., the practice of one's own religion without decrying that of others, and since the only way to bring this about here is to make religion a private affair, the aforesaid course seems to be the most likely to serve the constitutions's end.

The Hindu culture and philosophy [as differentiated from its mythology] is perhaps the oldest in the world and has won high praise from even non-Hindus such as Max Müller, Paul Deussen, Schophenhaeur and many other. Aldous Huxley says the *Bhagavadgita* is 'perhaps the most systematic scriptural statement of the Perennial Philosophy....it stands pointing, clearly and unmistakably, to the only road of escape from the self-imposed necessity of self-destruction',[258] and Schopenhauer called the *Upanisads* 'the products of the highest wisdom which are destined sooner or later to become the faith of the people'. India is prized in the west not for its imitative westemized manners, the adoption of pop, jazz, western habits and dresses, cabarets dances and discos and so forth, but for its ancient culture and immortal philosophy. But that is just where we err. We think we impress by being modern and western, while our westernism is only a cheap copy, coming nowhere near the real commodity, whether in language, behaviour, dress, make-up or manners; while we have lost track of our valuable culture. Whatever chance of a revival of this precious heritage there is, is nullified by our political leaders who prefer [if a cliche' be pardoned] to beat their drums and blow their trumpets, calling themselves messiahs, champions of the downtrodden and poor, 'goddess' and even 'Virgin Mary'!,[259] and seem to ignore the glorious traditions and philosophies which evoked the admiration of foreigners; and by the craze for lurid sex and prono given preference over the ancient wisdom by 'publishers who aren't preachers'. If India is to be really respected in the world we need to resurrect this moribund culture.

We were dominated first by the Turk invaders and then by the British. After getting freedom we are now coming under economic domination. No country can gain prominence unless it has wealth and power of its own. It should be like the sun shining with its own light, not like the moon by light that is borrowed. The beggar's bowl may have many coins dropped in it, but it can't give anyone self-respect. So instead of caving in to such things as borrowings, Dunken GATT, Patents, debt and so forth we should endeavour to be on our own. That implies a lot of fiscal discipline a term which our rulers keep on repeating once in while, but seldom observe, for with three-fourths of Indians in low water, the remaining are on the beano, with crores going to pot in the sprees of politicians, non-plan spending and lordly extravagance. Curiously the cost of preserving our democracy itself is quite a shucks, with repeated elections and many of those who are elected on the block for the highest bid. To have power we should forget wranglings and have a strong defence and of course [as we are finding to our discomfiture because we haven't paid it the attention it deserves] a competent espionage. As for the form of government as the popular saying is 'that which is best governed is best'. So without good administration, a sense of strict discipline and the building of character, mere change in government would be no good. It would be like putting the same water in a different vessel. So let us have democracy by all means but democracy which is democratic, and such a one, as T.N. Seshan, the chief election comissioner says, does not come cheap. It also does not also come the easy way.

NOTES

1. Estimated population figures according to the Registrar General of Census, India.

2. *Shevatashavatara Upanishad* 1. 1-2 [Trans, Author's]

3 *Katha Upanishad.* 5. 5-15. (Trans, Author's]

4. *The Bhagavadgita.* 11-12 —divi *suryasahastrasya bhavedyugapadusthita*

5. The Holy Bible, Exodus 3. 2-6- 'And the angel of the Lord appeared unto him in a flame of fire out of the midst of a bush: and he looked, and, behold, the bush burned with fire and the bush was not consumed. And Moses said, I will now turn aside and see this great sight, why the bush is not burnt.....God called unto him out of the midst of the bush and said.......I am the God of the Father the God of Abraham and the God of Jacob. And Moses hid his face; for he was afraid to look upon God'.

6 *Ibid,* 20. 3-5

7. The Holy Quran. 9.28 'The idolaters are nothing but unclean...? Trans, Muhammad Ali, Lahore, Ahmadiyya Anjuman - I.

8. These researchers are Doctor Kiibler-Ross, Dr Raymond A.Moody, Dr Russell Noyes Jr., Dr Grafield, Albert Heim, Dr R.C.A. Hunter, Dr Robert Crookall and Father Herbert Thurston. Some of the books on the subject are: Oliver Fox, Astral Projection: *A Record of Out-of-the-Body Experiences;* Muldoon and Carrington. *The Phenomens of Astral Projection* and *The Projection of Astral Body;* Monroe. *Journeys Out - of-the-Body;* Nils O. Jacobson M.D., *Life without Death?* (New York: Dell Publishing Co. Inc, 1947); Crookall. *Out-of-the-Body Experiences* : A *Fourth Analysis;* Celia Green. *Out-of-the-Body Experiences* (London; Hamish Hamilton Ltd., 1968); Ian Currie. *You Cannot Die.* London: The Hamlyn Publishing Group, 1978; Guy Lyon Playfair. *the Indefinite Boundary.* London: Souvenir Press Ltd., 1976; Arnold Toynbee and others. *Man's Concern with Death*, Hodder & Stoughton, 1968.

9. Shelley, P.B. *Prometheus Unbound* iii. iii. 113.

10. Ceny Lyon . Playfair. *The Indefinite Boundary* London: Souvenir Press, 1976, p., 288.

11. *Bhagvadgita,* 4.34 'When you go to the saints humbly and pay homage to them, and question them thus about truth, they will teach you wisdom'.

12. Guy Lyon Playfair. *The Indefinite Boundary.* London: Sovenir Press, 1976. p., 289.

13. *Bhagavadgita. 2. 56.*

    dukheshv anudvignamanah

    sukhesu vigatasprhah

    vitaragabhaya krodhah

    sithidhir munir ucyate,

14. *Bhagavadgita* 18.61.

15. Idem, 2.47.

16. *As You like it.* Act 2, Scene 7.

17. Arthur Osborne. *Ramana Maharshi, the Path of Knowledge.* New Delhi. B.I. Publications, 1954

18. ibid.

19. ibid.

20. Robert Browning. *Rabbi ben Ezra,* xii, [Browning is the English poet, who I think is unequalled among the Romantics. There is complete fusion of poetry and, philosophy in what he wrote].

23. The *Yoga-sutras* of Patanjali, chapter 4 [Attainments] The yogi, he says, can hear divine sounds (cf, Joan of Arc's voices and visions), know divine touch and colour and is able even to enter other bodies temporarily. But Patanjali's yoga has to be assiduously practised for several years strictly according to the method prescribed. The so-called holy men who promise powers like levitation by short courses are really frauds and money-sprinners.

24. George Gordon Byron, Lord. *Don Juan* C.I CXCIX

25. She never told her love,

    But let copncealment, like a worm i' the bud,

    Feed on her damask cheek: she pin'd in thought;

    And with a green and yellow melancholy,

She sat like patience on a monument,

Smiling at grief'.

Shakespeare. *Twelfth Night ii. iv.*

26. Algernon Charles Swinburne. *Dolores.*

 'No thorns go as deep as a rose's

 And love is more cruel than lust'.

27. William Shakespeare. *A Midsummer Night's Dream* Act scene 1, line 233.

28. *Shiva Purana. Rudra Samhita,* section 2, chaptaer 21. Narrative of Shiva.

29. *Bhagavata Purana.* Description of the *'Rasa'* (Circular) Dance of Krishna and the Gopis.

30. *The Rasikpriya of Keshavadasa.* Trans. K.P.Bahadur. Delhi! Motilal Banarsidass (UNESCO Collection) 1972. p.229.

31. *Brihadaranyaka Upanishad.* 4.3.

32. ibid. 6 (Procreation Ceremonies).

33. Derek Brown, writing in *The Guardian. Is it English or Hinglish?*

34. John Keats, *Hyperion.* Canto I.

35. Mahatma Gandhi. *To the Students* Gandhi Series vol. 1 ed. Anand T. Hingorani. Karachi: 1935 pp., 20 and 184.

36. *India* 1981. Ministry of Information . Government of India.

37. UNI 25 March 1991. *Population Touches 843.93 m mark.*

38. *Is it English or Hinglish*? Derek Brown writing in *The Guardian.*

39. James Russel Lowell. Democracy. Address, Birmingham, England, 8 October 1884.

40. Mahatma Gandhi. *To the Students.* ed. & published Karachi: Anand T. Hingorani, 1935. Gandhi Series Vol.1 p., 128.

41. John Keats. *Sleep and Poetry.*

42. The *Pioneer.* Pulse. 9 October 1994. Boom time for Publishers.

43. Robert Browning. *The Pied Piper of Hamelin.*

44. A *kabariwallah* is a collector of trash, things like old newspapers, books, tins, bottles and so forth.

45. the book has been translated by me into English: *The Parrot and the Starling*. Delhi: Motilal Banarsidass (UNESCO Collection of Representative Works Indian Series) 1977.

46. Megasthenes. *Ancient India.* J.W. McCrindle.

47. Francis Williams. *A Prime Minister Remembers*. London: Heinemann, 1961, pp., 204 and 209.

48. Memorial of 8 March 1833. *Select Documents* 1858-1947. C.H. Philip & others, London: Oxford University PRess, 1962, p., 124.

49. The amending article of the Indian constitution which provides for its amendment is 368. According to this on ordinary matters a simple majority in parliament is enough, for more important matters a two-third majority and for certain specified articles, apart from the two third majority in parliament, ratification by at least half of hte state legislatures. The right to the seven freedoms was protected but the 25th amendment took away this protection. The seven freedoms are: 1. Of speech and expression, 2. Of assembling peacefully without arms, 3. Of forming associations or unions, 4. Free movement within the territory of India, 5. To reside anywhere in the territory of India, 6. To acquire, hold and dispose of property, and 7. To practise any profession or to carry on any trade or business.

    With the protection of these freedoms guaranteed by the constitution, gone, the first freedom to get the hatchet was the right to property, 'Compensation' for [acquiring such property] was subsitituted by the word 'amount', so that a man could be deprived of a property of a crore rupees by giving him money amounting to a couple of lakhs! The legal tussle over the 25th amendment resulted in the stipulation the seven freedoms (guaranteed by article 19 of the constitution) shall remain protected but '*Subject to reasonable restricions*' (AIR 1978, SC 771). Thus governments were left free to curtail these freedoms for what 'a reasonable restriction' would be is anybody's guess.

50. Chester Bowles. *Ambassador's Report*. London and USA: Harper & Row, 1954, p., 10.

51. *The Advanced Learner's Dictionary of Current English* London: Oxford University Press, 1968.

52. *Chambers Etymological English Dictionary* New York: Pyramid Books, 1968.

53. *Kama Sutra of Vatsyayana* Trans. Richard Burton, London: Luxor Press, 1963. Chapter 3 'On Kissing'.

54. ibid. p., 72

55. Alfred, Lord Tennyson. *Fatima* iii.

56. Christopher Marlowe., *Faustus* I., 1324-25.

57. Biswajeet Banerjee. *The Pioneer* 'Poverty Alleviation Scheme Fails to Deliver Result'.

58. Pran Chopra. *Uncertain India.* Bombay: Asia Publishing House, 1968, p., 226.

59. Chester Bowles. *Ambassadors' Report* London & USA : Harper & Row, 1954, p., 94.

60. Keshav Chaturvedi. 'Villages Continue to Swelter in Fifth' *Pioneer* 15 December 1994.

61 *The Times of India.* 31 August 1986.

62. *The Pioneer* II January 1988 'Which way we are Heading?' Somnath Sapru.

63. Chester Bowles. *Ambassador's Report.* London: Harper & Row 1954, p., 157 op.cit.

64. Vera Micheles Dean, *New Patterns of Democracy in India.* Harvard University Press 1969, pp., 20-21.

65. *Muntakhan-ut-Tawarikh.* 'Abul Qadir Badauni.pp., 428-9.

66. K. P. Bahadur. *A History of Indian Civilization* vol, 3 part 3. New Delhi: Ess Ess Publications, 1983, p., 63. op.cit.

67. Bhowani Sen. *Rural Bengal in Ruins.* Quoted in Ram Gopal. *British Rule in India,* Asia, 1963, pp., 55-56.

68. Quoted in *the History and Culture of the Indian People* ed. R.C. Majumdar. Bhavan, vol., ix, p., 835.

69. The export of food-grains, particularly rice and wheat, rose from

853,000 in 1848 to 3.8 million in 1858, 7.9 million in 1877, 9.3 million in 1901 and 19.3 million in 1914 [R. Palme Dutt. *India Today*. Bombay 1947. Quoted in *The History and Culture of the Indian People* ed. R.C. Majumdar. Bhavan, 1963, vol. ix, p,, 836].

70. V.M. Dean. *New Patterns of Democracy in India,* Havard. 1969, p., 20.

71. Mahatma Gandhi. *To the Students.* 'At the Bihar Vidyapith'. Gandhi Series ed. Anand T. Hingorani, Karachi, 1935, p., 61.

72. Only 1.18 crore village people were employed in 1981 out of more than 29 crore of those idle in village industries. *India* 1981 Publications Division Government of India.

73. 'Per Capita Land Declining' U.N.I. New Delhi Reported in *The Pioneer* 16 November 1994.

74. Chester Bowles. *Ambassador's Report.* London & U.S.A Harper & Row. 1954, p., 95.

75. S. Sharma. 'Is India on the Brink of a Manmade Famine?' *The Pioneer.* 16 December 1994.

76. Mahatma Gandhi. *To the Students* Gandhi Series, Vol., 1 ed. Anand T. Hingorani. Karachi, 1935, p., 280

77. *The Times of India* 30 April 1988.

78. Biswajeet Banerjee. ' U.P. Villagers say no to Nirodh' The *Pioneer* 18 November 1994.

79. Washington. 'Violence against women Pervasive'. P.T.I (Reported in *The Pioneer* 16 December 1994).

80. Pradeep Mehta writing in *the Pioneer.* 'Can the "king" do no Wrong', qv.

81. *Sunday* 1-7 March 1987 'An End to the Telephone Tangle'.

82. Gauhati High Court. Shillong Bench. Civil Role No. 72 (SH) of 1989 Sardar Santokh Singh vs. Divisional Engineer Telephones and others, decided on 26 September 1989. Judgment delivered by Hon'ble Justice Dr B.P. Saraf.

83. B.N. Ganguli. *Indian Economic Thought*. Tata McGraw-Hill. 1977, p., 148 op.cit.

84. Taya Zinkin. *Challenges in India.* Chatto & Windus, 1966, p., 51.
85. Chester Bowles. *Ambassador's Report* London & U.S.A. Harper & Row. 1954, p., 9.
86. *Daily Telgraph.* 9 May 1986.
87. *Ramacharitamanasa. Bala kanda* 57 (B)
88. Phaedrus. *Fables.* I. 15. I.
89. *The History and Culture of the Indian Peole* ed. R.C. Majumdar, Bhavan, 1965, vol., 10 p., 90.
90. *India Today* 31 October 1986 p., 28 Gobind Thukral: 'Hitting Deep".
91. *To the Students.* Mahatma Gandhi. Gandhi Series Vol. 1. Anand T. Hingorani ed. Karachi 1935, p., 37.
92. *The Northern India Patrika* 17 April 1987 'Thesis Experts'.
93. The *Pioneer.* 29 October 1987.
94. AIFI study UNI 25 August 1986.
95. Larry Collins and Dominique Lapierre. *Freedom at Midnight* New Delhi: Vikas Publishing House 1976, p., 217.
96. Pyare Lal. Mahatma Gandhi. *The Last Phase* Vol. 2, p., 383; *Freedom at Midnight,* p., 287
97. *To the Students.* Mahatma Gandhi. Gandhi Series vol. 1 Karachi: Anand T. Hingorani, 1935 pp., 292-93.
98. ibid, pp. 214-216 'Heading for Promiscuity'.
99. *The Harijan* 6 July 1942.
100. Francis Williams. *A Prime Miister Remembers.* London: Heinemann, 1961 p., 207.
101. John Milton. *On his Blindness.*
102. Rudyard Kipling. *If.*
103. W.B. Yeats. *When you are old.*
104. Shakespeare. *Julius Caesar* iv. iii. 217
105. *The Bhagavadgita.* 16. 13-14.

106. Tennyson. *In Memoriam*. liv.

107. The Holy Bible. *Exodus*. 20. 5.

108. Shakespeare. *Macbeth*. Act 4. Scene 1.

109. Larry Collins and Dominique Lapiere. *Freedom at Midnight*. New Delhi: Vikas, 1976, p., 289.

110. ibid. p., 214

111. Pyarelal. *Mahatma - the Last Phase*. Navjivan vol. 2, p., 209

112. Collins and Lapure. *Freedom at Midnight*, Vikas p., 105.

113. Ziegler Philip. *Mountbatten. The Official Biography*. London: Collins, 1985. Letter of 12 March 1957, p., 473.

114. ibid. p., 474. op.cit., Letter dated 8 February 1952.

115. Terence. *Eunuchus* Act II. Scene 1. l., 19 Adeone homines immutarier Ex amore, ut non cognoscas euidem esse?

116. Maulana Abul Kalam Azad. *India Wins Freedom*. Orient Longkan. 1959 p, 186.

117. Collins and Lapiere. *Freedom at Midnight* New Delhi: Vikas. 1976, p., 157.

118. Euripedes. *Iphigenia in Aulide*, 1142.

119. Lucknow used to be the city of nabobs and so its citizens are noted for their tenderness and delicacy.

120. Collins and Lapiere. *Freedom* at *Midnight*. New Delhi: Vikas, 1976, p., 378.

121. ibid. p., 445.

122. *A History and Culture of the Indian People*. Bhavan ed. R.C. Majumdar, 1969, vol., XI, p., 361.

123. The *Pioneer* 13 January 1995. Newsmaker 'Economic Reforms Implementataion Poor, says Paul'.

124. Bhargava's HIndi-English Dictionary.

125. The following is quoted from *Jizyah* and *the Spread of Islam* by Harsh Narain. New Delhi: Voice of India 1990, p., 1, 'The Muslim psyche is of a peculiar making, vis-a-vis the attitude towards non-Muslims. According to the Prophet every child is born in Islam, but its parents make iat a non-Muslim. The

Qur'an also says that the earth belongs to Allah. He causes it to be inherited by whom of His servante He will. On the basis of it all the Prophet rules that all land. belongs to God or himself, the natural corollary being that all land belongs, through God and the Prophet, to the Muslims'.

126. The Holy Quran 9:28 and 25:52 Trans. Muhammad Ali President Ahmadiyya. Anjuman-I-Ishaat-I-Islam Lahore. Lahore Ahmadiyya Anjuman-I-Ishaat-I-Islam 1928. In the footnotes to these verses the translator says that the permission to fight is given to Moslems when some enemy attacks them and *jizyah* was leived on non-Moslems as protection charges as they were exempt from military service. But military service was never compulsory under Moslem rule and as for taking up the sword when attacked, the text (in translation) doesn't clear that this was the sense. And even if it was, history shows *jihads* were not when provacation was given but only as a kind of Crusade.

Also as regards the second passage the translator says in the footnote that chastisement (*jihad*) as not by the sword but by the Holy Quran. In practice, however, the history of Moslem India and the present day acts of Moslems seem to point out otherwise [For *jihad* and *jizyah* see also Harsh Narain's booklet published by Voice of India. New Delhi].

127. *Freedom at Midnight* p., 171.

128. ibid. p., 170.

129. Dasgupta, Dr. J.B. *Indo-Pakistan Relations 1947-1995* Jaico, 1959, p., 188.

130. ibid. p., 189.

131. ibid. p., 190.

132. Essay on Agra. 'Jesting Pilate' Aldous Huxloy *Stories, Essays & Poems*. Everyman's Library. London: J.M. Dent & Sons Ltd. 1937, p., 209.

133. Niccolao Manucci. *Storio Do Mogor*. Trans., Irvine, London: John Munay, 1906 vol. 1, p., 194.

134. ibid. pp., 194-5.

135 *Sri Ramakrishna Paramahasa.* Prem Lata: New Delhi Sumit Publicationis, 1991, P., 93 op.cit.

136. Aldous Huxley. 'Jesting Pilate' in *Stories, Essays & Poems. London:* John Dent. Benares. p., 216.

137. *Health & Nutrition* ed. Nirmala Ferrao. November 1991. Vol. 3 no. 8 'Beyond Physical Well-being' p., 27.

138. ibid.

139. *Health and Nutrition.* August 1992, vol., 4 No. 5 'How to Stop Worrying'. p., 27.

140. *The Pioneer.* 30 January 1995.

141. Chester Bowles. *An Ambassador's Report.* London & U.S.A: Harper & Row, 1954, p., 156.

142. *Local Government in India* ed., M. Venkatarangaiya and M. Pattabhiram. New Delhi: Allied Publishers, 1969, p., 39

143. *The Pioneer*, 17 December 1994 'Sugar Crisis: Full blame on Rai'.

144. UNI. *Pioneer.* 5 February 1995.

145. The *Pioneer.* 7 February 1995

146. *ibid.* 16 December 1994. Sudhirendra Sharma. 'Is India on the Brink of a Manmade Famine?'

147. Nirmal Mitra from New York. IANS. Reported in *Pionerr* 15 December 1994.

148. A.K. Bhattacharya. New Delhi Diary. 'Bureaucrats are Worried'. The *Pioneer* 6 February 1995.

149. *India 1976.* Publicationis Division, Ministry of Information Government of India p., i, 'why Emergency?'

150. *Violation of Democratic Rights in India* ed. A.R. Desai. Bombay: Popular Prakashan 1986 Gobinda Mukhoty. 'The Indian Constitution and Civil Liberties'. vol. 1 p., 82.

151. ibid. pp. 82-83.

152. ibid. p., 83. Gopalan's case.

153. Henry D. Thoreau, *Selected Writings on Nature and Liberty.* ed. Oscar Cargill, New York: The Liberal Arts Press, 1952, pp., 10-11. Essay on Civil Disobedience.

154. *Violation of Democratic Rights in India.* en. A.R. Desai. Bombay: Popular Prakashan, 1986, p., 74.

155. *The Analects of Confucius.* trans., William Edward Soothill. London: Oxford University Press, 1910.

156. Ralph Waldo Emerson. *Journals* (1861-1865).

157 Study conducted by H.K. Paintal Lecturer, Development of Psychology, Lucknow University. Journal of Correctional Work 1974 Jail Training School Lucknow.

158. Statistics got compiled by the author.

159. Madhur Mala. Problems of Women Offenders in Nari Bandi Niketan, Lucknow

160. H.K. Paintal's study 'Crime Responsibility in Women Murderers?

161 Ram Akshaibat Yadav 'Woman who kill' Indian J. Clini-Psychol. (1976) 3:122.

162. Dr(Miss) Majory F.Foyle MBBS(Lond.) DRCOG, DPM, MRC Psych.Clinical Director Nur Manzil Psychiatric Centre, Lucknow. 'Psychology of Particular Crimes'. Journal of Correctional Work, 1976. Jail Trainning School U.P. Lucknow, p., 109,

163. John Dowson. *A Classical Dictionary of Hindu Mythology and Religiion, Geography, History and Literature.* London: Routledge & Kegan Paul Ltd, 1961, pp., 373-74.

164. Shakespeare. *King Lear.* VII. 44-46

165. Menander, *Dis Exaparaton, Fragment* 4. and Hypsaeus. *Stobaeus Florilegium,* CXX., 13.

166. G.K.Chesterton. *Ecclesiastes.*

167. Antiphanes. Fabulae Incertae, Fragment 64. 'Methinks that grief is madness' next door neighbour'.

168. William Wordsworth. *The Borderers*

169. *Bhagavadgita* 5:14-15.

170. *Health and Nutrition.* August 1992.

'How to Stop Worrying.'

171. *Guide to Madras.* Tourist Division, Ministry of Transport & Communications, Neew Delhi, introduction, p.,3.

172. *Sunday.* 12-18 July 1987.

173. Delivering the Dr Rajendra Prasad Memorial Lecturc on 'Law'. *The Times of India.* 4 December 1987.

174. Speaking at the Silver Jubilec Celebrations of the Andhra Pradesh High Court. *The Pioneer.* 2 November 1981.

175. Speaking at the Silver Jubilee Celebrations of Andhra Pradesh High Court in 1981.

176. *The Times of India.* 23 November 1986. Sunday Review, p.,4.

177. ibid.

178. Anacharsis. *Solon.*

179. *Brihadaranyaka Upanishad*,4.

180. *The Pioneer.* 2 February 1995.

181. Vijay Sharma writing in *The Pioneer* 2 March 1995 'Bid to Protect' Guilty 'Offiers'.

182. Reported in *The Pioneer* 25 January 1995. 'Public Exposure of Crimes Against Women'.

183 *The Pioneer* 3 March 1995. Editorial. 'Policemen as Criminals'.

184. *The Pioneer,* 3 January 1995. PTI. '1994-A Saga of the Bizzare and the Unusual'.

185. ibid. 30 December 1994. Editorial.

186. ibid. 1 March 1995. 'It is unfair to expect fair polls in Laloo Yadav's Bihar'. Kanchan Gupta, deputy editor.

187. ibid. 30 January 1995. 'Police in league with house and land grabbers. Senior SP Leader's Sons on House-grabbing Spree. Reported by Archana Srivastave/Bishwadeep Ghosh.

188. Inder Malhorta. *India Trapped in Uncertainty* New Delhi: UBSPD, 1991, p., 158.

189. *The Pioneer* Editorial. 'Wither UP?'

190. *Hindustan Times.* 18 February 1995.

191. *Frontier* 180 October 1969, p., 31

192. *Sunday* 12-13 April 1987 'The Golder Mile' (cover story).
193. *The Times of India* 9 May 1988 "National Briefs'.
194 *Sunday.* 19-25 April 1987 The Impoverished Society'
195. ibid. 22-28 March 1987. 'A March for Survival'.
196. *India Today.* 15 January 1988,p.,112.
197. Reported in *The Pioneer* 7 March 1995
198. *India Today.* 15 January 1988 p,.95. 'The Coming Crunch'
199. L.Collins and D.Lapiere. *Freedom at Midnight.* New Delhi: Vikas, 1976, p,.314.
200. *The Pioneer.* Editorial. 23 February 1995.
201. The facts mentioned are from *Violation of Democratic Rights in India.* ed, A.R.Desai vol., 1 Bombay: Popullar Prakashan, 1986, pp., 336-38.
202. *The Analects of Confucius.* trans. William Edward Soothill, ed. Lady Hosie. London: Oxford University Press. The World's Classics, 1910, p.,144.
203. *The Pioneer* 11 March 1995 Anuradha Vashisht 'Is Privatarion the Answer?'
204. *Sunday.* 1-7 March 1987. pp., 12 and 15
205. *The Pioneer.* 11 March 1995 '10-year old boy thrashed'.
206 ibid. 4 December 1994. 'Is that what you call VIP security?' Report by Ketan Narottam Tanna.
207. ibid. 5 March 1995 "The Human Shield'.
208. ibid. 3 March 1995. 'Bypassing childhood' Upala Devi.
209. ibid.
210. ibid. 14March 1995 Mahout rapes minor girl?
211. ibid. 8 March 1995 'Women's Day'.
212. ibid. 14 March 1995 'The trauma of being a girl child-how long more?
213. ibid. 2 March 1995. 'Rise in crime against women, SC persons'.
214. ibid. 25 January 1999 'Public Expose of Crimes against

Women'.

215. *The Times of India* 4 October 1987. Rajiv Gandhi at the Centenary Celebrations of the New English High School, Nagpur.

216. *India Today* 30 November 1987, p.,47.

217. *The Pioneer* 31 March 1988.

218. *The Northern India Patrika.* 17 April 1987 'Thesis Expert'.

219. Henry Peter [1778-1868] Broughman: The Present State of Law.

220. Aristotle. Quoted by Diogenes Laertius.

221. *Front Line* 21 October 1994. Cover story. 'The Purge'.

222. *Health & Nutrition.* January 1992 'A Slice of Life'. p.,91.

223. ibid. February 1994. p., 36.

224. Lewis Carroll. *Alice in Wonderland.*

225. *The Pioneer.* 20 February 1995. Darry D'Monte, "The kidney racket is part of a larger malaise'.

226. *Health & Nutrition* October 1992. p.,69.

227. *The Pioneer* 28 February 1995 "Surgery abandoned midway'.

228. *India* 1981 Government of India. Ministry of Information. Publications Division, p.,248

229. William Blake. *Songs of Experience. The Tiger.*

230. PTI. The *Pioneer* 21 March 1995. 'Neglect chokes Hampi's heritage. The Vijaynagar empire monuments lie in shambles'.

231. *The Pioneer* 17 March 1995. 'Extortation with impunity' by a correspondent-Mohanlalganj

232. ibid. 12 March 1995. 'Supporters of minister, MLC exchange fire'.

233. ibid. 'Crimes soar in Lucknow Police playing a passive role'.

234. John Keats. *Ode on a Grecian Urn*

235. *The Daily Telegraph.* 'When sex lesson fail.' Ray Honeyford.

236. *The Pioneer.* 21 March 1995. Editorial, 'Distrgarding national security'.

237. Shakispeare. *Macbeth.*4.3
238. Dilip Hiro. *Inside India Today.* London: Routledge & Kegan Paul, 1976, p.,46.
239. Charles Bettelheim. *India Independent* trans., W.A.Caswell. Mac Gibbon & Kee, 1968 p., 107.
240. *The Pioneer.* 24 March 1995 'Policemen enforce their own laws'.
241. ibid. 'Making a living from the dead'.
242. In the author's personal knowledge.
243. *The Pioneer* 26 February 1995'. US firm quits capping work'.
244. Washington April 4(AP). *The Pioneer,* 5 April 1988.
245. Geoffery Tyson. *Nehru, the Years of Power,* Pall Mall Press, 1966, p.,44.
246. *The Analects of Confucius.* trans., W.H.Soothill. ed., Lady Hosie. London: Oxford University Press 1941, p.,141.
247. John Ruskin. *Stones of Venice*, 1853.
248. *The Pioneer.* 'Touts promising govt houses to officers'. Paranjoy Guha Thakurta.
249. ibid. 6 March 1995 'Most Delhites feel paying bribes is justified'.
250. ibid. The full quotation from the write-up is 'Sociologist SC Dubey, former director of the Indian Institute of Advanced Study, feels power has been the most corrupting factor. "When we have accepted Arjun Singh's marble palace, Chandra Shekhar's Bhondsi farm and Satish Sharma's marble tiles, how do these things matter any more." he asked,. The views of three prominent persons about corruption follow (a politician, Madhu Dandavate, former finance minister, understandably has an excuse of the Indira Gandhi brand, namely that all the world has it, so why not we).
251. ibid. 17 December 1994 and 20 January 1995 'Sugar Crisis: Full blame on Rai' and 'Kalpnath vows he will delthrone Rai'.
252. *Essays* by Francis Bacon

253. John Ruskin. *The Crown of Wild Olives*. Work.

254. *The Pioneer* 27 March 1995. 'Suffocating Bihar may no longer be Laloo's fiefdom-state of disarray where work without salary, extortion, abduction, have become a rule rather than an exception'. reported by Sanjay K.Jha.

255. Rudyard Kipling. *If.*

256. Forrest. *A History of the Indian Mutiny*, Vol., 2 P., 13.

257. Thomas Browne. *Hydriotaphia,* or *Urne-Buriall,* 1658.

258. Introduction to the *Bhagavadgita* The New American Library (Mentor Book) edition, 1954.

259. *The Pioneer.* 15 March, 1995 'Jayalalitha not acceptable as 'idol' P T.I.

BIBLIOGRAPHY

Bowles, Chester. *Ambassador's Report.* Lendon and USA : Harper & Row, 1954

Chopra, Pran. *Uneertain India.* Bombay: Asia Publishing House, 1963.

Cellins, L. and Lapierre, D. *Freedom at Midnight* New Delhi: Vikas Publishing House, 1976.

Dean, V.M., *New Patterns in Democracy in India.* Havard, 1969.

Desai, A.R. ed. *Violation of Democratic Rights in India.* Bombay: Popular Prakashan, 1986. 2 Vols.

Hire, Dilip. *Inside India Today.* London : Routledge and Kegan Paul, 1976.

Lacy, C. *Indian Insights.* New Delhi: Orient Longman, 1979.

Malhotra, Inder. *India Trapped in Uncertainty.* New Delhi: UBSPD, 1991.

Philip, C.H. and others. *Select Documents* 1858-1947. London: Oxford University Press, 1967.

Stern, Robert W. *The Process of Opposition in India.* University of Chicago, 1976.

Venkanta Rao, V. and Niru, H. *Local Self Government in India.* New Delhi : S. Chand and Co., 1980.

Ziegler, Philip. *Mountbatten, the Official Biography.* London: Collins, 1985.

Zinkin, Taya. *Challengers in India.* Chatto & Windus, 1966.

INDEX